New Constitutional Horizons

OXFORD CONSTITUTIONAL THEORY

Series Editors

MARTIN LOUGHLIN,
JOHN P. MCCORMICK, AND
NEIL WALKER

Oxford Constitutional Theory has rapidly established itself as the primary point of reference for theoretical reflections on the growing interest in constitutions and constitutional law in domestic, regional, and global contexts. The majority of the works published in the series are monographs that advance new understandings of their subject. But the series aims to provide a forum for further innovation in the field by also including well-conceived edited collections that bring a variety of perspectives and disciplinary approaches to bear on specific themes in constitutional thought and by publishing English translations of leading monographs in constitutional theory that have originally been written in languages other than English.

ALSO AVAILABLE IN THE SERIES

Constitutionalism and the Paradox of Principles and Rules
Between the Hydra and Hercules
Marcelo Neves

Constituent Power in the European Union
Markus Patberg

Religion, Law, and Democracy
Selected Writings
Ernst-Wolfgang Böckenförde

Edited by Mirjam Künkler and Tine Stein
Constituent Power and the Law
Joel Colón-Ríos

Euroconstitutionalism and its Discontents
Oliver Gerstenberg
Beyond the People

Social Imaginary and Constituent Imagination
Zoran Oklopcic

The Metaethics of Constitutional Adjudication
Boško Tripković

Carl Schmitt's State and Constitutional Theory
A Critical Analysis
Benjamin A. Schupmann

Law and Revolution
Legitimacy and Constitutionalism After the Arab Spring
Nimer Sultany

Constitutional and Political Theory
Selected Writings
Ernst-Wolfgang Böckenförde

Edited by Mirjam Künkler and Tine Stein
Constitutionalism
Past, Present, and Future
Dieter Grimm

Europe's Functional Constitution
A Theory of Constitutionalism Beyond the State
Turkuler Isiksel

Post Sovereign Constitution Making
Learning and Legitimacy
Andrew Arato

Popular Sovereignty in Early Modern Constitutional Though
Daniel Lee

The Cultural Defense of Nations
A Liberal Theory of Majority Rights
Liav Orgad

The Cosmopolitan Constitution
Alexander Somek

The Structure of Pluralism
Victor M. Muniz-Fraticelli

Constitutional Courts and Deliberative Democracy
Conrado Hübner Mendes

Fault Lines of Globalization
Legal Order and the Politics of A-Legality
Hans Lindahl

The Cosmopolitan State
H Patrick Glenn

After Public Law
Edited by Cormac Mac Amhlaigh, Claudio Michelon, and Neil Walker

The Three Branches
A Comparative Modelz of Separation of Powers
Christoph Möllers

The Global Model of Constitutional Rights
Kai Möller

The Twilight of Constitutionalism?
Edited by Petra Dobner and Martin Loughlin

Beyond Constitutionalism
The Pluralist Structure of Postnational Law
Nico Krisch

Constituting Economic and Social Rights
Katharine G. Young

Constitutional Referendums
The Theory and Practice of Republican Deliberation
Stephen Tierney

New Constitutional Horizons
Cormac S. Mac Amhlaigh

New Constitutional Horizons

Towards a Pluralist Constitutional Theory

CORMAC S. MAC AMHLAIGH

OXFORD
UNIVERSITY PRESS

OXFORD
UNIVERSITY PRESS

Great Clarendon Street, Oxford, OX2 6DP,
United Kingdom

Oxford University Press is a department of the University of Oxford.
It furthers the University's objective of excellence in research, scholarship,
and education by publishing worldwide. Oxford is a registered trade mark of
Oxford University Press in the UK and in certain other countries

First Edition published in 2022

Impression: 1

Published in the United States of America by Oxford University Press
198 Madison Avenue, New York, NY 10016, United States of America

British Library Cataloguing in Publication Data

Data available

Library of Congress Control Number: 2021951276

ISBN 978–0–19–885233–9

DOI: 10.1093/oso/9780198852339.001.0001

Printed and bound by
CPI Group (UK) Ltd, Croydon, CR0 4YY

Til Signe, Oscar, Isolde og Nóra;
agus mo thuismitheoirí;
Míle buíochais!
(Tusind Tak!)

Contents

Acknowledgements

I have collected many debts in the writing of this book. I first came across some of the problems considered in the book as a doctoral student at the European University Institute in Florence, Italy, where I was expertly tutored in the conceptual and theoretical problems posed by constitutional pluralism by my then doctoral supervisor, Neil Walker. As well as being fortunate enough to benefit from his wisdom and insights, but perhaps more importantly, his persistent but gentle probing of my thoughts and ideas, I benefitted and learned from the advice, encouragement, discussions, and friendships within the then wider EUI community—staff, colleagues, and friends—including Stine Andersen, Daniel Augenstein, Matej Avbelj, Pedro Barretto, Maria Cahill, Gráinne de Búrca, Bruno de Witte, Alun Gibbs, Andrew Glencross, Jen Hendry, Christian Joerges, Karine Kaunes, Jo Murkens, Miguel Poires Maduro, Pontus Rendahl, Thomas Roberts, Masimo Rospocher, Wojciech Sadurski, Kathrin Scherr, Mike Wilkinson, and Jacques Ziller.

I traded one beautiful city for another after leaving the EUI to take up a position at Edinburgh Law School where I benefitted further from discussions with colleagues and friends in Edinburgh's terrific research environment on the topics covered in this book. Neil Walker was, again, a protagonist in many of those discussions, this time as a colleague and friend rather than a supervisor. However, discussions with many others in the broader Edinburgh community helped the project along, particularly those with Zenon Bańkowski, Christine Bell, Dan Carr, Leonardo Cofré, Andrew Cornford, Sharon Cowan, Luís Duarte d'Almeida, Anthony Duff, Filippo Fontanelli, James Harrison, Chris Himsworth, Chloe Kennedy, Tobias Lock, Neil MacCormick, Euan Mac Donald, Claudio Michelon, Elisa Morgera, Amalia Amaya Navarro, Niamh Nic Shuibhne, Maggie O'Brien, and Jo Shaw.

More generally, others have made significant interventions which helped my thinking at different junctures including Maks del Mar, Adil Haque, Mattias Kumm, Hans Lindahl, Martin Loughlin, Philip Pettit, Mikael Rask Madsen, Nicole Roughan, Paul Schiff Berman, Michael Sevel, Adrienne Stone, Brian Tamanaha, Kevin Walton, and Marlene Wind.

Various parts of some of the chapters of the book were tested on audiences at seminars at the Free University of Amsterdam, IDC Herzliya, Radzyner

Law School, the London School of Economics, the National University of Singapore, Trinity College Dublin and the Universities of Bristol, Cambridge, Copenhagen, Leeds, Leuven, Melbourne, Milan, and Sydney. I am grateful for the engagement and feedback from those audiences on those occasions. I would also like to thank the students of my Law, Legitimacy and Globalization course at Edinburgh Law School who were often unwitting sounding-boards for some of the ideas developed in the book. Thanks also to Pravar Petkar for his superlative editorial assistance during the final drafting stages of the manuscript and for helping with the index. I would also like to thank Rebecca Lewis at OUP and Mohith Singh Dubey at Newgen for their efforts to ensure the timely production of the book.

Finally, I am grateful for the love and support of family over the years. Academia, and writing more generally, can be a solitary and, at times, frustrating, experience and my family have never wavered in their love and support—especially at the most frustrating times—and for that I will ever be grateful. My parents Brian and Kathleen have always provided a bedrock of support for my endeavours and have been unfailing in their encouragement. My wife, Signe, and our children Oscar, Isolde, and Nóra, along with providing love and moral support, also provided welcome and much-needed distraction from this project at critical junctures. This book is dedicated to them.

* * *

Parts of Chapters 2, 4, and 6 are based on material published elsewhere. Chapter 2 is based on the chapter 'Does Legal Theory have a pluralism problem?' in P Schiff Berman (ed), *The Oxford Handbook of Global Legal Pluralism* (Oxford University Press 2020). Chapter 4 is based on the article 'Taking Identity Seriously: On the Politics of the Individuation of Legal Systems' (2021) *Oxford Journal of Legal Studies*. Chapter 6 is based on the chapter 'Who's Afraid of Supra-state Constitutional Theory?: Two Reasons to be Sceptical of the Sceptics' in K Walton, W Sadurski, and M Sevel (eds), *Legitimacy: The State and Beyond* (Oxford University Press 2019). I am grateful for the permission to republish the material here.

List of Abbreviations

ECB	European Central Bank
ECHR	European Convention of Human Rights
ECJ	European Court of Justice
ECtHR	European Court of Human Rights
EU	European Union
FRY	Federal Republic of Yugoslavia
GAL	Global Administrative Law
GFCC	German Federal Constitutional Court
ICANN	Internet Corporation for Assigned Names and Numbers
IMF	International Monetary Fund
TFEU	Treaty on the Functioning of the European Union
UK	United Kingdom
UN	United Nations
UNSC	United Nations Security Council
US	United States
WTO	World Trade Organization

1
The Circumstances of Constitutional Pluralism

1. A Pluralist Tale

In April 1992, a small, recently incorporated Turkish airline charter company entered into an agreement with a Yugoslav-owned airline company to lease two aircraft with a view to operating charter flights to and from Turkey for the upcoming summer holiday season. The ensuing complex legal and institutional web in which this simple commercial leasing agreement became ensnared speaks clearly to the pluralism of our contemporary law and governance.

The company, Bosphorus Hava Yollari Turizm ve Ticaret A. S. ('Bosphorus Airlines'), leased two aircraft from JAT (Jugoslovenski Aerotransport—the flag airline carrier of the former Yugoslav state) for the use and control of the aircraft which was registered under Turkish law pursuant to the Chicago Convention on International Civil Aviation of 1944.[1] In 1993, the company entered into an aircraft maintenance agreement with TEAM Aer Lingus, an Irish aircraft maintenance company indirectly owned by the Irish state based in Dublin, Ireland. In May 1993, one of the aircraft operated by Bosphorus Airlines arrived in Dublin for maintenance, a service contract under Irish law was signed, and, by the end of the month, the company had been informed that the aircraft would be released on payment of a service fee due under the contract. Payment was duly made and the aircraft was released by TEAM Aer Lingus. However, while awaiting air traffic clearance for take-off on the tarmac at Dublin airport, the aircraft was stopped by Dublin airport air traffic control. TEAM Aer Lingus had been advised by the Irish government that allowing the aircraft to leave could constitute a breach of United Nations (UN) Security Council

[1] The facts are mainly drawn from Part I of the judgment of the European Court of Human Rights (*Bosphorus Airways v Ireland* [2005] European Court of Human Rights 45036/98.) as well as the Opinion of the Advocate General and the European Court of Justice's (ECJ) decision in the Irish Supreme Court's preliminary reference (Case C-84/95 *Bosphorus Hava Yollari Turizm ve Ticaret A. S. v Minister for Transport, Energy and Communications, Ireland and the Attorney General* [1996] ECR 1-3953).

New Constitutional Horizons. Cormac S. Mac Amhlaigh, Oxford University Press. © Cormac Mac Amhlaigh 2022.
DOI: 10.1093/oso/9780198852339.003.0001

Resolution 820 (1993) as interpreted by the UN Sanctions Committee. This was one of a series of sanctions taken by the United Nations Security Council (UNSC) against the Federal Republic of Yugoslavia (Serbia and Montenegro) (FRY) to address the armed conflict and human rights violations there during the Balkan conflict of the early 1990s. The Sanctions Committee itself was established by UNSC Resolution 724 (1991) under Chapter VII of the United Nations Charter to administer the various subsequent resolutions of the UNSC relating to the war in the former Yugoslavia.

The Irish government's notification of Dublin air traffic control was confirmed in a subsequent letter by the Irish government of June 1993 which stated that in its view, allowing the aircraft to depart would breach UN sanctions as well as Council Regulation (EEC) no 990/93 of the Council of the European Union aimed at implementing the sanctions of the UN Security Council for Member States of the European Union. In the same month, the Irish government adopted regulations pursuant to Irish law authorizing the impounding of the aircraft until further notice.[2] Attempts by the airline and the Turkish government to release the aircraft (including an offer to impound the aircraft in Turkey) were unsuccessful in the light of the direction of the UN Sanctions Committee.

Bosphorus Airlines sought a judicial review in Ireland of the Irish government's decision to impound the aircraft in November 1993. Various actions before the Irish High Court in 1994 and 1995 found that the law applicable to the case was the attempted implementation of the UN sanctions by the European Union (EU) in the form of EU regulations, rather than the sanction measures under the UN Charter directly which could not, the High Court found, have binding effect on the Irish government unless implemented into Irish law. The first of those decisions was appealed to the Irish Supreme Court regarding the interpretation of the EU regulation which implemented the sanctions. The Supreme Court referred the interpretation of the regulation to the ECJ[3] in 1995. The ECJ found that the Irish High Court's interpretation of the EU regulation as not relating specifically to aircraft (thereby making the impounding unlawful) was incorrect and then considered the proportionality of the measure in the light of EU fundamental rights law (which was partly based on the law of the European Convention of Human Rights (ECHR)), concluding that the requirement to sequester the aircraft was a proportionate

[2] The European Communities (Prohibition of Trade with the Federal Republic of Yugoslavia (Serbia and Montenegro)) Regulations 1993 (Statutory Instrument no 144 of 1993).

[3] As it then was.

interference with the right to peaceful possession of property protected by the ECHR.[4] This was remitted to the Irish Supreme Court which ordered that the impounding order be reinstated. Ultimately, the UNSC suspended the regulations pursuant to which the aircraft was impounded in the light of the improving situation and peace negotiations in the FRY and released the aircraft back to the proprietor of the planes, JAT, in 1997.[5] Bosphorus Airlines then launched an action against Ireland before the European Court of Human Rights (ECtHR) in 1997, alleging that it had breached its Convention obligations not to interfere with the peaceful enjoyment of possessions under Article 1 of the First Protocol of the Convention. The ECtHR delivered its judgment in 2005, finding that Ireland could not be considered in breach of its Convention obligations where it was acting pursuant to a directive from an organization of which it was a member, provided that the human rights protections provided by that organization were comparable with those under the Convention. In the event, the Court found that EU law contained sufficient rights guarantees such that Bosphorus Airlines' rights had not been violated when Ireland followed EU law in this case.

This legal saga, is, perhaps, best remembered for the judgment of the ECtHR which clarified the human rights obligations of Convention states in respect of their membership of international organizations, as well as endorsing a doctrine of 'equivalent protection' in international human rights law more generally.[6] However the fact pattern of the case also provides a particularly graphic example of the pluralistic nature of law and governance in the contemporary world. If we focus on the judgment of the ECtHR, we can see that the case before this particular Court had, by this stage, implicated a variety of distinct legal systems and political institutions. In terms of legal systems, the case had implicated Turkish law, Yugoslav law, elements of conventional public international law (the Chicago Civil Aviation Convention 1944, the UN Charter and bodies and decisions set up and taken under its authority), elements of conventional private international law (the leasing agreements between JAT and Bosphorus Airlines and the aircraft service maintenance agreements between Bosphorus Airlines and TEAM Aer Lingus), as well as supranational law (EU law in the form of the UN sanction-implementing regulations, EU fundamental rights

[4] Case C-85/95, ECR I-3978, Judgment of 30 July 1996.

[5] Bosphorus Airlines in the interim had shut down due to financial trouble. BI Hengi, *Airlines Remembered; Histories and Operations of 204 Airlines of the Last 30 Years* (Midland Publishing 2000).

[6] *Bosphorus Airways v Ireland* (n 1) paras 155–156. See Tobias Lock, 'Beyond Bosphorus: The European Court of Human Rights' Case Law on the Responsibility of Member States of International Organisations under the European Convention on Human Rights Recent Development' (2010) 10 Human Rights Law Review 529.

law incorporating, in part, ECHR law, and ECHR law directly), and the national constitutional and administrative law of Ireland. Moreover, the plurality of institutions included judicial institutions (the Irish High Court, the Irish Supreme Court, the ECJ, and the ECtHR) as well as political and administrative institutions of the Irish state (the Departments of Transport and Foreign Affairs as well as its Permanent Mission to the UN), the Turkish State (the Turkish Foreign Ministry and Ministry of Transport, the Turkish Central Bank, the Turkish ambassador to Ireland as well as its Permanent Mission to the UN), the United Nations (the Security Council and the Sanctions Committee), and the EU legislature.

Of course, complex transnational litigation is hardly new and legal pluralists have for decades highlighted the complex social realities of law involving various types of norms and authorities.[7] However, this case presents an example of the increasingly complex legal realities involving overlapping legal systems and authority claims involving *transnational* law and governance that form the focus of this particular book.[8] These realities have conventionally been captured in terms of a shift from a simple 'Westphalian order' of sovereign states to something altogether more complex, where the state as the supreme (or even exclusive) legal and political actor is demoted from the centre of the political and legal universe to one among a number of actors in a broader setting, where suprastate governing and adjudicatory bodies rival states for authority and influence.[9] These 'new constitutional horizons' constitute what, in the present volume, we call the circumstances of constitutional pluralism.

[7] For a comprehensive overview of recent debates, see generally Paul Schiff Berman, *The Oxford Handbook of Global Legal Pluralism* (Oxford University Press 2020).

[8] Thus, from the perspective of legal pluralism, the focus of the current volume lies in what Michaels has termed the 'third wave' of legal pluralism. Ralf Michaels, 'Global Legal Pluralism' (2009) 5 Annual Review of Law and Social Science 243. 'Transnational law' here, taking a pluralist ethos, encapsulates the broad range of legal systems captured within Jessup's well-known definition of 'all law which regulates actions or events that transcend national frontiers'. Philip Jessup, *Transnational Law* (Yale University Press 1956) 1. Each context of legal pluralism raises its own discrete set of questions for theories of law and political authority (for discussion in the transnational context see Gregory Shaffer and Carlos Coye, 'From International Law to Jessup's Transnational Law, from Transnational Law to Transnational Legal Orders' in Peer Zumbansen (ed), *The Many Lives of Transnational Law: Critical Engagements with Jessup's Bold Proposal* (Cambridge University Press 2020)). However, this does not necessarily imply a methodological 'pluralism of legal pluralisms' where the distinctiveness of each instance of legal pluralism requires entirely novel concepts and methods. For a discussion of this possibility see Cormac Mac Amhlaigh, 'Pluralising Constitutional Pluralism' in Andrew Halpin and Nicole Roughan (eds), *In Pursuit of Pluralist Jurisprudence* (Cambridge University Press 2017). Rather, given that our theoretical inquiry remains at a general level—in what we might call a 'general jurisprudence' of constitutional pluralism—the theoretical approach is of relevance to all contexts of legal pluralism.

[9] Nico Krisch, *Beyond Constitutionalism: The Pluralist Structure of Postnational Law* (Oxford University Press 2010) 5.

2. The Circumstances of Constitutional Pluralism

The idea of the circumstances of constitutional pluralism draws upon Hume's idea of the conditions for justice, as developed and elaborated by Rawls in terms of the 'circumstances of justice'.[10] Hume first posited the facts about the world which give rise to the need for theories of justice in human relations in terms of individual 'selfishness' and the finitude of 'possessions'.[11] For Hume, 'tis only from the selfishness and confin'd generosity of man, along with the scanty provision nature has made for his wants, that justice derives its origin'.[12] Rawls's development of these ideas in the form of 'limited altruism'[13] and 'moderate scarcity'[14] constituted his 'circumstances of justice', which are the 'normal conditions under which human cooperation is both possible and necessary'.[15] For Rawls, the circumstances of justice represent 'background conditions' that 'define the role of justice', which obtain 'whenever mutually disinterested persons put forward conflicting claims to the division of social advantages under conditions of moderate scarcity'.[16] Hume and Rawls's approach to justice, then, involves stipulating the conditions under which a theory of justice is *relevant*. A world without scarcity and limited altruism would not, in Hume and Rawls's view, be justice-apt.[17]

This idea is developed by Weale and Waldron to elaborate on the conditions under which theories of *democratic legitimacy* are necessary.[18] Like the assumptions of Hume and Rawls regarding the circumstances of justice—that humans have, in reality, limited levels of altruism, and that resources are, in fact, finite—Weale and Waldron elaborate the 'circumstances of politics',[19] involving particular facts about the world that become the conditions of their theories of political legitimacy. For Weale, these assumptions are constrained generosity, bounded rationality, and path dependence, and they set feasibility constraints

[10] John Rawls, *A Theory of Justice* (Harvard University Press 1973) 109.

[11] David Hume, *A Treatise of Human Nature*, vol I (David Fate Norton and Mary J Norton eds, Clarendon Press 2007) 318.

[12] ibid.

[13] Rawls, *A Theory of Justice* (n 10) 146.

[14] ibid 109–10.

[15] ibid 126.

[16] ibid 110.

[17] 'Encrease to a sufficient degree the benevolence of men, or the bounty of nature, and you render justice useless, by supplying its place with much nobler virtues, and more valuable blessings. The selfishness of men is animated by the few possessions we have, in proportion to our wants; and 'tis to restrain this selfishness, that men have been oblig'd to separate themselves from the community, and to distinguish betwixt their own goods and those of others.' Hume (n 11) 317–18.

[18] Albert Weale, *Democracy* (2nd edn, Palgrave Macmillan 2007); Jeremy Waldron, *Law and Disagreement* (Oxford University Press 1999).

[19] Weale (n 18) 12–18; Waldron (n 18) 101–03.

on our accounts of legitimate political decision-making.[20] For Waldron, the circumstances of politics emerge from the desire to reap the rewards of coordinated action while disagreeing, sometimes radically, about how those goods should be achieved.[21] Like the circumstances of justice, the elements of the circumstances of politics come together. If there were no need to act in concert, then disagreement would not matter; similarly, a 'felt need' for concerted action would not give rise to politics if there was no disagreement on how to act.[22]

The 'circumstances' of justice and politics serve a variety of roles in theory building. They stipulate the conditions under which the theory is necessary. Moreover, they also serve to inject an element of realism into our theorizing by paying attention to feasibility constraints to ensure that our theories adequately explain the world and are not radically counterfactual or utopian depending on the specific purposes of our theorizing.[23] Thus, the various circumstances of justice and politics attempt to set the conditions for theorizing society as it is, as opposed to how it 'might be', to paraphrase Rousseau.[24] Finally, they set the conditions for the development of the normative standards of the particular theory in question. These circumstances provide the basis for theorizing how decisions should be made, for Hume and Rawls justly, or for Weale and Waldron legitimately.

Here we draw on these observations regarding the 'background conditions' which give rise to the circumstances of justice and politics to argue for the *circumstances of constitutional pluralism* as establishing the conditions for theorizing contemporary legal and political practices, as exemplified by the *Bosphorus Airlines* case considered earlier. The circumstances of constitutional pluralism involve an *institutional* and *multilevel plurality* of *applicable law and institutional authority claims* at different levels of governance, including the transnational level.[25] It is not only the case that law and governance in the contemporary world are made up of different norms, sources of law, and institutional actors claiming authority[26]—including, but not limited to, the *trias*

[20] Weale (n 18) 17.
[21] Waldron (n 18) 102.
[22] ibid. For a discussion and critique of Waldron's view see Alexander Latham-Gambi, 'Jeremy Waldron and the Circumstances of Politics' (2021) 83 The Review of Politics 242.
[23] Weale (n 18). See further Chapter 7.
[24] 'My purpose is to consider if, in political society, there can be any legitimate and sure principle of government, taking men as they are and laws as they might be.' Jean-Jacques Rousseau, *The Social Contract*, as cited in John Rawls, *The Law of Peoples: With, the Idea of Public Reason Revisited* (Harvard University Press 1999) 13. For further discussion see Chapter 7.
[25] Neil Walker, 'The Idea of Constitutional Pluralism' (2002) 65 The Modern Law Review 317, 339. See also Nicole Roughan, *Authorities: Conflicts, Cooperation, and Transnational Legal Theory* (Oxford University Press 2013).
[26] What Roughan calls 'same-domain' plurality. Roughan (n 25) 46.

politica of states—but also that these diverse sets of norms and authority claims are applicable to, and made over, the same fact patterns and sets of subjects.[27] Furthermore, these authority claims elicit, in turn, disagreement as to what legitimate authority requires and what sorts of institutions can make authentic claims to legitimate authority, which is redolent of the reasonable pluralism of philosophical and moral views which Rawls sets as one of his constraints on theories of liberal democracy,[28] and also forms the basis of Weale and Waldron's accounts of the circumstances of politics.[29]

Thus, like the circumstances of justice and the circumstances of politics, the circumstances of constitutional pluralism are made up of the 'background conditions' which inform our understanding of the world as it is which set the conditions for our theorizing. In this respect, our 'background conditions' of the circumstances of constitutional pluralism involve a constitutional *plurality* of applicable legal systems and plausible authority claims over the same sets of facts and norm-subjects, as illustrated by the *Bosphorus Airlines* case, as well as disagreement borne of a value pluralism about what legitimate constitutional authority requires and whether we can pick out a 'correct' authority claim among the plurality. Moreover, our normative conclusions regarding what we should do in the face of such plurality is our theory of constitutional *pluralism*.[30] Under the circumstances of constitutional pluralism, then, *plurality* denotes a *descriptive account* of our contemporary world in terms of multiple applicable legal systems and authority claims alongside a second-order disagreement about which authority claims are correct which set the 'background conditions' for a normative account of pluralism; while *pluralism* denotes our *normative account* of how we should act in the face of such plurality.[31] Like the circumstances of justice and the circumstances of politics, the circumstances of constitutional pluralism reflect the need for legitimate decision-making in the face of a plurality of values as well as authority claims at different levels of governance over the same set of subjects. In this way, the circumstances of constitutional pluralism force us to think of law and authority in a non-monistic way; that is that our contemporary accounts of law and legitimate authority do

[27] Building on the accounts of legal pluralism advanced by Griffiths and Engle Merry in terms of the co-existence of two or more legal systems in the same 'social field'. See John Griffiths, 'What Is Legal Pluralism?' (1986) 18 Journal of Legal Pluralism and Unofficial Law 1, 2. Sally Engle Merry, 'Legal Pluralism' (1988) 22 Law & Society Review 869, 870.

[28] John Rawls, *Political Liberalism* (Columbia University Press 1993) 36; Rawls, *The Law of Peoples* (n 24).

[29] Weale (n 18); Waldron (n 18).

[30] In adopting the plurality/pluralism distinction as tracking the descriptive and normative dimensions of transnational legal pluralism, I follow Roughan (n 25) 44.

[31] Roughan (n 25).

not assume that all valid and applicable law belongs to the same legal system, nor that justified political decision-making is reducible to a single ultimate and final form of authority which makes a more 'authentic' or 'correct' claim to legitimate political authority in all cases.[32]

3. New Constitutional Horizons: Between Constitutional Plurality and Constitutional Pluralism

The challenges posed by the circumstances of constitutional pluralism therefore prompt us to think in terms of a pluralist account of legality and legitimacy.[33] In order to explore these questions, in the current volume we exploit the field of constitutional theory as a particularly useful 'way of world-making'[34] which can serve to capture the descriptive and normative questions which the circumstances of constitutional pluralism pose for our understanding of law and governance in the contemporary world.

In its analytical register, constitutional theory offers a 'purely descriptive'[35] account of law where a 'constitution' is a 'conceptual necessity of every legal system'[36] whose 'function' is the 'grounding of [the] validity'[37] of law. Thus, the idea of a constitution for the descriptive part of our enterprise is equated with the idea of legal system or *legality*,[38] particularly as developed primarily by the 'canon' of analytical legal theory.[39] In this sense, then, a *constitutional* plurality involves a plurality of *constitutions*; that is, a plurality of legal *systems* potentially

[32] See ibid. A similar idea to the circumstances of constitutional pluralism as presented here is captured by Walker's 'epistemic pluralism' which involves acknowledging that 'the underlying symbolic work involved in representing each [authority site] as units—and so also as *unities*—requires a different way of knowing and ordering, a different epistemic starting point and perspective with regard to each unit(y); and that so long as these different unit(ies) continue to be plausibly represented as such, there is no neutral perspective from which their distinct representational claims can be reconciled.' Walker (n 25) 338.

[33] See generally Nicole Roughan and Andrew Halpin (eds), *In Pursuit of Pluralist Jurisprudence* (Cambridge University Press 2017).

[34] Nelson Goodman, *Ways of Worldmaking* (Hackett Publishing 1978).

[35] Charles McIlwain, *Constitutionalism: Ancient and Modern* (Liberty Fund 1947) 26, emphasis added.

[36] John Gardner, *Law as a Leap of Faith* (Oxford University Press 2012) 89.

[37] Hans Kelsen, 'The Function of a Constitution' in Richard Tur and William Twining (eds), *Essays on Kelsen* (Clarendon Press 1986) 199.

[38] Where 'legality' here equates with the criteria of validity of law as contained within a legal system. See Jules Coleman, *The Practice of Principle: In Defence of a Pragmatist Approach to Legal Theory* (Oxford University Press 2003) Lecture 7. See also Scott J Shapiro, 'What is Law (and Why Should We Care)?' in Scott J Shapiro, *Legality* (Harvard University Press 2011).

[39] Paradigmatically that advanced by Raz; Joseph Raz, *The Concept of a Legal System: An Introduction to the Theory of a Legal System* (Oxford University Press 1980); Joseph Raz, *The Authority of Law* (2nd edn, Oxford University Press 2009). Of course, what, precisely, we mean by 'analytical legal theory' and what is included in its 'canon' is something which itself requires further consideration. This is taken up in Chapter 2.

applicable to the same fact patterns and sets of legal subjects. However, unlike, say, moderate scarcity and limited altruism which give rise to the circumstances of justice, the circumstances of constitutional pluralism raise a series of questions regarding our understanding of the 'background conditions' of our account of constitutional pluralism in terms of our pluralist account of legal systems. These questions primarily relate to the compatibility of our account of legal systems with the constitutional plurality which features in our circumstances of constitutional pluralism. They have been the subject of considerable attention in discourses of legal pluralism in recent decades, and the first part of the book is focused on examining the ways in which constitutional plurality can be theorized under the circumstances of constitutional pluralism. In particular, theorizing the circumstances of constitutional pluralism raises two conceptual questions for an account of constitutional plurality: the first relates to the question of whether our concepts of law and legal system, particularly in the analytical tradition, are apt to theorize non-state forms of law; and the second, whether the tendency in accounts of legal systems to assume a 'perspectival monism' of valid law[40]—what we call here a 'monist manner'—can be overcome to capture the circumstances of constitutional pluralism in a better way. These questions regarding the theorization of the circumstances of constitutional pluralism itself, that is the conceptual assumptions about a world of constitutional plurality, take up the first part of the book.

Our normative theory of *pluralism* draws on the idea of *constitutionalism* which has a particular storied 'tradition'[41] as a 'standard',[42] 'touchstone',[43] or 'code'[44] of political legitimacy. Here our circumstances of constitutional pluralism loom large in terms of disagreements about the relationship between the concept of constitutionalism and legitimate authority as well as whether the diverse authority claims within the constitutional plurality can be organized into 'true' or 'false' authority claims, or more or less authentic claims to legitimate authority depending on the level at which it is made. In particular, the circumstances of constitutional pluralism elicit considerable disagreement as to whether non-state sites can make claims to legitimate constitutional authority,

[40] See Kaarlo Tuori, 'Perspectivism in Law' in Rain Liivoja and Jarna Petman (eds), *International Law-Making: Essays in Honour of Jan Klabbers* (Taylor & Francis Group 2013).

[41] Martin Loughlin, *Foundations of Public Law* (Oxford University Press 2010) 158.

[42] Gordon J Schochet, 'Introduction: Constitutionalism, Liberalism and the Study of Politics' in James R Pennock and John W Chapman (eds), *Constitutionalism* (New York University Press 1979) 2.

[43] Daniel Bodansky, 'Is There an International Environmental Constitution?' (2009) 16 Indiana Journal of Global Legal Studies 565, 583.

[44] Neil Walker, 'Postnational Constitutionalism and the Problem of Translation' in Joseph HH Weiler and Marlene Wind (eds), *European Constitutionalism beyond the State* (Cambridge University Press 2003) 38.

a disagreement which is exemplified by the 'no demos' thesis which attaches itself to non-state constitutional authority claims.[45] In this part of the book we explore the ways in which we can develop a normative theory of constitutional pluralism by addressing these questions.

In constitutional theoretical terms then, the book approaches the circumstances of constitutional pluralism in terms of a constitutional 'plurality', a pluralist theorization of the concept of law and legal system and authority claims,[46] as well as a constitutional 'pluralism' which looks at the ways in which the constitutional tradition can be pluralized to provide a normative standard of legitimate decision-making under the circumstances of constitutional pluralism.[47]

In this respect, the focus of the current volume is primarily a theoretical one, examining the methodological and other questions which the circumstances of constitutional pluralism pose for our mainly state-based toolkit of constitutional theory.[48] Our conceptual tools of law and authority, particularly the ways in which we understand law as a systemic form of normative social practice, and our disagreements about what legitimate constitutional authority requires have tended towards monism both in terms of adopting a singular view on law and authority[49] and basing that singular view on a particular historic instance of law and authority: the legal systems and authority claims of states.[50] Whether this was ever warranted, as Raz has argued on the grounds that the state was the 'most comprehensive legally based social organization of the day',[51] or not, as legal pluralists such as Griffiths have argued,[52] is not of immediate interest to us here.[53] Rather, our interest lies in what challenges must be overcome to convert our monistic accounts of legal system and normative accounts of legitimate constitutional authority into pluralist ones.

The analysis in each part of the book is not, then, oriented towards predetermined conclusions that constitutional plurality and constitutional pluralism are 'oxymoronic'[54] based on an unalloyed monistic (in both senses) view of

[45] For discussion see Nico Krisch, 'The Promise and Perils of Postnational Constitutionalism' in Nico Krisch, *Beyond Constitutionalism: The Pluralist Structure of Postnational Law* (Oxford University Press 2010). See further Chapter 7.

[46] Roughan (n 25) 44.

[47] See for example, Krisch (n 45).

[48] Christian List and Laura Valentini, 'The Methodology of Political Theory' in Herman Cappelen, Tamar Szabó Gendler, and John Hawthorne (eds), *The Oxford Handbook of Philosophical Methodology* (2016).

[49] Neil Walker, 'Constitutional Pluralism Revisited' (2016) 22 European Law Journal 333, 337.

[50] Joseph Raz, 'Why the State?' in Nicole Roughan and Andrew Halpin (eds), *In Pursuit of Pluralist Jurisprudence* (Cambridge University Press 2017).

[51] ibid 137.

[52] Griffiths (n 27). See further Chapter 3.

[53] But see the discussion in Chapter 2.

[54] Martin Loughlin, 'Constitutional Pluralism: An Oxymoron?' (2014) 3 Global Constitutionalism 9.

legal and political ordering. It is not clear what kind of contribution to the puzzles of the circumstances of constitutional pluralism such an attempt would make. Rather, the ensuing chapters are aimed at exploring the pluralist potential of constitutional theory, clarifying more precisely the particular puzzles which the circumstances of constitutional pluralism raise, as well as offering potential solutions to these puzzles in the 'pursuit',[55] more broadly, of a pluralist constitutional theory. They constitute an attempt to respond to the question of how to turn the conceptual and methodological monism of constitutional theory into a pluralist one to explore the new constitutional horizons of constitutional pluralism.

4. ... Really? This? Now?

Some eyebrows may be raised at the publication of a book on transnational constitutional pluralism in the early 2020s. It is a virtual cliché of international and domestic politics that events over the past decade have shattered the complacent belief in a global 'rules-based order',[56] potentially posing a serious blow to the future of many of the transnational legal and governing structures which contribute to our circumstances of constitutional pluralism. The aftermath of the global financial crash and the 'great recession' of 2008, the refugee crisis sparked by the Syrian civil war (and many states' shameful responses to it), as well as the global pandemic sparked by the lightning-quick spread of the SARS-CoV-2 virus, each, in their own way, it could be argued, represents a turning point in the legal and political contexts which gave rise to the circumstances of constitutional pluralism. Amidst these economic and social crises, political populists who have been in the ascendency in the second decade of the second millennium have trained their cross-hairs on sites of transnational law and governance in their more general attack on 'corrupt elites' undermining the will of the 'pure people' whom they claim uniquely to represent.[57] This was showcased in the populist movement which took the United Kingdom out of the European Union in 2016 (the first state to leave the organization in its more than sixty-year history), ostensibly 'taking back control'

[55] Roughan and Halpin (n 33).

[56] G John Ikenberry, *A World Safe for Democracy: Liberal Internationalism and the Crises of Global Order* (Yale University Press 2020).

[57] Cas Mudde, 'Populism: An Ideational Approach' in Cristóbal Rovira Kaltwasser and others (eds), *The Oxford Handbook of Populism* (Oxford University Press 2017).

towards a legal and political monism.[58] Similarly, the increasingly populist authoritarian governments of remaining Member States such as Hungary, Poland, and Slovenia have used the European Union as a target to drum up support for their authoritarian brand of politics centred around a monistic national identity.[59] Beyond Europe, populists have promoted a rhetoric around the structures of transnational law and governance as a form of imperial domination controlled by hegemonic global powers or, alternatively, as a story of freeloading states, trading on the wealth and power of others.[60] That this latter form was a rhetoric promoted by the United States during the Trump administration, traditionally a robust supporter of transnational law and governance (even if it proved particularly reluctant to participate in those structures and be bound by their norms in practice), accompanied by steps to withdraw from transnational structures such as the Paris Climate Agreements and the World Health Organization during a global pandemic, seemed a particularly menacing development.[61] These issues were further exacerbated by the global pandemic caused by the rapid spread of the SARS-CoV-2 virus beginning in late 2019. The ensuing border closures, jealous hunting and stock-piling of medical equipment by (mainly wealthy) states, as well as the subsequent 'vaccine rows' about access to and distribution of the various vaccines seem to suggest that ultimately, when the chips are down, states are what matters.[62]

The potential significance of these events for our current inquiry is that they could signal a new direction of travel towards not more but less pluralism of law and governance. They suggest that the need for the practices, institutions, and structures which gave rise to the circumstances of constitutional pluralism in the first place are being replaced by a clamour for a resurgent state, reclaiming its authority and position in global law and politics in times of crisis, necessitating a return to a more traditional state-based form of legal and political monism. It is ironic, it might be suggested, that a book on a transnational pluralist constitutional theory should appear in the midst of such turmoil which seems to herald a return to monism.

[58] Ralf Michaels, 'Does Brexit Spell the Death of Transnational Law?' (2016) 17 German Law Journal 51.

[59] See, for example, in the Polish context Wojciech Sadurski, *Poland's Constitutional Breakdown* (Oxford University Press 2019).

[60] See generally Frank A Stengel, David B MacDonald, and Dirk Nabers (eds), *Populism and World Politics: Exploring Inter- and Transnational Dimensions* (Springer 2019).

[61] Robert Jervis and others, *Chaos in the Liberal Order: The Trump Presidency and International Politics in the Twenty-First Century* (Columbia University Press 2018); Elijah Wolfson, 'Trump Said He Would Terminate the U.S. Relationship with the W.H.O. Here's What That Means' [2020] *Time Magazine* <https://time.com/5847505/trump-withdrawal-who/> accessed 11 May 2021.

[62] See Florian Bieber, 'Global Nationalism in Times of the COVID-19 Pandemic' [2020] Nationalities Papers 1.

We could, in response to these claims, justify the publication of the current volume at this juncture with some sort of 'owl of Minerva' claim; that it is precisely at the end of a historical epoch that we truly understand it.[63] However, we do not need to refer to recondite Hegelian philosophies of history to reject the premise upon which this scepticism is based. It is undeniable that many of the dominant structures that have given rise to the circumstances of constitutional pluralism over the past number of decades have been swept up in global events and have been subject to unprecedented political attacks. It is also undeniable that a significant trope in these attacks has been a 'return' to the nation state, whether in the pursuit of some project of national renewal or as a purely practical observation that the historic achievement of the state remains the most plausible form of law and governance to provide and protect individual security and safety.[64] There is thus a superficial attraction to the idea that Minerva's owl has taken wing on the circumstances of constitutional pluralism and that governing arrangements in the next decades will be based more and more around less and less legal and political pluralism.

However, looking more closely, we have strong reasons to seriously doubt whether Minerva's owl has even woken up from her daytime slumber, let alone taken wing. It is beyond the scope of this introduction to provide an exhaustive overview of the developments to tackle the various crises of the past decades. However, focusing exclusively on Europe for brevity and simplicity, we can point to three particular trends which suggest that the various crises of the past decade prognosticate *more* rather than *less* legal and political pluralism.

The aftermath of the global financial crisis has resulted in *increased* rather than *decreased* regulation and governance in the form of both primary EU treaty law and secondary EU law bolstering legal and political pluralism between state and EU levels of governance.[65] This has, in turn, had the effect of boosting judicial pluralism within the context of EU law, with the German Federal Constitutional Court, a traditional protagonist in judicial pluralism in the EU context, making a series of resolutely pluralistic landmark decisions based on the measures taken to dig the Eurozone out of its crisis.[66]

[63] 'When philosophy paints its grey in grey, a shape of life grown old . . .; The owl of Minerva begins its flight only with the onset of dusk'; Georg Wilhelm Fredrich Hegel, *Hegel: Elements of the Philosophy of Right* (Allen W Wood ed, HB Nisbet tr, Cambridge University Press 1991) 23.

[64] See Martin Loughlin, 'In Defence of Staatslehre' (2009) 48 Der Staat 1; Martin Loughlin, 'The State: Conditio Sine qua Non' (2018) 16 International Journal of Constitutional Law 1156.

[65] See generally Kaarlo Tuori and Klaus Tuori, *The Eurozone Crisis: A Constitutional Analysis* (Cambridge University Press 2015); Alicia Hinarejos, *The Euro Area Crisis in Constitutional Perspective* (Oxford University Press 2015).

[66] See Sabine Saurugger and Fabien Terpan, 'Integration through (Case) Law in the Context of the Euro Area and Covid-19 Crises: Courts and Monetary Answers to Crises' (2020) 42 Journal of European Integration 1161.

In a similar way, the EU's rule of law crisis has resulted in (belated) enhanced EU scrutiny of domestic constitutional reforms in Poland and Hungary, resulting in infringement procedures being brought based on the threat to the rule of law.[67] These have occurred within the context of a legal and political pluralism professed, strategically, by the increasingly authoritarian institutions of these states.[68] The pandemic has seen further enhanced concerted action by the EU institutions both in terms of vaccine procurement and distribution (even if with mixed success) and major developments in EU-level management of the European economy in the form of an EU Recovery fund agreed in July 2020 under the banner of 'next-generation EU'.[69] Even Brexit, ostensibly the most portentous harbinger of the end of the circumstances of constitutional pluralism (at least in a European context),[70] has resulted in *more*, rather than *less*, legal and political pluralism in Europe. The structures which were established in the withdrawal arrangements and the future Trade and Cooperation Agreement have merely *added to*, rather than subtracted from, Europe's pluralistic complex regulatory structures. Now, alongside the complex edifice of the EU's legal and political structures for its Member States and the various legal frameworks for dealing with third countries can be added a bespoke novel architecture of the particular arrangements put in place by the agreement between the European Union and the United Kingdom on the terms of the latter's withdrawal as well as the subsequent Trade and Cooperation Agreement governing the future relationship between the bloc and the United Kingdom.[71] Moreover, the conditions of the UK's withdrawal have established a particularly baroque form of legal and political pluralism between the European Union and one corner of the United Kingdom, Northern Ireland, in the form of the Northern Irish Protocol.[72]

[67] See, for example, European Commission, 'European Commission Refers Poland to the Court of Justice' (2021) <https://ec.europa.eu/commission/presscorner/detail/en/ip_21_1524> accessed 6 May 2021.

[68] R Daniel Kelemen and Laurent Pech, 'The Uses and Abuses of Constitutional Pluralism: Undermining the Rule of Law in the Name of Constitutional Identity in Hungary and Poland' (2019) 21 Cambridge Yearbook of European Legal Studies 59.

[69] See Special European Council Conclusions 17–21 July 2020, <https://www.consilium.europa.eu/en/meetings/european-council/2020/07/17-21/> accessed 21 June 2021.

[70] Michaels (n 58).

[71] Most remarkably with the retention of the doctrine of supremacy within the UK's legal system for EU law passed prior to Brexit and with respect to certain aspects of the Withdrawal Agreement. See Cormac Mac Amhlaigh, 'Back to a Sovereign Future?: Constitutional Pluralism after Brexit' (2019) 21 Cambridge Yearbook of European Legal Studies 41; Steve Peers, 'The End—or a New Beginning? The EU/UK Withdrawal Agreement' (2020) 39 Yearbook of European Law 122.l. On the EU/UK Trade and Cooperation Agreement see: <https://ec.europa.eu/info/relations-united-kingdom/eu-uk-trade-and-cooperation-agreement_en> accessed 21 June 2021.

[72] Katy Hayward and Emmanuel Brunet-Jailly, '"Flexible and Imaginative": The EU's Accommodation of Northern Ireland in the UK–EU Withdrawal Agreement' (2021) 58(2) International Studies 201–18.

Futurology is a fool's game. However, it is possible to state with reasonable certainty that the trend in responses to the various crises which have emerged over the past decade or so have involved *more* rather than *less* transnational pluralism. A pluralism of law and governance has become an increasingly consistent response to the various recent regional and global crises, and we can expect this trend to continue into the immediate future with further crises looming on the horizon. As Chapter 8 of our current volume emphasizes, some form of state cooperation and coordination establishing transnational legal and governance structures is an inevitable feature of our contemporary world and our responses to global problems. In the light of the inertia of that need, it seems a reasonably safe bet to argue that it will displace rhetorical calls for a 'return to state sovereignty' (whatever that might mean) for the foreseeable future, not least in the context of the ever-looming climate crisis.

* * *

As noted earlier, this book is divided into two parts based on the two dimensions of constitutional theory: legality and legitimacy. Chapter 2, which opens the part on legality exploring the first of our 'background conditions' of our theory of constitutional pluralism, situates our idea of a constitution within a tradition of thinking about fundamental law and its connection to analytical legal theory. It takes a hard look at the question of whether the fact that our dominant descriptive accounts of constitution-as-legal system which have been developed within the context of the state pose insurmountable obstacles to the co-option of this idea of constitution to examine constitutional plurality as a 'circumstance' of constitutional pluralism. Framing the question in terms of legal theory's 'plurality problem', it examines in detail the attacks on these state-centred accounts of law and legal system from legal pluralists who argue that the tools of analytical legal theory are not up to the task of analysing legal plurality. These attacks are presented as a strong claim that legal theory assumes that all law is state law, an intermediate claim that state law is the best or 'paradigmatic' form of law, and a weak claim, that legal theory has neglected non-state forms of legal ordering. Parsing each claim and analysing each one in detail in the light of different accounts of legal system from the analytical tradition, it argues that whereas there may be some truth to the legal pluralist critique of analytical accounts of law and legal system, particularly with regard to the weak claim, the critiques do not present insurmountable obstacles to theorizing constitutional plurality using these primarily state-developed analytical tools in principle. Following on from the conclusions of Chapter 2, Chapter 3 focuses on the particular case of international law, reviewing in particular the objections to characterizing international law in terms of a 'constitutional' legal system. These are presented as a series of reasons revolving around the existence of a 'world state gap'; that is the absence of a single centralized coercive international authority which makes, adjudicates, and enforces norms of international law. It examines the ways in which analytical legal theory has wrestled with the problems associated with the 'world state gap', particularly through a focus on the accounts of international law advanced by Hans Kelsen and HLA Hart, as well as more contemporary contributions to the debate on the systemic nature of international law, concluding that that analytical legal theory has found imaginative solutions to the problem such that it is meaningful to speak of an international legal system. Whereas the case of international law is, in some sense, the 'well established, low-hanging fruit'[73] of this type of constitutional plurality, the chapter argues that the solutions developed to manage the 'world state gap' in respect of international law offer resources to the systemic theorization of other, particularly transnational, non-state legal contexts which similarly operate in the absence of a singular and unified coercive legal and bureaucratic authority, or which operate within a context where the authority of different systems and sites of governance are contested. Based on the conclusions of the previous two chapters, Chapter 4 goes on to examine how extant analytical accounts of legal systems account for constitutional plurality. It examines a puzzle which constitutional plurality poses for recognition-based accounts of legal systems: how to move beyond the 'monist manner' of collapsing constitutional plurality into a perspective-based form of constitutional monism. Standard validity-based accounts of legal systems fail to recognize plurality given that, for these accounts, everything that is valid according to the system constitutes part of the legal system. In this chapter, alternative criteria of individuation are advanced and defended based on political reasons for individuating norms in a particular way, which presents an account of the individuation of legal systems more conducive to constitutional plurality than existing approaches.

Chapter 5 opens the second part of the book on our normative account of constitutional pluralism by exploring the different meanings which have been attributed to the idea of constitutionalism as a normative theory of legitimate governing authority in its history. This survey reveals how conceptual disagreement about the concept of constitutionalism betrays a disagreement about substantive values regarding what legitimate authority requires. Chapter 6 focuses on two particular problems associated with the concept of constitutionalism as

[73] Roughan (n 25) 69.

a normative theory of legitimate authority in the light of the plurality of constitutional values surveyed in the previous chapter. The first is a critique of the language of constitutionalism which questions the utility of constitutionalism as a normative theory of legitimate authority in the light of the considerable 'definitional conundrums'[74] which affect the concept. These conundrums reflect disagreement regarding the value of constitutionalism as normative theory which, in turn, potentially opens up a space among the resulting 'cacophony'[75] for the hegemonic capture of the language of constitutionalism to give a cover of legitimacy to otherwise illegitimate norms and structures. The second critique considered in this chapter, the 'illegitimacy' critique, questions the value of constitutionalism based on democratic considerations. It examines an influential seam of constitutional theory which critiques the tendency towards legal entrenchment and judicial supremacy in constitutional theorizing on democratic grounds, a trend which is amplified at the transnational level where the idea of 'new constitutionalism'[76] potentially oppresses and dominates democratic political communities.

Chapter 7 interrogates a further 'category error' critique of transnational constitutionalism as legitimacy based on the 'no demos' thesis. This well-known critique of constitutionalism beyond the state argues, at root, that transnational governance is not 'constitutionalism-apt' in the light of the significant social, institutional, and political *dis*analogies between the state and transnational level of governance. In particular the absence of a *demos* in the latter context, a key hallmark of legitimate authority in the state constitutional tradition, makes attempts to think of legitimate authority at transnational level in constitutional terms either 'oxymoronic'[77] or 'utopian'.[78] The chapter interrogates the latter charge of utopianism implicit in the 'no demos' critique of transnational constitutionalism, arguing that the question of idealism in normative theory is context-specific and contingent upon the purposes of our theorizing. It is not, therefore, a necessarily problematic feature of normative theory.

[74] Jeffrey L Dunoff and Joel P Trachtman, 'A Functional Approach to International Constitutionalization' in Jeffrey L Dunoff and Joel P Trachtman (eds), *Ruling the World?: Constitutionalism, International Law, and Global Governance* (Cambridge University Press 2009) 9.

[75] Cormac Mac Amhlaigh, 'Harmonising Global Constitutionalism' (2016) 5 Global Constitutionalism 173.

[76] Stephen Gill and A Claire Cutler (eds), *New Constitutionalism and World Order* (Cambridge University Press 2014).

[77] Loughlin, 'Constitutional Pluralism: An Oxymoron?' (n 54).

[78] Nico Krisch, 'Pouvoir Constituant and Pouvoir Irritant in the Postnational Order' (2016) 14 International Journal of Constitutional Law 657.

Our final chapter, Chapter 8, pulls together the different threads of the discussion on constitutionalism as a normative theory of legitimate authority in the previous chapters of this part of the book and attempts to address the various critiques to advance a normative theory of transnational constitutional pluralism. It takes as its starting point Dworkin's 'interpretive' approach to political value in the face of conceptual disagreement, arguing that it helps to makes sense of and improve the characterization of disagreement considered in the previous chapters around the political value of constitutionalism.[79] Taking an interpretive approach to conceptual disagreements surrounding the concept of constitutionalism as well as the question of whether it can be 'exported' to the 'foreign climate' of transnational law and governance shows how these disagreements are a form of disagreement about what legitimate authority requires, as well as reflecting concerns about problems of idealization in normative theory. It also, moreover, helps address these disagreements in a convincing way to provide a more substantive normative account of constitutional pluralism. It achieves this, in part, by resolving what it identifies as the 'first constitutional question' of constitutional theory: the resolution of its 'definitional conundrums' in a non-arbitrary way by focusing on the value of the concept in terms of legitimate governing authority. This helps answer the various critiques canvassed in the preceding chapters. With regard to the cacophony critique, an interpretivist approach brings our disagreement onto the 'same page' of a shared political value while simultaneously encouraging us to think of political value (such as constitutionalism) in holistic terms. Moreover, the holistic tendency in Dworkin's interpretivist approach to concepts of political value contains the basis for a resolution of the illegitimacy critiques of constitutionalism and transnational constitutionalism respectively, through the unity of value. The unity of value discourages accounts of political value based on 'lopsided' or 'partially' worked out normative theories which are, the chapter argues, the basis of the illegitimacy critique. Furthermore, with regard to the question of idealism in transnational constitutional pluralism, it argues that an interpretive conception of transnational constitutional pluralism tailored to the purposes of practical reasoning is not only feasible but can provide a useful approach to thinking about questions of legitimate authority under the circumstances of constitutional pluralism.

[79] Ronald Dworkin, 'Interpretive Concepts' in Ronald Dworkin, *Law's Empire* (Belknap Press 1986).

In conclusion, the aim of the current volume is to make a contribution to the field of pluralist constitutional theory by examining in detail some of the puzzles and problems associated with constitutional plurality and pluralism. The hope is that it will support further avenues of inquiry into the past, present, and future of constitutional theory in our evolving and increasingly challenging circumstances of constitutional pluralism.

PART I
LEGALITY

2

The Possibility of Constitutional Plurality

1. Introduction: Legal Theory's Plurality Problem

The Latin root *constitutio*, along with its Greek cognate concept *politea*, connote, as McIlwain argues, '*purely descriptive*'[1] terms encapsulating the 'legal framework'[2] of a society 'as it actually is'.[3] As a descriptive term, 'constitution' in our modern sense provides us with a concept with which to describe, understand, and explain extant forms of legal and political organization. This descriptive use of constitution, moreover, reflects broader and narrower approaches to legal and political organization.

The broader understanding, which has a stronger affinity with the Ancient Greek notion of *politea*, involves the idea of constitution as the 'natural frame of the state'[4] and can be very capacious indeed, including not only the basic norms of government but also the social and historical condition of a particular governing arrangement. Rather than constituting a 'code of rules' contained in a canonical written constitution, this broader notion of constitution, understood as a 'discourse of political right',[5] is presented, following Bolingbroke, as a 'set of rules, principles, canons, maxims, customs, usages, and manners that condition, sustain, and regulate the activity of governing the state'[6] through the '*conferral of authority and legitimacy on modern governmental ordering*'.[7] This capacious understanding of the idea of a constitution, as Loughlin explicitly notes, bleeds into the idea of a constitution as a feature of the legitimacy of authority, and particularly the political legitimacy of state authorities. We take up

[1] Charles McIlwain, *Constitutionalism: Ancient and Modern* (Liberty Fund 1947) 26, emphasis added.
[2] ibid 23.
[3] ibid 26.
[4] ibid 24.
[5] Martin Loughlin, *Foundations of Public Law* (Oxford University Press 2010) 10.
[6] ibid. 'By constitution we mean, whenever we speak with priority and exactness, that assemblage of laws, institutions and customs, derived from certain fixed principles of reason, erected to certain fixed objects of public good, that compose the general system, according to which the community hath agreed to be governed ... We call this a good government, when ... the whole administration of public affairs is wisely pursued, and with a strict conformity to the principles and objects of the constitution.' Bolingbroke, 'A Dissertation upon Parties (1733–43)', in *The Works of Lord Bolingbroke* (1841) II, p 88 cited in McIlwain (n 1), 2–3.
[7] Loughlin (n 5), 2, emphasis added.

New Constitutional Horizons. Cormac S. Mac Amhlaigh, Oxford University Press. © Cormac Mac Amhlaigh 2022.
DOI: 10.1093/oso/9780198852339.003.0002

the relationship between constitution and legitimacy in the second part of the book through the idea of *constitutionalism*. Rather, in thinking about constitutional plurality for current purposes we will focus on the narrower meaning of constitution as a descriptive account of the fundamental laws of a governing regime.

The narrower sense of constitution is arguably the most predominant in contemporary usage and reflects the tradition of constitutional thinking which equates a constitution with '*ius publicum*', that is the public law of the realm, and in particular, the fundamental laws of a governing regime.[8] Most modern definitions of constitution have tended to implicitly focus on this *ius publicum* sense of constitution. Thus, for example, AV Dicey's definition of a constitution as 'all rules which directly or indirectly affect the distribution or the exercise of the sovereign power in the state', including 'all rules which *define the members* of the sovereign power, all rules which *regulate the relation* of such members to each other, or which *determine the mode* in which sovereign power, or the members thereof, exercise their authority'[9] clearly captures this idea. Other accounts of a constitution express this *ius publicum* idea of a constitution in terms of the '*codes* of rules which aspire to regulate the allocation of functions, powers and duties among the various agencies and offices of government, and define the relationship between these and the public',[10] or 'the law that establishes and regulates the main organs of government, their constitution and powers, and *ipso facto* it includes law that establishes the general principles under which the country is governed: democracy, if it establishes democratic organs of government, federalism, if it establishes a federal structure, and so on.'[11]

This particular understanding of constitution involves an account of a variety of rules of governing based on a fundamental norm or norms providing the validity of all the other laws of a legal system.[12] On this view the term 'constitution' becomes the 'conceptual necessity of every legal system'.[13] As Gardner writes:[14]

[8] McIlwain (n 1), 24.

[9] Albert Venn Dicey, *Introduction to the Study of the Law of the Constitution* (3rd edn, Macmillan 1889) 22–23, emphasis added.

[10] Samuel E Finer, *Five Constitutions* (Humanities Press 1979) 15.

[11] Joseph Raz, 'On the Authority and Interpretation of Constitutions: Some Preliminaries' in Larry Alexander (ed), *Constitutionalism: Philosophical Foundations* (Cambridge University Press 1998) 324. Raz goes on to provide a list of common features of constitutions: they are constitutive of the organs and powers of governing organs, they are stable, they are canonical (usually written), they are superior law, they are justiciable, they are entrenched, and they express a common ideology. (324–25).

[12] Joseph Raz, *The Authority of Law* (2nd edn, Oxford University Press 2009) ch8, 'Legal Validity'.

[13] John Gardner, *Law as a Leap of Faith* (Oxford University Press 2012) 89.

[14] Gardner (n 13), emphasis added.

> In every legal system there are rules that specify the major institutions and officials of government, and determine which of them is to do what, and how they are to interact, and how their membership of succession is to be determined ... *These rules* without which there would be no legal system ... *make up the constitution of that system.*

In thinking about the idea of a constitution in terms of a valid legal system, and in particular the fundamental law of a legal system, legal theory offers us a variety of possibilities. Perhaps the most well-known are Kelsen's basic norm presupposed in relation to the 'historically first' constitution which provides successor constitutions, and the laws created under them with their validity;[15] Hart's account of secondary rules, and particularly a rule of recognition which contains the criteria of validity of other rules of the legal system;[16] or Raz's expansion of Hart's account involving a possible plurality of rules of recognition.[17] What all these accounts have in common is the idea of a constitution in this descriptive *ius publicum* sense founding the validity of the norms of a legal system. In this respect, as Kelsen argues, the 'function' of a constitution is the 'grounding of [the] validity'[18] of law.

The simple conjunction of constitution and legal system belies a series of further questions, particularly relating to constitutional plurality; for example, whether the idea of legal validity is sufficient to account for constitutional plurality in the form of distinct, individuated legal systems.[19] However, prior to addressing those more specific questions, in focusing on the idea of a 'constitution' in terms of the concept of a legal system as advanced by analytical legal theory to get our analysis of constitutional plurality off the ground, we encounter an initial 'threshold' objection. This objection takes the form of a trenchant critique of these analytical accounts of legal system from legal pluralists.[20] In summary, the critique of legal theory's 'plurality problem' involves the idea that analytical accounts of law are obsessed with the idea of law being made up of individual laws or norms, connected together through a chain of

[15] Hans Kelsen, *General Theory of Law and State* (Anders Wedberg tr, Harvard University Press 1945) 115.

[16] HLA Hart, *The Concept of Law* (Joseph Raz and Penelope Bulloch eds, 2nd edn, Clarendon Press 1994).

[17] Joseph Raz, *The Concept of a Legal System: An Introduction to the Theory of a Legal System* (Oxford University Press 1980).

[18] Hans Kelsen, 'The Function of a Constitution' in Richard Tur and William Twining (eds), *Essays on Kelsen* (Clarendon Press 1986) 199.

[19] Raz, *The Authority of Law* (n 12). See further Chapter 4.

[20] Which Roberts described in terms of 'a rude, in-your-face, mocking assault on what was presented as a blindly self-absorbed condition ("a kind of legal Ptolmaism").' Simon Roberts, 'After Government? On Representing Law Without the State' (2005) 68 Modern Law Review 1, 11.

validity, and ultimately traceable to a single source of validity whether it is a sovereign,[21] a basic norm,[22] or a social rule of recognition,[23] which is necessarily ultimate in that it is not reliant on another, external, source for its validity. Legal pluralists complain that while this may account for some of the prominent features of *state* law, it cannot be exhaustive of the category of law more generally because many of the types of law experienced in the world do not meet several, or even any, of these criteria. This challenge to legal theory has been given a renewed vigour in the context which forms the focus of the current volume: transnational legal plurality.[24] As with their anthropological forebears, these 'third wave' critiques, primarily, but not exclusively from more sociological approaches to law, continue to criticize legal theory for its 'plurality problem' which renders it incapable of documenting, analysing, and addressing the novel challenges and puzzles posed by the circumstances of constitutional pluralism.[25]

This chapter therefore explores whether, in attempting to theorize a constitutional plurality with the tools of analytical legal theory, we find ourselves in the position of the proverbial driver who, upon asking a local the best way to get to a particular destination, receives the reply, 'I wouldn't start from here'. It interrogates the allegation of legal theory's 'plurality problem' by breaking down the general critique launched by legal pluralism into three, more specific, claims: two attributed to legal theory by legal pluralists (a strong and an intermediate claim), and one made by legal pluralists about legal theory (a weak claim). The first (the strong claim) is that legal theory assumes that all law is, ultimately, reducible to state law; the second (the intermediate claim) is that while legal theory may accept that other forms of law can exist, it implicitly assumes that state law is the 'best' or 'paradigmatic' form of law; and the third (the weak claim) is that legal theory has neglected analysis of non-state law. The chapter locates each of the distinct claims within the general legal pluralist literature and reviews key ideas or works in the legal theory canon most relevant to the claim to assess the extent to which each claim can be said to be true of legal theory. Reviewing each specific claim as well as its corresponding idea in legal theory reveals, the chapter concludes, that if legal theory does have a

[21] John Austin, *Austin: The Province of Jurisprudence Determined* (Wilfrid E Rumble ed, Cambridge University Press 1995).

[22] Kelsen, *General Theory of Law and State* (n 15), x.

[23] Hart (n 16), 110.

[24] Ralf Michaels, 'Global Legal Pluralism' (2009) 5 Annual Review of Law and Social Science 243, 245.

[25] Brian Z Tamanaha, *A Realistic Theory of Law* (Cambridge University Press 2017); William Twining, *General Jurisprudence: Understanding Law from a Global Perspective* (Cambridge University Press 2009); Michael Giudice and Keith Culver, *Legality's Borders: An Essay in General Jurisprudence* (Oxford University Press 2010).

plurality problem, and there is some evidence that it may, it is not a particularly serious one. It argues that most of the resources of analytical legal theory can capture and account for most of the phenomenon that legal pluralists wish to emphasize, particularly 'third wave' pluralists, and that at any rate, legal theory itself has become much more aware of the need to think about non-state law than it has done in the past. As such, the tools of legal theory provide a promising point of departure for the development of a pluralist constitutional theory which responds to the circumstances of constitutional pluralism.

2. Approaching Legal Theory's Plurality Problem

Contemporary legal pluralism emerged from work of legal anthropologists in post-colonial such as Malawi, Zambia,[26] and Papua New Guinea[27] where they discovered that the social reality of such societies was not the simple monistic model of law and legal system where all law was ultimately traceable to one source in the state but was, rather, pluralistic, commonly defined as a situation where two or more legal systems coexist in the same social field.[28] This early engagement with legal pluralism in legal discourse has been identified as a 'first wave' of legal pluralism in legal scholarship which subsequently gave way to a second, sociological 'wave' of legal pluralism where the emphasis shifted from the multiple normative orderings of non-Western post-colonial societies to the contemporary societies of industrialized states.[29] Here, legal pluralism was not limited to the coexistence of indigenous law and imposed colonial law but extended to a variety of different legal forms such as those of clubs, associations, gangs, workplaces, and commercial relationships.[30] More recently still, we are experiencing a 'third wave' of legal pluralism corresponding with the circumstances of constitutional pluralism. Perhaps more than the other two waves of legal pluralism, this third wave presents a more pressing challenge to state-based accounts of law given that it involves forms of law which ape

[26] Martin Chanock, *Law, Custom and Social Order: The Colonial Experience in Malawi and Zambia* (Cambridge University Press 1985).

[27] Leopold Pospisil, *Kapauku Papuans and Their Law* (Yale University Press 1958).

[28] Sally Engle Merry, 'Legal Pluralism' (1988) 22 Law & Society Review 869, 872. For a contemporary account, see Alex Green and Jennifer Hendry, 'Non-Positivist Legal Pluralism and Crises of Legitimacy in Settler-States' (2020) 14 Journal of Comparative Law 267.

[29] What Merry writing in the 1980s called the 'new legal pluralism'. Merry (n 28), 872. See also Gunther Teubner, 'The Two Faces of Janus: Rethinking Legal Pluralism Closed Systems and Open Justice: The Legal Sociology of Niklas Luhmann' (1992) 13 Cardozo Law Review 1443.

[30] Teubner (n 29). See also Sally Falk Moore, 'Law and Social Change: The Semi-Autonomous Social Field as an Appropriate Subject of Study' (1973) 7 Law & Society Review 719.

to a considerable degree the laws of states, resulting in a direct challenge to the supremacy and comprehensiveness of state law.[31] Previous waves of legal pluralism tended to juxtapose state law with other kinds of law such as indigenous law or social customs or practices which could be dismissed by some as either not law, or what John Griffiths called 'weak pluralism':[32] forms of law whose status as law depended on their being 'tolerated' as such by the state and therefore being ultimately subject to it.[33] However, the challenges of the circumstances of constitutional pluralism are thrown into sharp relief by the coexistence of types of law that, when compared with other forms of legal pluralism, seem to replicate to a considerable degree the hallmarks of official state law including a systemic nature, a hierarchy of norms, claims to authority and supremacy, and robust and developed institutional structures such as those that exist at transnational level.[34]

In this chapter we will examine the extent to which this 'third wave' plurality in particular requires substantial revisions and adaptation of (primarily state-based) legal theory to reflect the new realities of globalization and transnationalism. It argues that the extent of the necessary revision of the legal-theoretical toolkit to capture these realities will be determined by the seriousness of its plurality problem. If the problem is not particularly serious, then minor adjustments would be in order; if more serious, a more radical overhaul might be required to address the circumstances of constitutional pluralism.[35] In order to determine how serious it is, the chapter parses the more general critique into the three more specific claims outlined earlier: the strong, intermediate,

[31] See, for example, Cormac Mac Amhlaigh, 'Concepts of Law in Integration Through Law' in Daniel Augentstein (ed), *'Integration through Law' Revisited: The Making of the European Polity* (Routledge 2012).

[32] John Griffiths, 'What Is Legal Pluralism?' (1986) 18 Journal of Legal Pluralism and Unofficial Law 1, 5.

[33] Griffiths (n 32).

[34] See, for example, in the EU context, Justin Lindeboom, 'Why EU Law Claims Supremacy' (2018) 38 Oxford Journal of Legal Studies 328.

[35] Existing contemporary approaches are divided on the question of how radical legal theory needs to be in revising its conceptions of law to address the circumstances of constitutional pluralism. MacCormick, for example, proposes a modestly revised Hartian account of law in his account of 'institutional normative order' to account of plurality. See Neil MacCormick, *Questioning Sovereignty: Law, State and Nation in the European Commonwealth* (Oxford University Press 1999); Neil MacCormick, 'Beyond the Sovereign State?' (1993) 56 The Modern Law Review 1. Others, such as Tamanaha and Culver and Giudice to be discussed in detail further 44–50, propose more radical reconstructions of legal theoretical conceptions of law to address the questions of legal plurality. For example, Tamanaha's pluralist-friendly 'folk conception'—where law is whatever social groups see as 'law'—represents a particularly radical departure from his initial Hartian starting point. Brian Z Tamanaha, *A General Jurisprudence of Law and Society* (Oxford University Press 2001). Similarly, Culver and Giudice's 'inter-institutional legality' is in stark contrast with the Razian conception of legal system upon which it is based, not least in its rejection of the systemic nature of law. See Giudice and Culver (n 25), ch5, 'An Inter-Institutional Account of Non-State Legality'.

and weak claims. In order to appraise these claims individually, however, two more aspects of the approach taken here require further clarification; first, clarifying what we mean by 'analytical legal theory' and secondly, the way in which the claims surrounding legal theory's 'plurality problem' will be tested. With respect to the definitional question, defining the different categories of jurisprudence, legal theory, and legal philosophy is one that has spawned its own literature and is not a debate with which we will engage in here.[36] Here the generic label 'legal theory' will be employed to capture what Twining calls 'Anglo-American jurisprudence'[37] which has traditionally been concerned with the central question of general jurisprudence: the nature of law.[38] This focus on the 'Anglo-American' jurisprudential tradition is explained both by reasons of practicality but also because it is the main target of the legal pluralist challenge.[39]

Of course, as Twining (a prominent pluralist and critic of the canon) notes, even limiting 'legal theory' to the primary voices in the tradition presents its own problems of selection given its 'extent and diversity'[40]. In this tradition, Twining notes, '[t]exts and authors become 'canonised' partly on perceived merit, but as often as not arbitrarily'[41] where '[i]nertia, fashion, ideology, power, self-promotion, and serendipity'[42] influence the choices that are made. However, notwithstanding these problems, he recognizes that 'surveys of jurisprudence courses'[43] and 'statistics of citation'[44] do converge on 'a fairly consistent shortlist of individual authors who are widely read and studied at any given time'[45] such that a 'mainstream and something approaching a canonical core'[46] does exist. It is this 'mainstream' or 'canonical core' which will serve as a basis of the generic label of 'legal theory' for the purposes of the current volume.[47] As such, the primary legal theorists under consideration here

[36] William A Edmundson, 'Introduction' in Martin P Golding and William A Edmundson (eds), *The Blackwell Guide to the Philosophy of Law and Legal Theory* (Wiley 2005).
[37] Twining (n 25), 11.
[38] See Andrei Marmor and Alexander Sarch, 'The Nature of Law' in Edward N Zalta (ed), *The Stanford Encyclopedia of Philosophy* (Fall 2019, Metaphysics Research Lab, Stanford University 2019) <https://plato.stanford.edu/archives/fall2019/entries/lawphil-nature/>, which perhaps tellingly doesn't refer to legal pluralism at all.
[39] Griffiths, for example, specifically targets Bodin, Hobbes, Austin, Kelsen, and Hart. Griffiths (n 32), 3.
[40] Twining (n 25), 11.
[41] Twining (n 25).
[42] ibid.
[43] ibid.
[44] ibid.
[45] ibid.
[46] ibid.
[47] Including in Chapters 3 and 4.

include those conventionally identified as analytical legal positivists such as Hans Kelsen, HLA Hart, Joseph Raz, Jeremy Waldron, and Neil MacCormick. However, given that the putative 'ideology of legal centralism' expands beyond the positivist credo, here non-positivists such as Lon Fuller and Ronald Dworkin are also included in the canon.[48] Moreover, the 'principle of selection' of which authors or works within that core form the basis of analysis will be determined, for the current chapter, by the extent to which a member of the canon is an explicit target of legal pluralists or the extent to which their work approximates or best illustrates one of the three claims entailed in legal theory's plurality problem. In the ensuing chapters, the 'principle of selection' is based on the extent to which a particular theorist within the canon has considered in depth the problems associated with a pluralist conception of law and legal system.

3. Reporting Legal Theory's Plurality Problem

This section will review the literature on legal pluralism to see how each of the three specific claims—that all law is state law, that state law is the best form of law, or that legal theory has neglected non-state forms of law—is made in legal pluralist literature. Each claim will be taken in turn, beginning with the strong claim.

3.1 The Strong Claim: All Law Is State Law

With regard to the strong claim, the idea here is that conceptually all law necessarily refers to the law of states. Perhaps the clearest version of the charge against legal theory by legal pluralism is made by John Griffiths, one of the protagonists in the legal pluralist critique of legal theory.[49] In an important contribution to the debate, he argued that a central tenet of legal theory's 'ideology of legal centralism' was the idea that 'law is and should be the law of the state, uniform for all persons, exclusive of all other law, and administered by a single set of state institutions'.[50] As an ideology, Griffiths argues, it makes a 'mixture of assertions'[51] about 'how the world ought to be and *a priori* assumptions about

[48] See also Chapter 4.
[49] Griffiths (n 32), 1.
[50] ibid 3.
[51] Griffiths (n 32).

how it actually and even necessarily is',[52] a central premise of which being that the 'factual power of the state'[53] provides the 'keystone'[54] of a normative system and therefore affords the empirical condition for the actual existence of 'law'.[55] This, for Griffiths, creates a necessary connection between the concept of law as a 'single, unified and exclusive hierarchical normative ordering'[56] and the state as the 'fundamental unit of political organisation.'[57] The problem with this, Griffiths maintains, is that the reality of law is an 'unsystematic collage of inconsistent and overlapping parts, lending itself to no easy legal interpretation'[58] very unlike the picture painted by the legal centralism of legal theory. As such, Griffiths concludes that '[l]egal centralism is a myth, an ideal, a claim, an illusion'[59] while 'legal pluralism is the fact'[60] such that 'not all law is state law nor administered by a single set of state institutions'.[61]

3.2 The Intermediate Claim: State Law Is The Paradigm of The Concept of Law

The intermediate claim that state law is the paradigm of the concept of law essentially holds that in conceptual terms state law is the 'center against which the periphery is modelled and evaluated'.[62] Thus, the intermediate claim recognizes that other types of law and even legal systems may exist, such as customary law, international law, or even less formal normative orders, however state law remains the benchmark against which other forms of law and legal orderings are to be measured.[63] Two recent interventions in the context of 'third wave' pluralism make the intermediate claim directly: Brian Tamanaha's critique of legal theory's claims about the nature of law, and Keith Culver and Michael Giudice's critique of 'bootstrapping' in legal theory.

For Tamanaha, the version of the intermediate claim that state law is a paradigm or the 'epitome'[64] of law is clear, not from explicit statements to that effect

[52] ibid.
[53] ibid.
[54] ibid.
[55] ibid.
[56] ibid.
[57] ibid.
[58] ibid 4.
[59] Griffiths (n 32).
[60] ibid.
[61] ibid 5.
[62] Martha-Marie Kleinhans and Roderick A Macdonald, 'What Is a Critical Legal Pluralism?' (1997) 12 Canadian Journal of Law and Society 25, 39.
[63] Griffiths (n 32), 5.
[64] Tamanaha (n 25), 92.

but rather in the methodology legal theory adopts in developing its theories of law and legal system. In adopting the methodologies of analytical philosophy, Tamanaha argues, conventional legal theory heavily and surreptitiously loads the dice in favour of state law in its general approach to theorizing law.[65] This is clear in the assertions of legal theorists that law is a natural kind like water as opposed to a social construction which is 'contingent on and shaped by human subjectivity and purposes'[66] as well as in the fact that legal theory makes universal truth claims about law drawn from explicitly parochial concepts where the statist bias of the parochial conception becomes 'entrenched in the theory of law produced'[67] and its 'parochial source'[68] is 'concealed in elaborate philosophical clothing'.[69] However the key feature of legal theory in terms of the intermediate claim for Tamanaha is the fact that it insists upon the fact that the nature of law is grounded in an *a priori* conception[70] and the fact that legal theory is not explicit about the 'dataset' which makes up that conception.[71] The fact that knowledge about law in legal theory stems from the pre-theoretical formulation of the definition of law rather than our empirical experience of it is an error, Tamanaha argues, because law is necessarily an *a posteriori* concept; that is, that knowledge of law stems primarily from the empirical experience of the phenomenon as practised in a particular society.[72] As an *a posteriori* concept, law does not lend itself to neat *a priori* definitions akin, for example, to geometric shapes.[73] Tamanaha contends that this is supported by the fact that the concept of law is deeply disputed within legal theory itself.[74] Given that the knowledge gained from the experience of law is diffuse, different experiences of law lead to different definitions and therefore contestation surrounding the concept itself. Furthermore, the assumptions or 'dataset' relied upon by legal theory in order to develop *a priori* concepts of law are merely assumed rather than justified.[75] That is, legal theory rarely, if ever, reveals what is included in the 'pre-theoretical understandings' which lead to their concepts of law nor the criteria for inclusion and exclusion of particular data into the set. This is

[65] Tamanaha does, however, believe, like Culver and Giudice (n 25), that analytical legal theory can provide a useful starting point for thinking about law in a pluralist way. However, it needs to undergo a quite dramatic reconstruction to make it adaptable to considering legal pluralism. Tamanaha (n 35).
[66] Tamanaha (n 25), 59.
[67] ibid 67.
[68] ibid.
[69] ibid.
[70] ibid 62–65.
[71] ibid 71–73.
[72] ibid 62.
[73] ibid.
[74] ibid 63.
[75] ibid 71.

problematic, Tamanaha argues, because different datasets of the experience of law will result in different accounts of the nature of law. As such, where the criteria for inclusion are not made explicit, the data included in pre-theoretical conceptions of law runs the risk of being arbitrarily included. Tamanaha contends that legal theory in particular, has arbitrarily included in its pre-theoretical dataset the key elements of state law creating a path-dependency between this pre-theoretical understanding and state law being a paradigm or central case of law. He argues, for example, that Hart's union of primary and secondary rules was an 'abstraction' devised after 'stripping away what [Hart] considered nonessential to the concept of *state* law'.[76] More generally, legal theorists make mere 'assertions about what lawyers or educated people think law is—*invariably state law*—without considering that people might hold other concepts of law as well'.[77] Thus, Tamanaha concludes with a clear statement of the intermediate claim:

> Proceeding on the assumption that state law is the paradigm form of law, various analytical jurisprudents assert law is unified and systematic (Hart), claims supreme legitimate authority (Raz), and solves complex moral problems (Shapiro). They do not contemplate that state law as they portray it is exceptional. Many legal systems past and present are contrary to the essential features identified by these theories of law.[78]

In a similar vein, Culver and Giudice critique legal theory for failing to capture the novel legal phenomena introduced by legal globalization and legal transnationalism due to its statist bias. This, they argue, is inexcusable in the contemporary world where a multitude of 'legalities' coexist with the state form including intra-state legality (complex forms of distributed governance within a state), trans-state legality (legal institutions established by state governments operating outwith the state but binding their citizens), supra-state legality (complex law-based governing arrangements operating at the supra-state level such as the European Union), and super-state legality (universally applicable norms such as *ius cogens* norms). To the extent that conventional legal theoretical accounts of law engage with novel normative phenomena, it holds the view that they are legal only 'to the extent that (i) they share the

[76] ibid 63.
[77] ibid 71, emphasis added.
[78] ibid 79.

characteristic features of state law or (ii) are in some way actually supported by or connected to state practice or recognition'.[79]

Like Tamanaha, Culver and Giudice identify methodological issues with the ways in which legal theory has approached the question of the nature of law, thus leading to its statist bias. Legal theory—at least in the Hartian tradition—usually claims to develop a (general) conception of law and legal systems from relevant empirical data; that is, empirical observations regarding practices of rule-following and subjection to authority. However, the resulting theories, Culver and Giudice maintain, are 'bootstrapped'[80] in that the concepts and theories of law do not obviously follow from the complex empirical realities upon which they are based.[81] Legal theoretical concepts of law result, they contend, not from the social realities of normative phenomena in all their complexity but from a 'few readily available examples of legality and law-states—or in Raz's case 'all intuitively clear' instances of *municipal* legal systems'.[82] The way in which concepts of law have been bootstrapped, then, has created an unwarranted statist bias in the concept of law, making 'the experience of the law-state'[83] the '*standard and measure of legality*'.[84] In claiming a statist bias in legal theory along the lines of the intermediate claim, Culver and Giudice even attack MacCormick's account of law as institutional normative order on the grounds that it, too, betrays an unwarranted statist bias.[85] This may seem surprising in the light of the fact that MacCormick saw the pluralist potential in legal theories such as that of Hart as well as the fact that MacCormick's account of law as institutional normative order explicitly embraced many types of non-state normative ordering.[86] They acknowledge that MacCormick's 'comparatively broader'[87] account of law as institutional normative order could succeed 'where Hart's and Raz's theories did not, addressing a broader range of phenomena using a broader range of explanatory categories while attending to the law-state at the same time'.[88] However, for Culver and Giudice, MacCormick's account also betrays a statist bias given that his focus is primarily on legal orders which ape to a considerable extent the law of states such as that of the

[79] Giudice and Culver (n 25), xxiv.
[80] ibid 81.
[81] ibid xxx.
[82] ibid 90.
[83] ibid xxiii.
[84] Giudice and Culver (n 25).
[85] ibid 95.
[86] MacCormick, *Questioning Sovereignty: Law, State and Nation in the European Commonwealth* (n 35), ch1, 'The Legal Framework: Institutional Normative Order'.
[87] Giudice and Culver (n 25), 97.
[88] ibid.

European Union, as well as, more problematically, his insistence on the systemic nature of law.[89] In relying particularly on the concept of system in his account of law as institutional normative order, they argue that his account also betrays an 'epistemological priority of state law'[90] and therefore an '*accidental* re-emphasis of the law-state as the mark and measure of legality'.[91]

3.3 The Weak Claim: Legal Theory Has Neglected Non-State Forms of Law

As a claim about legal scholarship and theorizing about law, the weak claim has a distinguished pedigree. For example, Eugene Ehrlich, writing in 1912, lamented the 'tragic fate of juristic science' and its devotion 'exclusively to state law'.[92] In more recent times, however, William Twining has provided a particularly pithy critique of legal theory based on the third claim.[93]

Twining argues that 'academic law'[94] has been obsessed with state law for over 150 years both in the Anglophone legal world as well as in continental Europe.[95] He berates Anglo-American legal theory in particular, for employing what he dubs its 'country and Western'[96] attitude of thinking almost exclusively about state law and the law of Western states at that, while 'only exceptionally'[97] looking at the rich variety of law and legal orders which exist in the world, including religious laws such as Hindu, Jewish, or Islamic law as well as non-Western legal traditions.[98]

More specifically, he accuses the legal theory tradition[99] of being 'narrow and parochial'[100] on three main grounds.[101] First, he argues that nearly all Anglo-American legal theorists, 'including those who claim to be doing general

[89] ibid 97–98.

[90] ibid 98.

[91] ibid 99. They therefore propose a radical overhaul of the concepts of law advanced by Hart and Raz in the form of inter-institutional legality, one which rejects a necessary connection between the concept of law and system. See 44–50.

[92] Eugen Ehrlich, *Fundamental Principles of the Sociology of Law* (Russell and Russell 1936) 13, 13.

[93] See William Twining, *Globalisation and Legal Theory* (Cambridge University Press 2000); Twining (n 25). The references here refer to the latter work.

[94] ibid 16.

[95] ibid 17.

[96] ibid 10.

[97] ibid 16.

[98] The 'few exceptions' Twining identifies are Ehrlich, Maine, and Llewellyn who are 'generally treated as marginal'. ibid 17.

[99] In which he includes 'canonical jurists' including Bentham, Austin, Dworkin, Raz, and Duncan Kennedy. ibid, 16–17.

[100] ibid 11.

[101] ibid.

jurisprudence',[102] work almost exclusively in the Western legal tradition. One of the primary self-understandings of this tradition, Twining notes, is its resolute secularism. To the extent that it does engage with religious traditions, it engages almost exclusively with Christianity, ignoring a rich global heritage of non-Western religious legal cultures and traditions.[103] Furthermore, and central to the weak claim, Twining argues that '*almost all of Western jurisprudence has focused on state law, especially the domestic (municipal) law of sovereign, industrialised nation states*'.[104] Hart is identified as a dominant figure in this tradition, and while Twining accepts that his conception of law is 'still useful in analysing the predominant legal orders of modern nation states',[105] it fares less well in considering other forms of law. It falls short, Twining argues, with respect to giving an account of custom, religious law, or 'normative orderings emerging from self-regulation or commercial practice',[106] as well as in accounting for the interactions between state and supra-state legal orders. Finally, Twining argues that Anglo-American jurisprudence suffers from a deficient agenda; that is that the problems and issues on which it has tended to concern itself are narrow and far removed from vast swathes of the legal experiences of most of the population of the globe.[107]

In short, he argues that the Anglo-American jurisprudential tradition is collectively open to charges of 'myopia, ignorance, parochialism, and irrelevance'[108] primarily due to its obsessive focus on state forms of law and legal ordering.

4. Locating Legal Theory's Plurality Problem

In this section, the key targets of legal pluralists, both specific authors and ideas, will be examined and appraised to assess the extent to which each claim is warranted. While it does not provide an exhaustive study of each idea or work, it provides, it is submitted, an analysis of sufficient detail to address the claim advanced by legal pluralists about legal theory and to permit preliminary conclusions as to whether the problems are serious enough to require radical revision of the concepts of law advanced by the legal theory canon.

[102] ibid 11.
[103] ibid.
[104] ibid 12, emphasis added.
[105] ibid.
[106] ibid 12.
[107] ibid.
[108] ibid 12.

4.1 Analysing the Strong Claim: Kelsen and the Unity and Identity Theses

Hans Kelsen is arguably the author in the legal theory canon whose work comes closest to resembling the first claim that all law is necessarily state law. This can be seen perhaps most obviously in his famous 'identity thesis'—that the state is nothing more than its legal system—but it is also discernible implicitly in his 'unity thesis' regarding the unity of state law and international law.

Kelsen develops his 'identity thesis' against the backdrop of 'dualist' conceptions of the state advanced by, for example, Georg Jellinek, who posited that the state was made up of two components, a legal system and a political collective.[109] Kelsen's theory of state was explicitly aimed at debunking this popular dualist myth. The core claim of the identity thesis is that the concept of the state is nothing more than its legal system.[110] For Kelsen, sociologically speaking, associations don't exist, people exist.[111] What makes associations possible is the fact that we *impute* the acts of individuals to the association through the legal system.[112] In the context of the state, our ability to impute sociological acts taken by the state such as authorizing, prohibiting, apprehending, imprisoning, even killing, exists by virtue of the law and the legal system of the state.[113] Thus, in terms of the strong claim, the idea that the state is nothing more than its legal system seems to provide an example *par excellence* of the claim that all law is ultimately state law.

The second of Kelsen's key theses about law—the unity thesis—similarly seems to support the contention that Kelsen defended the strong view. The unity thesis—which entails the idea that state law and international law are part of one and the same system—comes in two forms: the primacy of international law and the primacy of state law.[114] The difference between them relates to the

[109] Hans Kelsen, *Introduction to the Problems of Legal Theory: A Translation of the First Edition of the Reine Rechtslehre, or, Pure Theory of Law* (Bonnie Litschewski Paulson and Stanley L Paulson eds, Clarendon Press 1992) 97.

[110] 'The state *qua* subject of the acts of state, which is really the state *qua* person, is nothing other than the personification of a system that, as a legal system, is a coercive system; and it is precisely as this coercive system alone that the state can be comprehended.' ibid 101.

[111] Alexander Somek, 'Stateless Law: Kelsen's Conception and Its Limits' (2006) 26 Oxford Journal of Legal Studies 753, 757.

[112] Kelsen, *Introduction to the Problems of Legal Theory: A Translation of the First Edition of the Reine Rechtslehre, or, Pure Theory of Law* (n 109), 101.

[113] 'All of the external displays in which on traditionally perceives the power of the state—the prisons and fortresses, the gallows and machine guns—all of these are in and of themselves lifeless objects. They become tools of state power only in so far as human beings make use of them in accordance with a certain system, only in so far as these human beings are governed by the notion of this system, by the belief that they ought to act in conformity with this system.' ibid 104.

[114] For further consideration of Kelsen's account of international law as a legal system, see Chapter 3.

viewpoint from which the relationship is observed. The unitary legal system can be observed from the viewpoint of international law, meaning that it enjoys primacy over state law, or from the viewpoint of state law, giving it primacy over international law. For Kelsen, the viewpoint from which the relationship is observed is a 'matter of political ideology, not law'[115] and is guided by 'ethical and political considerations'.[116] However, this does not change the basic idea that they are both part of a single legal system such that 'the legal rights and obligations of states and individuals remain the same whichever of the two alternative systems is adopted'.[117] The unity thesis is explicitly presented by Kelsen as a refutation of '*pluralistic*'[118] theories of law and in particular, the positing of state law and international law as two distinct legal systems.[119] With regard to the strong claim being considered here, if it is the case that state law and international law are all part of the same system, then clearly all law is, in some sense, state law. This can be the case directly, if the relationship is viewed from the viewpoint of the state resulting in the primacy of state law, or indirectly, if the relationship is viewed from the viewpoint of international law resulting in the primacy of international law. (Of course, this also entails the idea that all law is necessarily also international law.) As such, it would appear that the unity thesis also provides further support to the contention that Kelsen supported the strong claim.

However, on closer inspection, it is not clear that either of these core tenets of Kelsen's concept of law support the strong claim, or at least preclude legal pluralism in a substantive sense. With regard to the identity thesis, *prima facie*, it appears to be the clearest statement of the strong claim to be found in legal theory.[120] If it is the case that the state is nothing more than its legal system, then this seems to suggest that the only legal systems that can exist are state legal systems (or at least state legal systems as entailed by the unified legal system of state law and international law when combined with the unity thesis). Significantly for present purposes, it emphatically excludes all the types of normative phenomena and normative ordering which legal pluralists wish to emphasize. However, this interpretation does not necessarily follow from Kelsen's view of the relationship between the state and its legal system.

[115] HLA Hart, *Essays in Jurisprudence and Philosophy* (Oxford University Press 1983) 312. See also Kelsen, *General Theory of Law and State* (n 15), 388.

[116] Hart (n 115), 312.

[117] ibid.

[118] Kelsen, *General Theory of Law and State* (n 15), 363.

[119] ibid 363–64. See also Kelsen, *Introduction to the Problems of Legal Theory: A Translation of the First Edition of the Reine Rechtslehre, or, Pure Theory of Law* (n 109), 328–29.

[120] With the possible exception of Austin's sovereign-based account of law. Austin (n 21).

The claim that the state is nothing more than its legal system does not rule out the possibility that other types of law and legal system can and do exist. This is because it can be interpreted as a claim about the concept of the *state* rather than the concept of *law* more generally. This is supported by the context within which the thesis was developed: as a critique of sociological accounts of the state as a social actor. In contending that the state is nothing other than its legal system, Kelsen does not make the related claim that the concept of law is necessarily the concept of state law. In fact, elsewhere in his discussion of the relationship between law and state he explicitly acknowledges that other types of law and legal system *can* and *do* exist.[121] He explicitly recognizes that 'not every legal system, ... is characterized as a state',[122] explaining that this characterization only holds when certain organs and functions form part of the legal system. However, other types of legal systems can exist such as those of a 'primitive, pre-state legal community'[123] where general norms evolve as part of custom. The lack of institutions and offices for enforcing norms through coercive means does not mean that these norms are not legal norms nor their systems legal systems. By contrast with state-based communities, the coercive element of enforcement in such systems is privatized in that the determination of the violation of legal norms and their consequences are left up to those whose interests have been violated.[124] In undertaking acts of interpretation and enforcement of legal norms, the members of such communities are 'acting as organs of the legal system and of the community constituted by that system'.[125] On this basis, he draws a distinction between different types of legal norms and legal systems, based on their methods of enforcement. 'Primitive' legal systems are decentralized, in that the enforcement of their norms in cases of violation are decentralized to the interested parties to the case.[126] More 'developed' legal systems, such as state legal systems, have centralized enforcement mechanisms with bureaucracies and specialized organs and agencies to determine cases of breach and determine and apply the consequences of violations of the norms of the system.[127] The distinction between more and less developed legal systems

[121] Kelsen, *Introduction to the Problems of Legal Theory: A Translation of the First Edition of the Reine Rechtslehre, or, Pure Theory of Law* (n 109), 99.

[122] ibid.

[123] ibid.

[124] ibid.

[125] ibid.

[126] For a critique of the association between 'primitive' and non-Western legal orders see Patrick Capps, 'International Legal Positivism and Modern Natural Law' in Jörg Kammerhofer and Jean D'Aspremont (eds), *International Legal Positivism in a Post-Modern World* (Cambridge University Press 2014).

[127] Kelsen, *Introduction to the Problems of Legal Theory: A Translation of the First Edition of the Reine Rechtslehre, or, Pure Theory of Law* (n 109), 100.

as distinguished by their methods of enforcement, is, Kelsen explicitly states, therefore *quantitative* and *not* qualitative;[128] while their methods of enforcement may differ, they are both undoubtedly types of law.

What of the unity thesis? The unity thesis seems to lead to the strong claim in that it objects to laws and their validity being severed into different systems—even minimally into state law and international law—as a logical impossibility. This is the result of an 'epistemological postulate'[129] adopted by jurisprudence which, in trying to 'present its object as a unity',[130] subsumes state law and international law 'under one and the same category of law'.[131] As such, the unity thesis is an explicitly anti-pluralist thesis. However, it is also possible to interpret the unity thesis in a more pluralist-friendly way. Even if it is the case for Kelsen that jurisprudence cognizes only one category—unitary valid law—whose existence is determined through presuppositions such as the basic norm,[132] this view is not necessarily incompatible with the types of normative phenomena which legal pluralists wish to emphasize. Whereas Kelsen limits his discussion on the unity thesis to international law and state law, there is nothing in principle precluding the extension of this to other forms of normative orderings including religious laws, customary laws, indigenous laws, and social laws, among others. This would simply require an augmentation of the viewpoints or 'poles' from which the single unitary legal system is observed.[133] Thus, rather than positing a simple bi-polar model of perspectives on the unitary legal system—state law and international law—the model could be augmented to include multi-polar perspectives on the unitary legal system, where it could be observed from the perspective of indigenous law, religious law, or transnational law, a move which, in the light of Kelsen's explicit acceptance of non-state legal systems shouldn't prove to be too problematic.

Moreover, this move is wholly compatible with the politics of observation of the unitary legal system. As noted earlier, Kelsen argued that the viewpoint from which the system is viewed is one of 'political preference'[134] and not dictated by 'the science of law'.[135] Thus, a refusal to expand the poles from which to observe the legal system to indigenous law or religious law could be criticized,

[128] ibid.

[129] Hart (n 115), 322.

[130] Hans Kelsen, *Pure Theory of Law* (University of California Press 1967) 328.

[131] ibid. See further Chapter 3.

[132] Kelsen, *General Theory of Law and State* (n 15), 115.

[133] For an example which includes EU law as a potential third type of law alongside international law and state law, see Catherine Richmond, 'Preserving the Identity Crisis: Autonomy, System and Sovereignty in European Law' (1997) 16 Law and Philosophy 377.

[134] Kelsen, *General Theory of Law and State* (n 15), 388.

[135] ibid.

on Kelsenian grounds, as a form of political ideology, and in particular an unwarranted 'dominant ideology' of state law. The Kelsenian model of the unitary legal system, and particularly the politics of the observation of the system, need not automatically privilege the 'contingent triumphs'[136] of the dominance of the statist viewpoint, and turn them into 'necessary truths'.[137] Rather, given that the viewpoint of observation is necessarily political, as Kelsen himself acknowledged, the 'ethical and political'[138] considerations which guide observation may (and arguably in many cases should) warrant an augmentation of the poles of observation to capture precisely the types of legal phenomenon emphasized by legal pluralists. Whereas such an interpretation of Kelsen's identity thesis cannot be directly equated with the standard account of legal pluralism as more than one legal system coexisting on the same social field given that under the unitary thesis, more than one legal system is a jurisprudential impossibility, the result of the interpretation is, in substantive terms, similar. Even if there is only one form of law and legal system, its susceptibility to being observed from multiple perspectives means that types of normative ordering both beyond and beneath the state are taken seriously as law.

In sum, Kelsen's identity and unitary theses, while superficially seeming to imply the strong claim that all law is state law, on closer inspection reveal that there are good grounds for interpreting Kelsen in a much more pluralist-friendly way.

The other dominant figure in the legal theory canon, HLA Hart, was less interested in the relationship between the law and the state than Kelsen was. His most famous work, *The Concept of Law*, was primarily concerned with giving an account of 'municipal law',[139] with international law being relegated to one chapter and defined as a 'set' of laws rather than a legal system.[140] Nonetheless, there are pluralistic elements in Hart's theory which seem to suggest he would not endorse the strong claim. At a preliminary level, as well as distinguishing between international law and municipal law, he also draws a distinction between 'primitive' and developed legal systems, as well as customary law and municipal law,[141] suggesting that he believes there are at least a number of analytically relevant distinctions to be made in thinking about law and legal systems. However, beyond these basic distinctions, Hart does not

[136] MacCormick, *Questioning Sovereignty: Law, State and Nation in the European Commonwealth* (n 35), 24.
[137] ibid.
[138] Kelsen, *General Theory of Law and State* (n 15), 388.
[139] Hart (n 16), 17.
[140] ibid 236. For discussion and analysis of Hart's view of international law, see Chapter 3.
[141] ibid.

spend much time thinking about non-state law and legal systems and there is no clear statement which points to his endorsement of the strong claim.[142] It is true that he does insist that legal officials, and particularly courts, have a central role to play in the existence of legal systems[143] and that most systems of law involve organized coercion.[144] It is also true that his account is not particularly demotic in that the relevant actors for the question of the existence of a legal system are elite officials, with no requirement of 'popular buy-in'[145] in terms of the recognition of the legal system.[146] However, as Cottrell notes,[147]

> nothing in Hart's books seems to indicate that 'officials' for this purpose must be state officials: certainly the judges of an international tribunal and perhaps the priests of a religious group [or] the elders of a cultural or ethnic group ... could qualify. Each of these kinds of group or association could thus have a kind of law of its own according to its members' concept of law.

Moreover, Hart's rejection of the centrality of the relevance of sovereignty to the concept of law, his insistence that law emerges from social practices rather than central commands, and his recognition that custom is a form of law properly so-called irrespective of its official recognition as such,[148] opens up possibilities for a pluralist reading of his concept of law which would militate against the strong claim.[149] These factors have led some to emphasize the 'pluralistic or polycentric potentialities'[150] of Hart's approach, even if they were not explicitly explored by Hart himself. As such, '[l]aw doesn't have to be state law on Hart's account'.[151]

[142] Nevertheless, some have attributed the strong claim to Hart. See for example Griffiths (n 32). See also Nick W Barber, 'The Rechtsstaat and the Rule of Law' (2003) 53 University of Toronto Law Journal 443, 450.

[143] Hart (n 16), 97–98.

[144] ibid.

[145] Leslie Green, 'Jurisprudence for Foxes' (2012) 3 Transnational Legal Theory 150, 157.

[146] Hart (n 16), 117.

[147] Roger Cotterrell, *Law, Culture and Society: Legal Ideas in the Mirror of Social Theory* (Ashgate Publishing, Ltd 2013) 37.

[148] Hart (n 16), 46. Jeremy Waldron, 'Legal Pluralism and the Contrast between Hart's Jurisprudence and Fuller's' in Peter Cane (ed), *The Hart–Fuller Debate in the Twenty First Century* (Hart 2010) 141.

[149] Waldron, 'Legal Pluralism and the Contrast between Hart's Jurisprudence and Fuller's' (n 148), 139. For discussion see also George Letsas, 'Harmonic Law: The Case Against Pluralism' in Julie Dickson and Pavlos Eleftheriadis (eds), *Philosophical Foundations of European Union Law* (Oxford University Press 2012).

[150] MacCormick, 'Beyond the Sovereign State?' (n 35), 9.

[151] Waldron, 'Legal Pluralism and the Contrast between Hart's Jurisprudence and Fuller's' (n 148), 139. See also Kenneth Einar Himma, 'Do Philosophy and Sociology Mix? A Non-Essentialist Socio-Legal Positivist Analysis of the Concept of Law' (2004) 24 Oxford Journal of Legal Studies 717.

Among others in the legal theory canon there is little evidence of the strong claim that all law properly so-called is necessarily municipal or state law. Raz, for example, has noted on a number of occasions the social and political importance of legal systems, with no claim that such society and politics be state society and state politics.[152] For example, he notes that '[l]egal systems are always legal systems of complex forms of social life, such as religions, states, regimes, tribes etc. Legal systems serve as one, but only one, of the defining features of these'.[153] Neil MacCormick has also exploited the pluralistic possibilities of Hartian-style legal systems in his conception of law as an 'institutional normative order'.[154] In developing this conception, MacCormick, following Hart, makes a point of severing the concept of law *qua* institutional normative order from the concept of sovereignty and the state.[155] He notes that a belief in the necessary relationship between the state and concept of law is possible but would mean marginalizing many other types of law including international law, canon law, customary law, social laws among others.[156] As such, he concludes that 'the law of the state is not the only law that human beings have'.[157] He argues that whereas the law of the state has been a predominant form of law, it has never succeeded in 'absolutely eliminating rival orders of one kind or another'[158] and that the dominance of state law has had 'serious distorting effects for legal theory'.[159] For MacCormick, whereas state law can be considered to be a 'principal'[160] example of law, it is 'by no means the only example'.[161] State law is merely a 'species of a genus'[162] of institutional normative order. Thus, he concludes, 'law is institutional normative order, and state-law is simply one form of law'.[163]

[152] Joseph Raz, 'Incorporation by Law' (2004) 10 Legal Theory 1, 15.
[153] Raz, *The Concept of a Legal System: An Introduction to the Theory of a Legal System* (n 17), 188.
[154] MacCormick, *Questioning Sovereignty: Law, State and Nation in the European Commonwealth* (n 35), ch1, 'The Legal Framework: Institutional Normative Order'.
[155] MacCormick, 'Beyond the Sovereign State?' (n 35), 10.
[156] ibid 14.
[157] MacCormick, *Questioning Sovereignty: Law, State and Nation in the European Commonwealth* (n 35), 11.
[158] ibid 9.
[159] ibid.
[160] ibid 1.
[161] ibid.
[162] ibid 1.
[163] ibid 15. For an examination of the affinity between MacCormick's legal pluralism that of Santi Romano, see Cormac Mac Amhlaigh, 'Constitutional Pluralism Avant La Lettre?: On Santi Romano's L'ordinamento Giuridico' (2020) 11 Jurisprudence 101.

4.2 Examining the Intermediate Claim: State Law Is a Paradigm Form of Law

With regard to the case of the second interpretation of the charge, the intermediate claim that state law is a paradigm or benchmark case of law, the picture is more ambivalent. Hart (and Kelsen before him) certainly seems to have intimated the sentiment of the intermediate claim in distinguishing between 'primitive' legal systems which enjoyed only primary rules, and more 'developed'[164] systems made up of the union of primary and secondary rules. However, as noted earlier, whereas his primary focus was on municipal or state legal systems, he did not explicitly claim any necessary relationship between 'developed' legal systems and state legal systems. The theorist that comes closest to making this type of claim explicitly is, perhaps somewhat surprisingly, Lon Fuller. At the outset, Fuller looks like an archetypal legal pluralist. He called on legal theory to examine 'not only the legal systems of states and nations'[165] but also 'the smaller systems—at least "law-like" in structure and function—to be found in labor unions, professional associations, clubs, churches, and universities'[166] calling them 'miniature legal systems'.[167] As such, law needed to be extracted from 'any connotation of the power and authority of the state'.[168] These statements seem to mark out Fuller clearly as a 'second wave' legal pluralist. However, scraping beneath the surface of this seeming celebration of legal pluralism, Waldron argues that in Fuller's endorsement of the 'inner morality of law', he ends up in a rather anti-pluralist place, at least as far as the claim that state law is a paradigmatic form of law is concerned. Whereas Fuller recognized that different systems, including the 'miniature legal systems' could, themselves involve the features of the 'inner morality of law',[169] his seeming endorsement of state law emerges when considering the effect on individuals of multiple legal systems applying to the same social field. As Waldron notes, the inner morality of law is concerned with the 'dignity and freedom of a person

[164] Hart (n 16), 214.

[165] Lon L Fuller, 'The Law's Precarious Hold on Life' (1968-1969) 3 Georgia Law Review 530, 542 cited in Waldron, 'Legal Pluralism and the Contrast between Hart's Jurisprudence and Fuller's' (n 148), 146.

[166] Lon L Fuller, 'Human Interaction and the Law' (1969) 14 American Journal of Jurisprudence 1, 2 cited in Waldron, ibid.

[167] ibid 1.

[168] Waldron, 'Legal Pluralism and the Contrast between Hart's Jurisprudence and Fuller's' (n 148), 147.

[169] Lon L Fuller, *The Morality of Law* (Yale University Press 1969) ch2, 'The Morality That Makes Law Possible'.

confronted with legal demands'.[170] However, where multiple legal demands are made upon individuals, such as in situations of legal pluralism, then the inner morality of law is compromised, especially where the demands are contradictory.[171] As such, where contradictory demands are made on individuals by different legal systems, Fuller seems to endorse an (anti-pluralist) statist resolution. He argues that in such circumstances the situation needs to be made more 'systematic' by setting out clear 'boundaries of competence'[172] or 'rules of *over-arching* adjudication'[173] which, as Waldron notes, reduces the effects of genuine pluralism.[174] Furthermore, Waldron argues that considerations relating to equality before the law, implicit in Fuller's 'inner morality' criteria of generality, militate against the celebration of legal pluralism where different individuals are subject to different standards emanating from different legal systems.[175] As such, a situation of genuine legal pluralism seems to offend Fuller's inner morality of law where there is an absence of an overarching authority—the state—which can systematize and order pluralism in order to achieve the aims of the inner morality of law. In such circumstances, it seems, ultimately that state law is the law which can best achieve the inner morality of law over other types of law existing in a social field, thereby rendering it 'paradigmatic' of law's inner morality.

Beyond this seemingly explicit, if ultimate, endorsement of state law as a paradigm of law, pluralists have, as noted earlier, accused legal theory of making the intermediate claim *implicitly* through the methodologies they adopt in developing their concepts of law. With regard to Tamanaha's charge in particular, it is not clear that his focus on methodology inexorably leads to a statist bias in legal theory. This is due to the fact that the question of whether law is a natural kind, whether the concept entails universal necessary and sufficient conditions or is an *a priori* concept, is a distinct one from whether state forms of law and legal ordering fulfil those conditions more than any other expression of the phenomenon. It is possible, and in some cases even perhaps probable, that state law was the main point of reference for extrapolating universal conditions for the concept of law among the theorists against which he makes this charge.[176] However, this doesn't mean that the methodology itself necessarily produces

170 Waldron, 'Legal Pluralism and the Contrast between Hart's Jurisprudence and Fuller's' (n 148), 152.
171 ibid.
172 Fuller (n 169), 124.
173 Waldron, 'Legal Pluralism and the Contrast between Hart's Jurisprudence and Fuller's' (n 148), 152.
174 ibid.
175 ibid 154.
176 Hart (n 16), 17.

a statist bias in the concept of law. We could extrapolate a robust criterion for the nature of law, involving an *a priori* conception, the stipulation of necessary and sufficient conditions and universal claims which ignored the relevance of state law in its entirety. Indeed, Tamanaha in his own approach to formulating a concept of law as a 'folk concept' seems to acknowledge this implicitly. His own view that law is a 'folk concept'—essentially that law is whatever a social group sees as 'law'[177]—could itself be said to employ a similar methodology to that of legal theory in that a 'folk concept' itself can be interpreted as a natural kind and/or a concept which is *a priori* and which captures a universal category.[178] Moreover, Tamanaha's criteria for a folk concept—whatever social groups designate as law—could itself be taken as necessary and sufficient criteria for his concept of law. The fact that any such minimalist definition would considerably broaden the types of phenomena that are captured as law as compared with many of the standard accounts of legal theory does not alter the fact that the methodological approach is very similar.

Problems of state bias (or indeed any other type of bias), if they do emerge, then, emerge at the point of loading up the theory with a pre-theoretical 'dataset' about the concept of law. As such, the strength of Tamanaha's version of the intermediate claim seems to lie in the contingent fact that legal theorists have tended to draw their *a priori* assumptions about law from state law rather than the fact that they make a priori assumptions about law *tout court*. However, even here, in order to be able to evaluate whether the 'dataset' relied upon by legal theory is a relevant one, we would need a clear criterion by which to evaluate whether the dataset over—or under—includes. Whereas Tamanaha

[177] Tamanaha (n 25), 48.

[178] Tamanaha distinguishes between 'folk' concepts and 'analytical' concepts by arguing that the former relates to ideas and concepts that 'social groups hold' whereas the latter are concepts which 'social scientists and philosophers formulate to study folk concepts and social phenomena'; however, this distinction is not developed in any detail; ibid. But surely this is too stark. The concepts developed by philosophers, not least recognition-based approach to law such as Hart and Raz's are precisely attempts at capturing the 'self-understandings' of social groups engaged in practices such as law (primarily legal officials). Whereas it is possible that the concept of law could be reduced purely to a heuristic—which is what Tamanaha seems to suggest in his account of analytical concepts—this is arguably not what most in the legal theory canon see themselves as doing. They see themselves as engaged in what Tamanaha himself is engaged in: identifying the concepts and understandings of those engaged in the practice. For example, Raz notes in this regard that '[t]he notion of law as designating a type of social institution is not ... part of the scholarly apparatus of any learned discipline. It is not a concept introduced by academics to help with explaining some social phenomena. Rather *it is a concept entrenched in our society's self-understanding*. It is a common concept in our society and one which is not the preserve of any specialised discipline ... In large measure what we study when we study the nature of law is the nature of our own self-understanding. The identification of a certain social institution as law is not introduced by sociologists, political scientists, or some other academics as part of their study of society. It is part of the self-consciousness of our society to see certain institution as legal. And that consciousness is part of what we study when we inquire into the nature of law.' Joseph Raz, *Between Authority and Interpretation: On the Theory of Law and Practical Reason* (Oxford University Press 2009) 31.

assumes that the 'dataset' relied upon by legal theory radically under-includes, leading to the intermediate claim, he does not offer criteria by which to evaluate whether this is the case to support the claim. One sensible way to start developing such criteria might be that the criteria involve, at least in part, the objectives of the development of the particular theory; that is that they examine and consider the practical questions that the concept is being employed to address. More specific objectives or questions such as those involved in a 'particular jurisprudence' might warrant a more detailed approach to the data that informs our assumptions and concepts, whereas more general questions such as those that come under the label of 'general jurisprudence' would seem to warrant more generous inclusion. As such, the extent to which a definition or account of law over- or under-includes would, in part, be dependent on an understanding of the object of the particular inquiry. Thus, for example, if we take Hart's objectives in developing his concept of law as advancing legal theory by providing 'an improved analysis of the *distinctive* structure of a *municipal* legal system',[179] the criterion to determine whether the concept over- or under-includes should reflect these specific purposes. When viewed in the light of much of the phenomena which make up the 'third wave' of legal pluralism, and in particular the prominence of international law, Hart's focus, and therefore the assumptions which feed into his concept of law will seem to under-include, leading to a municipal law bias in his concept of law.[180] However, whereas he does seem to stray beyond this initial focus in various parts of his book, especially on his comments on 'primitive' and international law which hint towards a defence of the intermediate claim, these were, Waldron argues, only ever incidental to his primary interest which was to develop a concept of municipal law.[181] Furthermore, recent revisions of Hart's approach show that he was simply mistaken in his views of, for example, international law and that his concept of law can, without much revision, account for other legal phenomena.[182] As such, if Hart's account does entail a statist bias, this is not directly attributable to the assumptions he loads into his theory of law but due to a limited ambition and a particular interest in municipal law as well as a lack of understanding of other forms of law and international law in particular,[183] which led to a relatively

[179] Hart (n 16), 17, emphasis added.

[180] See further 51.

[181] Jeremy Waldron, 'International Law: "A Relatively Small and Unimportant" Part of Jurisprudence?' in Luis Duarte d'Almeida, James Edwards, and Andrea Dolcetti (eds), *Reading HLA Hart's 'The Concept of Law'* (Hart Publishing 2013) 210.

[182] Mehrdad Payandeh, 'The Concept of International Law in the Jurisprudence of H.L.A. Hart' (2011) 21 European Journal of International Law 967. For more detailed analysis, see Chapter 3.

[183] Waldron, 'International Law: "A Relatively Small and Unimportant" Part of Jurisprudence?' (n 181), 210.

parsimonious selection of pre-theoretical data for his dataset. This could, of course, constitute grounds for independent criticism of Hart's approach (see further below); however, it provides relatively weak grounds for criticizing Hart based on the intermediate claim, at least in terms of his methodology.

With regard to Raz's account of law—a particular target of Tamanaha's—beyond the issue of methodology, it is not clear that the intermediate claim holds. We have already seen that Raz is in principle open to the coexistence of different types of law.[184] Furthermore, even if his stipulation of criteria for the concept of law as supreme, comprehensive, and open,[185] and making claims to legitimate authority could be seen to fit the state particularly well, as he himself notes, it also fits other non-state legal systems such as the Jewish legal system and that this is the case even if Jewish law does not even have a concept of law.[186]

In sum, in linking the intermediate claim specifically to the question of methodology, as Tamanaha does, it appears that a statist bias in legal theory—where it exists—is not one of methodology *per se* but rather relates to contingent matters of the interests or knowledge of the theorists writing at a particular time.

As a version of the intermediate claim, Culver and Giudice's critique of legal theory is a weaker one than Tamanaha's. This is primarily because they seem to accept that legal theory's statist bias is, in principle, justified. As such, they actually agree with much of what legal theory has to say about law and legal system as well as accepting that the focus on municipal law is a valid way of doing legal theory. The problem, they argue, emerges where legal theory clings rigidly to concepts of law based on state law in the face of changing circumstances—in particular those of the 'third wave' of legal pluralism—and a failure to revise state-based concepts of law in the light of these changing circumstances.

Culver and Giudice's justification of legal theory's (at least initial) focus on municipal law and their subsequent critique is based primarily on epistemological considerations, and particularly on an epistemological tendency in legal theory traceable as far back as Austin. Austin argued that in developing concepts of law we should only look at a limited number of systems given that 'it is only a few systems with which it is possible to become acquainted, even imperfectly'.[187] This limited ambition entails, Culver and Giudice argue, a rejection of the epistemic closure principle which holds that 'we can extend our

184 Raz, *The Concept of a Legal System: An Introduction to the Theory of a Legal System* (n 17), 188.
185 Raz, *The Authority of Law* (n 12), 116.
186 Raz, *Between Authority and Interpretation: On the Theory of Law and Practical Reason* (n 178), 40.
187 Giudice and Culver (n 25), 88.

knowledge by recognising, and accepting thereby, things that follow from our knowledge'.[188] Thus, unlike Tamanaha who, following his 'folk concept' idea, assumes that a vast array of normative orderings and conceptions of law from radically diverse contexts are, in principle, cognizable, legal theorists start, according to Culver and Giudice, with a much more parsimonious methodology whereby the primacy of central cases of law provide the initial steps in understanding and accounting for legal phenomena. According to Culver and Giudice then, legal theorists develop conceptions of law based on alternative epistemologies involving the possibility of evaluating concepts by their ability to explain social phenomena.[189] On this approach, the validity of concepts is predicated not on the concept having the 'right kind of evidentiary links'[190] to 'complex social phenomena whose amount and variety outstrip our descriptive capacities'[191] but rather their '*explanatory value* with respect to a wide range of social situations'.[192] Adopting this approach to the concept of law does not require a 'thoroughly specified body of "descriptive sociology" '[193] encompassing a wide variety of normative practices. It is for this reason that the general claims that legal theorists make about law are *bootstrapped* according to Culver and Giudice.

Moreover, they argue that such bootstrapping in developing conceptions of law is justifiable on the basis that the particular epistemology adopted is a sound one. That is, that it is plausible to assert that a concept of law based on the epistemic closure principle fails to recognize concerns about the cognitive limitations to what we can know about complex and prolific social phenomena such as law.[194] To ask for more of a concept of law is to ask for 'unavailable and unnecessary precision'.[195]

Their issue with legal theoretical accounts of law is not, then, the bootstrapping methodology *per se* but rather the *way* in which it is employed within legal theory.[196] In a similar charge to Tamanaha's, they argue that legal theorists tend not to be explicit about the empirical basis of their bootstrapped concepts,

[188] ibid 89. Steven Luper, 'Epistemic Closure' in Edward N Zalta (ed), *The Stanford Encyclopedia of Philosophy* (Summer 2020, Metaphysics Research Lab, Stanford University 2020) <https://plato.stanford.edu/archives/sum2020/entries/closure-epistemic/> accessed 17 May 2021. Thus, if we know something, 'p', and we also know that some other piece of knowledge 'q' is entailed in 'p', then we can claim to know 'q'.

[189] A 'reliabilist' conception. Giudice and Culver (n 25), 90.

[190] ibid 91.

[191] ibid.

[192] ibid.

[193] ibid 90.

[194] ibid 91.

[195] ibid.

[196] ibid xxx.

leading them to fail to revise the empirical basis in the light of new social realities. Whereas they argue that Austin was explicit and justified in his bootstrapping in terms of the empirical basis of his conception of law, Hart, in particular, is not. He was not particularly forthcoming about the 'experiential basis'[197] of his concept of law, which was 'tacit and incomplete'.[198] For example, as noted by number of critics, his lack of engagement with international law as a form of normative ordering is a rather obvious deficiency in this regard.[199] From this basis, Culver and Giudice argue that legal theoretical bootstrapped accounts of law following in the Hartian tradition have become 'static'[200] and have therefore responded in an unsatisfactory way to emergent legalities.[201] They accuse legal theory of failing to acknowledge the key feature of contingency in empirical realities of legal phenomena, leading to an obsession with state forms of legal ordering which is no longer justifiable. Thus, they argue that legal theoretical accounts of law need to 'rediscover their inner contingency' and revise their concepts accordingly to make them suitable to account for emergent legalities in the contemporary world.

They conclude that it is possible to address novel legal phenomena such as those posed by the 'third wave' of legal pluralism using the conventional tools of analytical legal positivism.[202] The trick, they contend, is to revise and develop these contingent conceptions to help fit new phenomena rather than remaining in thrall to their prescriptions based on limited and contingent data.[203]

4.3 Examining the Weak Claim: Legal Theory Has Neglected Non-State Forms of Law

Intuitively, the weak claim seems to be the only one of the three specific claims regarding legal theory's plurality problem which seems to be clearly warranted almost without exception. Whereas it is true that legal theorists have mentioned other types of law (such as Raz on religious or other laws)[204] or even discussed them in reasonable detail (such as Kelsen on international law,[205]

[197] ibid 92.
[198] ibid 91.
[199] Giudice and Culver (n 25); see also Waldron, 'International Law: "A Relatively Small and Unimportant" Part of Jurisprudence?' (n 181).
[200] Giudice and Culver (n 25), 81.
[201] ibid 93.
[202] ibid xviii.
[203] Giudice and Culver (n 25).
[204] Raz, *The Concept of a Legal System: An Introduction to the Theory of a Legal System* (n 17); Raz, *Between Authority and Interpretation: On the Theory of Law and Practical Reason* (n 178).
[205] Kelsen, *General Theory of Law and State* (n 15), vi.

Fuller on 'miniature-legal systems',[206] or Hart on 'primitive' legal systems),[207] it seems true that the primary interest of legal theorists has been the law of the state or municipal law; and primarily that of industrialized Western states[208] where non-state laws are either marginalized or whose status as law depends on state law recognizing them as such.[209] Indeed, legal theory seems to have been particularly candid about this. MacCormick, for example, in one of his last works, exclaimed that he would 'make no apology for giving priority to expounding a theory about law in its state and state-like contexts'.[210] However, as it happens, we don't need to look too far into these matters because the mantle of investigating and responding to the third claim—that legal theory has had an unwarranted focus on state law—has already been taken up *by the canon of legal theory itself*. Prominent theorists of the canon such as Jeremy Waldron and Joseph Raz have recently been engaged in a sort of self-criticism of the field of legal theory based on precisely the fact that it has neglected non-state forms of legal ordering.

Jeremy Waldron has taken legal theoretical conceptions of law, and in particular that of HLA Hart for his neglect of international law in his concept of law, to task for ignoring non-state forms of legal ordering.[211] Waldron identifies Hart's neglect of international law as one of several 'shortcomings'[212] in his seminal book *The Concept of Law*, which, he argues, is particularly problematic in the light of the fact that the book has had such a significant impact on subsequent thinking in legal theory. The omission is presaged early in Hart's book, where Hart clearly states his intention to provide an account of the 'distinctive structure of a municipal legal system'.[213] Given this emphasis, Waldron observes that international law 'was always going to be a distraction from this task'[214] and was therefore treated 'from the outset as a borderline case'.[215] Thus,

[206] Fuller (n 169), 1.

[207] Hart (n 16).

[208] Kelsen, *Introduction to the Problems of Legal Theory: A Translation of the First Edition of the Reine Rechtslehre, or, Pure Theory of Law* (n 109), 101–03.

[209] Griffiths (n 32), 5.

[210] Neil MacCormick, *Institutions of Law: An Essay in Legal Theory* (Oxford University Press 2007) 2.

[211] Jeremy Waldron, 'Hart and the Principles of Legality' in Matthew Kramer and others (eds), *The Legacy of H.L.A. Hart: Legal, Political and Moral Philosophy* (Oxford University Press 2008); Waldron, 'International Law: "A Relatively Small and Unimportant" Part of Jurisprudence?' (n 181).

[212] Waldron, 'Hart and the Principles of Legality' (n 211), 68.

[213] Hart (n 16), 17.

[214] Waldron, 'International Law: "A Relatively Small and Unimportant" Part of Jurisprudence?' (n 181), 210.

[215] Waldron, 'International Law: "A Relatively Small and Unimportant" Part of Jurisprudence?' (n 181).

the general impression left by Hart's treatment of international law was that he didn't believe 'there was any such thing'.[216]

From the perspective of legal theory, Waldron argues, the impact of Hart's neglect is that legal theory has concluded that international law is of 'marginal significance'[217] and 'not worth the attention of serious legal philosophers'[218] leaving major gaps in legal theory.[219] He argues that this neglect of international law by legal theory is 'nothing short of scandalous'[220] given that theoretically it is 'the issue of the hour'.[221] However, Waldron notes that 'no leading modern positivist saw fit to try to map onto these controversies what Hart said in Chapter X of his book',[222] leaving a 'deafening silence'[223] in analytical legal theory.

For Waldron, the main problem with Hart's approach to international law is his intimation that the lack of institutions predicated on secondary rules comparable with those of state law create problems in considering international law as law. Waldron argues that whereas it is trivially true that international law does not have the institutions predicated on secondary rules of the same type as those of state systems, this does not mean that international law has no secondary rules at all.[224] He argues that the account of secondary rules is drawn sufficiently broadly in Hart's concept of law to be able to include types of institutions discharging the functions of secondary rules distinct from those found in municipal legal systems.[225] As such, the lack of compulsory jurisdiction of the International Court of Justice or the lack of a global legislature, for example, is not evidence of the lack of secondary rules of adjudication and change as Hart contended, because compulsory jurisdiction is not necessary for the existence of rules of adjudication nor a formal legislature necessary for rules of change.[226] Furthermore, Hart's argument that international law lacks a rule of recognition and is therefore not systemic in the same way as municipal law, based on the fact that the primary rules of international law conflict is, Waldron contends, overdone. The fact that rules of international law conflict without having a clear, rule-based way of resolving such conflict is not

216 Waldron, 'Hart and the Principles of Legality' (n 211), 69.
217 Waldron, 'International Law: "A Relatively Small and Unimportant" Part of Jurisprudence?' (n 181), 210.
218 ibid.
219 Waldron, 'Hart and the Principles of Legality' (n 211), 68.
220 ibid 69.
221 ibid.
222 ibid 211.
223 ibid.
224 ibid 216.
225 ibid 215.
226 ibid 216–17.

evidence that it lacks a systemic nature. Waldron points out that the laws of municipal systems conflict, and that it has been shown that the unifying role of a single rule of recognition to settle all conflicts is not necessary, even in municipal legal systems.[227] As such, as with the rules of international law, the rules of municipal law frequently contradict each other and their strict priority is never perfectly worked out. Thus, if international law is not a system for this reason, then neither is municipal law, a conclusion which Hart himself clearly rejected.[228] Waldron concludes that whereas there are clear differences between municipal legal systems and the international legal system, these were exaggerated by Hart with the unfortunate consequence that legal theory neglected the field of international law and therefore deprived us of insights that legal theory could bring to this increasingly important area of law.

Joseph Raz has also, in a recent essay, reflected upon the substance of the third claim: that is whether and why legal theory has tended to focus almost exclusively on state law and whether this is something that can be expected to continue into the future.[229] The essay represents a sustained reflection on the reasons for, and appropriateness of, the centrality of state law to legal theory, whether it is justified and how and whether it will remain the case into the future.

Raz begins his essay by asking why so many theories of law focus on state law and why it is that the state has formed a special place in our social arrangements. He argues that theorizing about law throughout history, including as far back as the *polis* of ancient Greece, has tended to focus on 'the most comprehensive legally based social organisation of the day'[230] as important and 'deserving of special theoretical attention';[231] what we can call a 'comprehensiveness condition'. The comprehensiveness condition means that law and systems that comply with it present 'more challenging theoretical puzzles'[232] than other forms of law. For historical reasons, and at least since the Peace of

[227] Referring to Raz's contention that municipal legal systems can have multiple rules of recognition, none of which unify the legal system in its entirety. ibid 221.

[228] 'My point is that, so far as recognition is concerned, Hart should not be making greater demands on international law than he makes on municipal law.' ibid 220.

[229] Joseph Raz, 'Why the State?' in Nicole Roughan and Andrew Halpin (eds), *In Pursuit of Pluralist Jurisprudence* (Cambridge University Press 2017).

[230] ibid 137. Here he defines comprehensiveness in terms of having 'extensive responsibility within its domain' and 'freedom from external legal constraints' (ibid 138). Furthermore, 'responsibility' involves three elements; normative powers, duties to exercise them under certain circumstances or for certain purposes, and acceptance of these duties as reason-giving by those subject to them (ibid 145). The condition of independence relates, simply, to institutions not acknowledging that any institutions or rules of other law-based systems bind it which of itself admits of degrees (ibid 146).

[231] ibid 147.

[232] ibid 137.

Westphalia and the development of the modern conception of state sovereignty with its ideas of equality and non-interference,[233] the organization that has fulfilled the comprehensiveness condition in society and therefore warranted such attention has been the state. In particular, it is the twin qualities of statehood in terms of (claims to) legitimacy and sovereignty that make states the most comprehensive legally based social organization of the day.[234] Even if other forms of law can and have coexisted with the state during this period such as canon law or EU law, they are not as comprehensive as state law given that their responsibilities within their domain have conventionally been more restricted than that of state law and they have been subject to external legal constraints.[235]

The question, then, Raz asserts, is whether this is likely to be the case into the future, such that the state should remain the primary focus of theorizing about law. On the future of the state fulfilling the comprehensiveness condition, Raz is less certain. He notes that various trends in contemporary law and politics seem to suggest that we will arrive at a point where the state no longer fulfils the comprehensiveness condition. These trends include many of the phenomena which are captured by our circumstances of constitutional pluralism including the autonomous development of international organizations, the novel ways in which international norms emerge, and the extended range of agents in international law, including individuals.[236] In particular, he emphasizes the ways in which contemporary international law, while formally treaty-based and preserving of the sovereign independence of states, in practice creates a form of external authority over states in that they are very difficult to leave and the consequences for doing so can be extreme.[237] As such, developments in the quantitative and qualitative scope of international law combined with its increasing autonomy mean that the conditions that gave rise to the prominence of states as forms of legal ordering are undergoing change.[238] This, in turn, impacts upon the standing of states, and in particular their role as the most comprehensive legally based social organization of the day. Developments in international law mean that the freedom of states is more limited, 'hemmed in by pervasive and invasive international regulations'[239] such that they are no longer free from external authorities which are not under their control.[240] In

[233] ibid 150.
[234] ibid 156.
[235] ibid 138.
[236] ibid 151.
[237] ibid 152.
[238] ibid 154.
[239] ibid 155.
[240] ibid.

light of this, Raz believes that there is room for doubt that states will retain their status as the primary entities fulfilling the comprehensiveness condition and, significantly from the perspective of the weak claim, the primary 'focus of legal philosophy'.[241] However, importantly this does not mean that states will disappear. States, Raz contends, face 'change but not displacement'.[242] Whereas the key characteristics of legitimacy and sovereignty which lead to the comprehensiveness condition are challenged by legal globalization and legal transnationalism, they are challenged in a 'special way'[243] by making them 'limited states'.[244] In terms of the comprehensiveness condition and legal theory, then, Raz argues that in the light of these developments it behoves legal theorists to 'revive and explore theories of a limited state'.[245]

Thus, the state will, in Raz's view, continue to fulfil the comprehensiveness condition into the future; however, the way in which it does so will change, something which must be tracked by legal scholarship. Raz's call for a new research agenda based on the limited state in legal theory is a clear, if reasonably tentative, acknowledgment that legal theory should broaden its horizons beyond the conventional models of state law. However, the more radical aspects of Raz's essay are a series of scattered remarks about legal theory's traditional focus on state law. In the essay he explicitly acknowledges the existence of other 'kinds of law'[246] and references a number of examples including international law, EU law, canon law, Sharia law, Scottish law, indigenous laws, the 'rules and regulations governing the activities of voluntary associations, or those of legally recognized corporations',[247] and even 'very transient phenomena, like neighborhood gangs'[248] which are worthy of scholarly attention. Furthermore, he argues that legal theory has an unwarranted and unjustifiable focus on state law. In a series of concluding comments, he explicitly endorses the weak claim against legal theory:

> exclusive concentration on state law was, it now turns out, never justified, and is less justified today. In part, though not only, we need to rethink the relations of state law to other legal systems, as the scope both of the authority and of the sovereignty of states has diminished and is likely to diminish still

[241] ibid 155.
[242] ibid 156.
[243] ibid 160.
[244] ibid.
[245] ibid.
[246] ibid 138.
[247] ibid.
[248] ibid.

further, and the ways states integrate within the emerging international law is going to confront us with practical and theoretical problems.[249]

5. Conclusion: Appraising Legal Theory's Plurality Problem

What, then, is our conclusion to the question which animated our inquiry at the outset: does legal theory have a plurality problem? Parsing the general claim into three specific claims—that all law is necessarily state law, that state law is the paradigm of law, and that legal theorists have focused unduly on state law—reveals a mixed picture. It seems reasonably clear that the attribution of the first claim to legal theory by legal pluralists is unwarranted. Few, if any scholars in the legal theory canon make the first claim.[250] Even Kelsen, who might be thought to imply the first claim given the centrality of the concept of state to his concept of law and legal system, can be interpreted in a more pluralist-friendly way which does not involve the strong claim. The attribution of the second, intermediate, claim to legal theory seems to be more plausible, even if it is made implicitly rather than explicitly by legal theorists. However, with the partial exception of Fuller, even here the evidence that legal theory assumes that state law is the 'best' or 'paradigmatic' form of law is not conclusive. A version of the intermediate claim can be read into some loose comments by legal theorists, such as, for example, Hart's distinction between 'primitive' law and municipal law or MacCormick's reference to state law being a 'paradigmatic' or 'principal' species of the genus law.[251] However, if one focuses, as many critics have done, on the methodology employed by legal theorists, then the picture becomes less clear. Much of what is attributed to legal theory as a claim that municipal law is a paradigmatic form of law can be justified in terms of the focus or research interests of particular members of the legal theory canon. We could fault them for their lack of curiosity or disinterest in other forms of law. However, this is distinct from the claim that they unwarrantedly claim that state law is a more paradigmatic form of law than other types of law. Moreover, the fact that many of these accounts of municipal law can be co-opted to theorize non-state forms of law would seem to undermine the case that the intermediate claim is a valid critique of legal theory.

[249] ibid 161.

[250] Again, with the exception of Austin (n 21).

[251] MacCormick, *Questioning Sovereignty: Law, State and Nation in the European Commonwealth* (n 35), 1.

Finally, the weak claim—that legal theory has been unduly focused on state law—is, perhaps, the charge that most clearly sticks. However, as noted earlier, it is something about which legal theory is aware as evidenced, for example, in the self-critique of the legal theory canon by some of its most prominent members. Furthermore, the burgeoning theoretical scholarship on non-state forms of law shows that legal theory is breaking free from this habit.[252] If the question were posed several decades ago it might have been more appropriate, but it is becoming an increasingly less valid critique in the twenty-first century.

Thus, our conclusion to the question with which this chapter is centrally concerned is that if legal theory does have a plurality problem—and the foregoing analysis illustrates that in some senses it has—it is not a particularly profound one. The legal theory canon still provides a useful set of conceptual tools to theorize constitutional plurality under the circumstances of pluralism without necessarily undergoing the radical reconstructions proposed, for example, by Tamanaha or Culver and Giudice.[253] In Chapter 3 we will consider in much more detail how the 'toolkit', and particularly the accounts of legal system advanced by Kelsen and Hart, have grappled with legal plurality in the context of the theorization of international law, even if, as a form of legal plurality, it is a relatively modest form.[254] In Chapter 4 we will look at how we can develop Raz's account of a legal system in particular, to tackle a particular 'monistic manner' in thinking about interactions

[252] It is impossible to capture the explosion in theorizing non-state legal systems in recent years. Some examples involving EU law, international law, global law, and indigenous law include: MacCormick, *Questioning Sovereignty: Law, State and Nation in the European Commonwealth* (n 35); Cormac Mac Amhlaigh, 'The Anatomy of Constitutional Pluralism in the European Union' in Gareth Davies and Matej Avbelj (eds), *Research Handbook on Legal Pluralism and EU Law* (Elgar 2018); Cormac Mac Amhlaigh, 'Pluralising Constitutional Pluralism' in Andrew Halpin and Nicole Roughan (eds), *In Pursuit of Pluralist Jurisprudence* (Cambridge University Press 2017); Mac Amhlaigh, 'Concepts of Law in Integration Through Law' (n 31); Mattias Kumm, 'The Jurisprudence of Constitutional Conflict: Constitutional Supremacy in Europe before and after the Constitutional Treaty' (2005) 11 European Law Journal 262; Julie Dickson, 'How Many Legal Systems?: Some Puzzles Regarding the Identity Conditions of, and Relations Between, Legal Systems in the European Union' (2008) 1 Problema. Anuario de Filosofía y Teoría del Derecho 9; Julie Dickson and Pavlos Eleftheriadis (eds), *Philosophical Foundations of European Union Law* (Oxford University Press 2012); Payandeh (n 182); Ronald Dworkin, 'A New Philosophy for International Law' (2013) 41 Philosophy and Public Affairs 2; Noppadon Detsomboonrut, 'International Law as a Constitutional Legal System' (PhD, University of Edinburgh 2015); Liam Murphy, 'Law Beyond the State: Some Philosophical Questions' (2017) 28 European Journal of International Law 203.; Samantha Besson and John Tasioulas (eds), *The Philosophy of International Law* (Oxford University Press 2010); Neil Walker, *Intimations of Global Law* (Cambridge University Press 2015); Benedict Kingsbury, 'The Concept of "Law" in Global Administrative Law' (2009) 20 European Journal of International Law 23; Nicole Roughan, 'The Association of State and Indigenous Law: A Case Study in "Legal Association"' (2009) 59 The University of Toronto law journal 135.; Nicole Roughan, *Authorities: Conflicts, Cooperation, and Transnational Legal Theory* (Oxford University Press 2013) ch13, 'A Case Study in Relative Authority'.

[253] Tamanaha (n 35); Giudice and Culver (n 25).

[254] Roughan, *Authorities: Conflicts, Cooperation, and Transnational Legal Theory* (n 252), 69.

between legal systems which has affected some recognition-based accounts of legal systems such as Hart's. Our current chapter, however, concludes that, in thinking about constitutional plurality under the circumstances of constitutional pluralism, the conventional toolkit of analytical legal theory really isn't a bad place to start.

3

Law Beyond the Shadow of the State

1. Introduction: Transnational Constitutional Plurality

In our contemporary condition of the 'circumstances of constitutional pluralism', the transnational conceptual 'space' between the state and global level is replete with a diverse array of norms and normative practices from the most institutionalized and formal such as international treaties, international courts, international legislative and administrative bodies to the most informal such as the transboundary practices of private agencies, to a variety of practices in between such as those of the Internet Corporation Assigned Names and Numbers or the development of *lex mercatoria*.[1] Moreover, these different normative practices have been classified in different ways.[2] Even among the most formalized and institutionalized examples of normative practices beyond the state, there is a diversity of forms and types with differing approaches to the efficacy and status of suprastate norms.[3] Thus, in focusing our lens on normative practices 'beyond the state' in the context of constitutional plurality, we should not automatically assume that this space is less pluralistic with a less diverse array of law-like forms than the potential legal plurality within the legal and political constructions of states.[4]

Notwithstanding the diversity of normative practices beyond the state, however, they all share one feature in common: a 'world state gap'. This relates to the fact that they exist in a context in which there is no overarching, all-encompassing authority which claims supreme legislative competence, ultimate adjudicative authority, or a coercive enforcement mechanism comparable to the state context. There is no supreme global legislature empowered

[1] See generally Neil Walker, *Intimations of Global Law* (Cambridge University Press 2015).

[2] See generally Peer Zumbansen, 'Transnational Legal Pluralism' (2015) 1 Transnational Legal Theory 141.

[3] Contrast, for example, the 'direct effect' of the law of the European Union and the more indirect effect of the law of the European Convention on Human Rights. For discussion see Cormac Mac Amhlaigh, 'Pluralising Constitutional Pluralism' in Andrew Halpin and Nicole Roughan (eds), *In Pursuit of Pluralist Jurisprudence* (Cambridge University Press 2017).

[4] For discussion, see Nico Krisch, *Beyond Constitutionalism: The Pluralist Structure of Postnational Law* (Oxford University Press 2010).

New Constitutional Horizons. Cormac S. Mac Amhlaigh, Oxford University Press. © Cormac Mac Amhlaigh 2022.
DOI: 10.1093/oso/9780198852339.003.0003

to make laws for the world, there is no central global government which can enforce norms beyond the state, and, relatedly, there is no organized coercive enforcement mechanism to enforce compliance with norms such as a global police or a global army nor a global Supreme Court to arbitrate disputes nor resolve conflicts between them.[5] Thus, normative practices beyond the state lack both normative and institutional 'authoritative hierarchies'[6] which distinguish them from municipal contexts and therefore potentially pose a serious challenge to the idea of constitutional plurality.[7] In pluralist terms, there is no 'global state' to 'contain' or 'manage' legal plurality comparable to the role of state law in potentially managing legal plurality in state-based societies as endorsed by some accounts of legal pluralism.[8]

This chapter will therefore focus on the ways in which analytical legal theory has approached the idea of legal system in the context of a 'world state gap'. Its primary engagement with this type of phenomenon has been with respect to public international law and it is this form of normative practice beyond the state which will form the focus of the ensuing analysis.

Even if the case of international law as an instance of constitutional plurality represents what Roughan has dubbed the 'well established, low-hanging fruit'[9] of legal plurality, the ways in which the analytical theorization of international law manages the problem of the 'world state gap' can provide methods and strategies for the theorization of other, more *sui generis* forms of suprastate legal ordering,[10] as well as, potentially, less formalized and institutionalized

[5] The extent to which one or several of these features presents puzzles for theorizing law beyond the state varies between commentators. For example, Hathaway and Shapiro parse the 'world state gap' into two related, but analytically distinct features; an 'internality objection' involving the idea that international norms are not enforced by sanctions contained within the international legal system itself, and a 'brute force objection' that international norms lack a means of physical coercion to be applied in cases of non-compliance. Oona Hathaway and Scott Shapiro, 'Outcasting: Enforcement in Domestic and International Law' (2011) 121 The Yale Law Journal 252, 268.

[6] Stephen D Krasner, *Sovereignty: Organized Hypocrisy* (Princeton University Press 1999) 42.

[7] This fact remains the case even if we focus on regional regimes such as the European Union which have more developed institutions than traditional international organizations. The frequent 'battles' between the EU Courts and national apex courts merely serve to highlight the fact that even the EU legal system has yet to have its claims to the supremacy of its law accepted in a settled manner analogous to the way in which municipal law has. See generally Gareth Davies and Matej Avbelj (eds), *Research Handbook on Legal Pluralism and EU Law* (Edward Elgar 2018).

[8] Such as 'weak pluralism'. See Cormac Mac Amhlaigh, 'Constitutional Pluralism Avant La Lettre?: On Santi Romano's L'ordinamento Giuridico' (2020) 11 Jurisprudence 101; John Griffiths, 'What Is Legal Pluralism?' (1986) 18 Journal of Legal Pluralism and Unofficial Law 1.

[9] Nicole Roughan, *Authorities: Conflicts, Cooperation, and Transnational Legal Theory* (Oxford University Press 2014) 69.

[10] For an illustration of these possibilities in respect of EU law, see Neil MacCormick, 'Beyond the Sovereign State?' (1993) 56 The Modern Law Review 1; Neil MacCormick, *Questioning Sovereignty: Law, State and Nation in the European Commonwealth* (Oxford University Press 1999).

normative practices.[11] The insights which can be gleaned from theorizing international law with respect to the 'world state gap' can therefore provide a foundation for theorizing and thinking about forms of constitutional plurality beyond the state which may be distinct from 'classic' international law, but which have the 'world state gap' in common.

2. International Law and the 'World State Gap'

The theorization of international law in the analytical tradition can trace its roots at least as far back as the 1700s[12] and has also been the subject of renewed interest by analytical legal theorists.[13]

In this context, the 'world state gap' has been a key preoccupation for the theorization of international law making, what Santi Romano an early twentieth-century legal pluralist, called the 'problem of international law' the 'litmus test for all definitions of law'.[14] The 'world state gap' has been the basis for questioning the status of norms beyond the state as *legal* norms as well as whether international law constitutes a legal *system*. For many, the lack of the necessary apparatus and hierarchies of government at the international level have proved to be fatal to considering any norms which happened to exist beyond the state as *law*.[15] The clearest articulation of this view in Anglophone legal theory is John Austin's well-known view on the subject. For Austin, rules were general commands backed by threats and legal rules were general commands issued by a sovereign backed by threats for non-compliance.[16] The sovereign

[11] Benedict Kingsbury, 'The Concept of "Law" in Global Administrative Law' (2009) 20 European Journal of International Law 23; Thomas Schultz, *Transnational Legality: Stateless Law and International Arbitration* (Oxford University Press 2014).

[12] In German, in the work of for example, Wolff and Kaltenborn, See Jochen von Bernstorff, *The Public International Law Theory of Hans Kelsen: Believing in Universal Law* (Cambridge University Press 2010) ch1, 'Method and construction of international law in nineteeth-century German scholarship'; in Italian in the work of Anzilotti and Romano, Santi Romano, *The Legal Order [L'ordinamento Giuridico]* (Mariano Croce ed, Mariano Croce tr, Routledge 2017); and in English in the work of Bentham and Austin Brian Z Tamanaha, *A Realistic Theory of Law* (Cambridge University Press 2017) ch6, 'What is International Law?'.

[13] See Jeremy Waldron, 'International Law: "A Relatively Small and Unimportant" Part of Jurisprudence?' in Luis Duarte d'Almeida, James Edwards, and Andrea Dolcetti (eds), *Reading HLA Hart's 'The Concept of Law'* (Hart Publishing 2013); Samantha Besson, 'Theorizing the Sources of International Law' in Samantha Besson and John Tasioulas (eds), *The Philosophy of International Law* (Oxford University Press 2010). Carmen E Pavel, 'Is International Law a Hartian Legal System?' (2018) 31 Ratio Juris 307.

[14] Romano (n 12), 25.

[15] Hedley Bull, 'Kelsen and International Law' in William Twining and Richard Tur (eds), Essays on Kelsen (Oxford 1986); John Austin, *Austin: The Province of Jurisprudence Determined* (Wilfrid E Rumble ed, Cambridge University Press 1995).

[16] ibid.

was, moreover, an entity to whom the subjects of the law were in a habit of obedience, which was itself not subject to a higher sovereign.[17] Thus, for the Austinian, the sticking points in considering international law as law were the fact that the subjects of international law—states—were not in a habit of obedience to a global law-making sovereign, the norms of international law—'improperly so called'[18]—could not, in the absence of a global law-making sovereign, be considered commands of a sovereign backed by threats of coercion and they could not, therefore be considered *legal* norms.[19] International law was therefore merely 'positive morality'.[20]

Since Austin's nineteenth-century views, however, analytical legal theorists have become more sanguine as to the status of international norms as law. They have, in the main, adopted three strategies to manage the challenges to the status of international norms as legal norms posed by the 'world state gap'. The first has been to argue that the missing elements at the international level of Austin's account of law are not necessary for the concept of law. In particular, this move dispenses with the need for any necessary relationship between the concept of law and coercion.[21] On this view, law is a social phenomenon which can be theorized without the necessity of a 'monopoly of coercive force' and is therefore qualitatively distinct from the sociological realities of coercion.[22] Another strategy to manage the 'world state gap' has been to co-opt the organs and coercive apparatus of states to the cause of the application and enforcement of international norms; what George Scelle called the '*dedoublement functionnel*' of states.[23] On this view, states are essentially 'double-hatted' legal actors. When they operate within the state legal system, they wear their 'state

[17] ibid 18–34, 210; MacCormick, 'Beyond the Sovereign State?' (n 10); Hathaway and Shapiro (n 5).

[18] Austin (n 15), 208.

[19] Austin (n 15).

[20] 'The law obtaining between nations is not positive law: for every positive law is set by a given sovereign to a person or persons in a state of subjection to its authors ... [T]he law obtaining between national is law (improperly so called) set by general opinion. The duties which it imposes are enforced by moral sanctions: by fear on the part of nations, or by fear on the part of sovereigns, of provoking general hostility, and incurring its probable evil, in case they shall violate maxims general received and respected.' ibid 208, 112, 124.

[21] For a discussion of the relationship between law and coercion generally, see Lucas Miotto, 'Law and Coercion: Some Clarification' (2021) 34 Ratio Juris 74.

[22] Hathaway and Shapiro identify three sorts of arguments for this strategy: first a 'society of angel's thought experiment, second, an observation that rule-following, on the whole does not involve coercion in practice due to the fact that most people believe they have a moral obligation to obey the law, and third, only certain branches of law rely on coercion (private law, criminal law) but others, such as public law, do not, such that coercion cannot be a necessary condition of the concept of law. Hathaway and Shapiro (n 5), 277–82.

[23] Georges Scelle, *Precis de Droit Des Gens. Principes et Systematique*, vol 1 (Sirey 1932). For an excellent overview of Scelle's account see Antonio Cassese, 'Remarks on Scelle's Theory of "Role Splitting" (Dedoublement Fonctionnel) in International Law' (1990) 1 European Journal of International Law 210.

organ' hat; however, when they operate in international law, they wear their 'agents of international law' hat. In this way international law can 'externalise'[24] or 'delegate'[25] some key functions such as the enforcement of international norms to state actors where appropriate, with the result that the world state gap is no impediment to considering international law as law, given the obvious bureaucratic and coercive enforcement measures available to states.

A third, related, strategy in tackling the problems posed by the 'world state gap' is to focus specifically on the *validity* of international law thereby ensuring the status of international law as a developed legal *system*. On this view, if international norms can be attributed to a valid law-making power, then their status as a legal system can be assured. This strategy, therefore, has focused on identifying the source of validity of an international legal system.[26]

Given that our interest in this part of our constitutional inquiry involves the idea of constitution as *legality* or *legal system*, the primary 'constitutional' question in respect of international law in the context of a 'world state gap' relates to the third of these strategies to support the legal quality of the norms of international law; that is, the extent to which it can be considered a legal (or constitutional) *system*. In this chapter, therefore, we will focus on the ways in which legal theorists have endorsed or critiqued this third strategy to contest the assertion that international law is not law by examining the question of the systemic nature of international law. In particular, we will look at perhaps the most sophisticated analytical account of the systemic nature of international law in the work of Hans Kelsen, as well as examining the reasons why others such as Hart refuted the systemic nature of international law as well as more recent rebuttals or revisions of Hart's account.[27]

Beyond the immediate intellectual interests of the current book, there are a number of reasons why this focus is in itself worthwhile, which relate both to the advantages of legal systems in general as well as the specific issues which emerge in the suprastate context. From a purely jurisprudential viewpoint, as noted in Chapter 2, Waldron lays the blame for a lack of engagement and serious reflection on international law from analytical legal theory at the feet of those who have endorsed its status as an inferior or primitive form of law based, in part, on its non-systemic nature.[28] It has, he argues, given international

[24] Hathaway and Shapiro (n 5).

[25] Hans Kelsen, *General Theory of Law and State* (Anders Wedberg tr, Harvard University Press 1945) 227.

[26] ibid 369.

[27] For a more wide-ranging account of the debate between Kelsen and Hart on international law, see Michael Giudice, 'Hart and Kelsen on International Law' in Leslie Green and Brian Leiter (eds), *Oxford Studies in Philosophy of Law*, vol 2 (Oxford University Press 2013).

[28] Waldron (n 13).

law a stigma among 'serious legal philosophers'[29] which has had the effect of impoverishing the field of international legal theory to a considerable degree.

Moreover, Hathaway and Shapiro argue that the question of whether international law is a legal *system* 'matters a great deal',[30] particularly from a moral point of view given that legal systems are 'morally valuable institutions'[31] which enjoy properties that make them 'worthy of our esteem and allegiance'.[32] In a similar way, Payandeh has argued that conceiving of international law in non-systemic terms, even where it is accepted that it is a type of *law*, can undermine its normativity in that the rhetoric of international law as an ersatz, that is a non-systemic form of law (but law nonetheless), can lead its subjects to view its directives as less than binding and therefore motivate non-compliance.[33] The 'esteem and allegiance' owed to a putative international legal system is also underpinned by an instrumental justification for viewing international law in 'constitutional' systemic terms. If we care about the problems which many international law norms are (however (un)successfully) aimed at addressing, such as global injustice, the management of manmade climate change, fair trade, the alleviation of extreme poverty, or the promotion of global health, then we should care about the means by which those aims are achieved. If it is the case that legal *systems* are a particularly effective means of achieving those ends, then we should be concerned about the fact that the best tools (in the form of an advanced legal system affording 'immense' gains of 'adaptability to change, certainty, and efficiency')[34] are available to us to achieve those goals.[35]

Concerns about the 'fragmentation' of international law also illustrate the problems with viewing international law in non-systemic terms.[36] If international law is not or cannot be centralized or systemic, then it can fail in its function to guide state behaviour and, where necessary, tame the more

[29] ibid.

[30] Hathaway and Shapiro (n 5), 255.

[31] Hathaway and Shapiro (n 5).

[32] ibid.

[33] Mehrdad Payandeh, 'The Concept of International Law in the Jurisprudence of H.L.A. Hart' (2011) 21 European Journal of International Law 967, 978. Indeed, he argues that notwithstanding Hart's recognition that international law was law, that his insistence that international law does not constitute a legal system 'seems almost as problematic as Austin's insistence that International law is not law at all'. (ibid 978).

[34] HLA Hart, *The Concept of Law* (Joseph Raz and Penelope Bulloch eds, 2nd edn, Clarendon Press 1994) 202.

[35] See generally Brian Z Tamanaha, *Law as a Means to an End: Threat to the Rule of Law* (Cambridge University Press 2006).

[36] See generally, Gerhard Hafner, 'Risks Ensuing from Fragmentation of International Law' (2000) ILC (LII)/WG/LT/L.1/Add. 1.

malignant impulses of states.[37] On this view, legal systems bring order to and control the exercise of political power: through constitutional law internally, international law externally.[38] If we lack the means to provide the efficiencies and certainties associated with a legal system at the international level, the interpretation of international norms or the resolution of conflicts between them can be captured by vested interests or manipulated by hegemonic or imperialistic interests.[39] Similarly, fragmentation and the lack of an overarching international legal system may lead to significant gaps in the regulation of matters at the international level, gaps which may be filled by international tribunals, thereby running the risk of exponential judicial empowerment. Judicial empowerment is also a risk where there are no clear methods of conflicts resolution between different forms of legal regulation at the global level. If the norms of international law are not organized in a systemic manner, then the resolution of conflicts can become arbitrary, undermining law's action-guiding function as well as further empowering judicial actors.[40]

3. Kelsen on the International Legal System

As we considered in Chapter 2, in thinking about the systemic nature of law in the analytical tradition, validity is key.[41] A series of norms constitute a legal system in virtue of the fact that all of the norms of the system can trace their validity back to some fundamental law containing criteria of validity of the legal system, whether single or multiple.[42] Thus, for international norms to constitute, or be considered part of, a legal system, it is necessary to determine candidate sources for their validity. This was precisely Kelsen's strategy in relation to international law as part of his support for his unity thesis considered at length in Chapter 2.[43]

37 Martti Koskenniemi and Päivi Leino, 'Fragmentation of International Law? Postmodern Anxieties' (2002) 15 Leiden Journal of International Law 553; Prosper Weil, 'Towards Relative Normativity in International Law' (1983) 77 American Journal of International Law 413.

38 Koskenniemi and Leino (n 37), 556.

39 Hafner (n 36); Cormac Mac Amhlaigh, 'Harmonising Global Constitutionalism' (2016) 5 Global Constitutionalism 173; Eyal Benvenisti and George W Downs, 'The Empire's New Clothes: Political Economy and the Fragmentation of International Law' (2007) 60 Stanford Law Review 595.

40 In this regard Koskiniemmi and Leino talk of a 'hegemonic struggle' by courts to have their 'special interests identified with the general interest.' Koskenniemi and Leino (n 37), 562.

41 Joseph Raz, 'Legal Validity', *The Authority of Law* (2nd edn, Oxford University Press 2009).

42 ibid.

43 Given that Kelsen bases the systemic nature of international law (by virtue of its basic norm) on the unity of the state and international legal systems, the question of the systemic nature of international law is part of Kelsen's unity thesis. It is but one feature of Kelsen's argument for the unity of state and international legal systems considered in Chapter 2.

For Kelsen, in order to establish whether a series of norms counts as a legal system, we need to establish the existence of a basic norm which is presupposed in relation to the legal system and serves the purpose of unifying the norms into a single legal system.[44] All the norms created in accordance with the basic norm are then norms of the system.[45] To consider international law as an international legal system, then, for Kelsen, we must establish the basic norm of international law. Kelsen does this in two stages: extrapolating from the systemic nature of state law by adopting an international legal perspective on states, and identifying the content of the basic norm of the international legal system based on the norms and practices of international law.

3.1 State Law as International Law

One way in which Kelsen establishes the systemic nature of international law involves, perhaps somewhat counterintuitively, focusing on the validity of the legal systems of *states*. For Kelsen, the efficacy of a state legal order is a necessary condition for the validity of all of its norms.[46] The constitution of a state is only valid if the legal order established in the territory of the state is 'on the whole, efficacious'.[47] This condition, Kelsen argues, amounts to a principle—a principle of effectiveness—which is itself a positive norm.[48] It is, however, a positive norm of the *international* legal system.[49] Thus, the validity and effectiveness of the legal systems of *states* depends on conformity with this principle of effectiveness of *international law*. The principle of effectiveness *qua* positive law of international law 'provides the individual basic norm of the *national legal order*'.[50] As such, the basic norms of state legal systems are 'themselves based on a *general norm of the international legal order*'.[51] It is according to the principle of effectiveness of *international* law that the 'Fathers' of the historically first constitution were empowered to act as the first legislators of the state legal order.[52] Thus, the international legal order establishes both the reason for the validity, as well as the sphere of validity, of *state* legal orders.[53]

[44] Kelsen, *General Theory of Law and State* (n 25), 111.
[45] Kelsen, *General Theory of Law and State* (n 25).
[46] ibid 119.
[47] ibid 121.
[48] Kelsen, *General Theory of Law and State* (n 25).
[49] ibid.
[50] ibid, emphasis added.
[51] ibid, emphasis added.
[52] ibid 116, 367. See also section 3.2.
[53] ibid 367. This is the basic implication of Kelsen's 'unity thesis' considered in more detail in Chapter 2.

In this way, then, Kelsen establishes the systemic nature of international law by trading on the unambiguous and uncontested systemic nature of the law of states and his particular approach to legal validity through his notion of the basic norm. It is clear that the law of a state constitutes a legal system. However, the law of states relies, ultimately, for Kelsen, on a positive norm of international law for its validity. Given that the basic norm of state legal systems is a positive norm of international law, then, we need to establish where the principle of effectiveness—a positive norm of international law—gains *its* validity.[54] The principle of effectiveness of international law, which provides the validity of state legal systems, then, itself needs to be validated by a higher norm of international law which itself needs to be validated by a superior norm and so on up the chain of validity to the ultimate criteria of validity of the norms of international law. This ultimate source of validity cannot itself be a positive norm on pain of circularity. Rather, the ultimate source—a basic norm—is 'presupposed'[55] in relation to the ultimate positive norm of the system. Thus, in order to establish the ultimate criteria of validity of state legal systems, we need to establish the basic norm of international law. In doing so we establish both the validity of state legal systems as well as the systemic nature of international law.

3.2 The Basic Norm of International Law

For Kelsen, to identify the basic norm of any legal system we must find the ultimate source of validity in a system. In the context of state legal systems, then, we should start with a norm applied by a court, for example. We trace the validity of an individual norm back through its parent statute to the constitution in force at the time of promulgation of the norm and ultimately the constitution which is the 'first historically'.[56] It is the validity of this first constitution that is the 'last presupposition, the final postulate'[57] upon which the validity of all subsequent valid norms created in relation to it rests. In this historically first constitution:[58] 'It is postulated that one ought to behave as the individual, or the individuals, who laid down the first constitution have ordained.' In looking for a basic norm of *international* law, we adopt the self-same approach. We start with a particular positive norm of international law such as the principle of

[54] Kelsen, *General Theory of Law and State* (n 25).
[55] ibid 111.
[56] ibid 115.
[57] Kelsen, *General Theory of Law and State* (n 25).
[58] ibid.

effectiveness or the decision of an international court. To determine the validity of these norms we work our way up the chain of validity of positive norms to, perhaps, an international treaty and beyond and ultimately to the 'general norm which obligates the States to behave in conformity with the treaties they have concluded', which Kelsen identifies as the norm of *pacta sunt servanda*.[59] From this Kelsen extrapolates that the basic norm of the international legal system is one which 'countenances custom as a norm-creating fact'[60] and which can be formulated in the following way: 'States ought to behave as they have customarily behaved.'[61]

Thus, in the light of the fact that state legal systems are undoubtedly valid legal systems, and the fact that their validity stems from a valid positive norm of international law, and the fact that this positive norm ultimately bottoms out in a basic norm of the international legal system, then the basic norm of the international legal system is the 'only true basic norm'.[62] On Kelsen's account, not only is international law undoubtedly a system of valid law, but it is in fact the 'legal system of legal systems' providing the ultimate source of validity of those unambiguously systemic forms of law: the legal systems of states.[63]

4. Hart Attacks

Kelsen's approach to the systemic nature of law and in particular, his idea of the basic norm and his conclusion that international law and state law are part of one legal system, has been the subject of a variety of attacks over the years.[64] Perhaps the most well-known of these attacks in the Anglophone world has come from HLA Hart, who directly challenged both Kelsen's approach to validity as well as his conclusions surrounding the systemic nature of international law.[65]

With regard to the first stage of Kelsen's argument for the systemic nature of international law based on the fact that international law provides the source

[59] ibid 369.

[60] Kelsen, *General Theory of Law and State* (n 25).

[61] ibid.

[62] ibid 121.

[63] In this regard he refers to the basic norm of the international legal system as the 'constitution' of international law in a 'transcendental-logical sense'. Hans Kelsen, *Pure Theory of Law* (University of California Press 1967) 216.

[64] Particularly from Carl Schmitt. See von Bernstorff (n 12), ch3, 'An "objective" architecture of international law: Kelsen, Kunz, and Verdross'.

[65] HLA Hart, *Essays in Jurisprudence and Philosophy* (Oxford University Press 1983) ch15, 'Kelsen's Doctrine of the Unity of Law'; Hart, *The Concept of Law* (n 38), chX, 'International Law'.

of validity of state legal systems, Hart argued that the conditions created by the perspective of international law on the validity of state law are at best necessary conditions rather than sufficient conditions for the success of the thesis that state legal systems are validated by international law.[66] What was more important in determining the validity of legal systems, and particularly an international legal system, were the reasons why states obey a provision of international law, which may or may not correspond with the content of provisions of international law such as the principle of effectiveness. What was missing from this account, Hart argued, were the circumstances surrounding the 'making and origins of laws, whether they are recognized as authoritative and by whom'.[67] What matters for determining whether state law is validated by international law—and ultimately therefore whether Kelsen's account of international law as a legal *system* is plausible—relates to the authoritative criteria of recognition internal to the state itself, rather than the claims made by international law over the behaviour of states. States may conform to the content of norms of international law for reasons other than claims that their legal systems are ultimately validated by norms of international law.[68]

Hart parses out Kelsen's account of the validation of state legal systems by international law into weaker and stronger versions. The weaker version of the thesis is that while the validation of state law by international law is not a necessary truth about law in general, it is a contingent truth about the relationship between international law and state law. Hart attributes Kelsen's claims surrounding the validation of state law by international law by reference to the existence of a 'completion relationship' and a relationship of 'validating purport' between international law and state law.[69] Further support for this view is provided by what Hart calls a weaker version of a 'no conflicts thesis': that international law and state law do not conflict in fact.[70]

The stronger version of the validation thesis involves a 'central positive contention' that all valid laws necessarily form a single system and a 'central negative contention' that valid laws cannot conflict.[71] This is supported by Kelsen's claims surrounding the necessary 'epistemological postulate'[72] of the juristic point of view of legal science.

[66] Hart, *Essays in Jurisprudence and Philosophy* (n 69), 313.
[67] Hart, *Essays in Jurisprudence and Philosophy* (n 69).
[68] ibid.
[69] ibid 318.
[70] ibid 314–21.
[71] ibid 309.
[72] ibid 322.

4.1 The Weaker Version of the Validation Thesis

The first element of the validation thesis which Hart attacks is the way in which many norms of international law delegate certain matters to state legal systems. One example Kelsen advances to support this contention is that international law requires that war must not begin without a formal declaration of war. Whereas this is a 'time-honored rule of common international law', the precise method of declaration and the actor which must make the declaration is 'delegated'[73] to the state legal system. In the United States, the Constitution states that it is Congress that must make declarations of war. In this way, Kelsen argues, the US Constitution 'completes' the norm of international law.[74] Without the 'completion relationship' between international law and state law, international legal norms would be an 'inapplicable fragment of a legal order'.[75]

Whereas Hart endorses Kelsen's claims that a reference to national law is 'inherent'[76] in the 'meaning of the norms of international law',[77] this is, by itself insufficient to support the thesis that international law validates state legal systems.[78] Rather, for the fact of the completion relationship to support this thesis, Hart argues that it would need to be shown on other grounds that legal plurality is impossible or that there is, in fact, only one system of rules. This is because the existence of a completion relationship between norms can hold both *within* as well as *between* legal systems.[79] As Hart points out, as much is admitted by Kelsen himself when he draws the analogy of the completion relationship between international law and state law and the norms of municipal law which 'delegate' their completion to corporations under certain circumstances.[80] Thus, the mere fact of a delegation of functions by the norms of a legal system is insufficient to support the view that the delegating norms and the entities to which certain functions are delegated are necessarily part of the same legal system and that the grounds of validity of the delegated entities stems from the delegating system.

Hart recognizes that the primary basis of the validation thesis lies not in the fact of the existence of a completion relationship between international law and state law but rather in the principle of effectiveness of international law

[73] Kelsen, *General Theory of Law and State* (n 25), 348.
[74] ibid 343.
[75] ibid 348.
[76] Kelsen, *General Theory of Law and State* (n 25).
[77] ibid.
[78] Hart, *Essays in Jurisprudence and Philosophy* (n 65), 315.
[79] ibid.
[80] Kelsen, *General Theory of Law and State* (n 25), 349.

providing the basis of the validity of state legal systems. However, this too, Hart argues, is insufficient to support the validation thesis.[81] In respect of the relationship between the principle of effectiveness and the validity of state legal systems in terms of 'validating purport',[82] it is not sufficient, Hart argues, in order to show that two rules form part of one system, to argue that 'one of them provides that rules of a certain description satisfied by the other are valid'.[83] For Hart, the mere fact that a rule claims to validate another rule cannot, without more, lead to a conclusion that the subordinate rule is validated by the superior rule because there may be other reasons why the purportedly validated rule is indeed valid, independently of the claims of the rule of validating purport.[84] What is decisive for determining the validity of norms are not the claims of particular laws purporting to validate them, such as the principle of effectiveness of international law in relation to state law, but the *attitudes of the officials of the system applying the relevant norms*.[85] Hart argues that the legal systems of states are validated primarily by the attitudes and acts of their officials, and in particular their courts, and not the fact that an international legal system makes claims to validate state legal systems through the principle of effectiveness.

The fact of validating purport *can*, however, serve a function of determining the validity of laws from the perspective of a particular legal system.[86] However this cannot be converted into a more universal claim about the basis of the validity of legal systems in general.[87] Moreover, given that for Hart, validity is a question for the attitudes of the officials of the system, it *is* possible that international law provides the basis for the validity of a state legal system, where the officials of the state legal system explicitly hold this attitude.[88] However, he argues that this is a contingent (and rare) feature of the validity of state legal systems.[89] Hart's view of the international legal world when he was writing in the early 1960s was that there was insufficient evidence to suggest that this was a widespread position. He acknowledged that this doesn't mean that the

[81] Hart, *Essays in Jurisprudence and Philosophy* (n 65), 318.
[82] ibid 319.
[83] Hart, *Essays in Jurisprudence and Philosophy* (n 65).
[84] Hart motivates this thought through the example of the fictional Soviet Laws Validity Act 1970 of the English legal system. The fact that a hypothetical English statute purported to validate the Soviet legal system could not provide the grounds for the validity of the Soviet legal system. Rather, it would be the attitudes of the courts and law enforcement agents in the Soviet Union which determined the question of validity. ibid 319.
[85] ibid.
[86] For example, in Hart's hypothetical example, it *is* possible to conclude, that *for the purposes of English law*, Soviet law is valid law.
[87] Hart, *Essays in Jurisprudence and Philosophy* (n 65), 320.
[88] ibid 321.
[89] ibid.

evidence could not change and legal practice could evolve such that the positing of a single source of validity of international legal rules could possibly be a good account of international rules.[90] However, until such a time, the reality remains that the rules 'which are *in fact* operative' constitute not a system but a 'set' of rules.[91]

Hart also critiques Kelsen's view that the fact that international law and state law do not conflict is evidence that the international legal system could be said to validate the legal system of states. This provides the 'negative criterion' of the validation thesis.[92] The 'no conflicts' thesis assumes that were there to be conflicts between international law and state law, the idea that international law validated state law 'could not be sustained'.[93] Thus, the no-conflicts theory of the relationship between international law and state law is a necessary condition of the unity thesis. If it does not apply, and if the norms of international law and state law do conflict, then the unity thesis is false.[94]

With regard to the weaker version of the no conflicts thesis, Kelsen argues that there are no conflicts *in fact* between international law and state law. Such a conflict would arise where the state legal system enacts a law whose content conflicts with the content of a norm of international law. However, this does not occur in practice, Kelsen argues. If the legal system of a state passes a law the content of which conflicts with the content of a provision of international law—say that international law requires that particular minorities should be provided with particular rights, but a state passes a law depriving the same minorities of those rights—Kelsen argues that no conflict emerges because international law simply serves to *outlaw* the act: the passing of a statute depriving minorities of rights. In such a scenario 'the rule of international law does not seek to determine directly the content of state statutes, but only the legality or illegality of their enforcement'.[95] Thus, conflicts do not emerge because

[90] 'Perhaps international law is at present in a stage of transition towards acceptance of this and other forms which would bring it nearer in structure to a municipal legal system. If, and when, this transition is completed the formal analogies, which at present seem thin and even delusive, would acquire substance, and the sceptic's last doubts about the legal "quality" of international law may then be laid to rest. Till this stage is reached the analogies are surely those of function and content, not form.' Hart, *The Concept of Law* (n 34), 236–37.

[91] ibid 236.

[92] Hans Kelsen, *Introduction to the Problems of Legal Theory: A Translation of the First Edition of the Reine Rechtslehre, or, Pure Theory of Law* (Bonnie Litschewski Paulson and Stanley L Paulson eds, Clarendon Press 1992) 328. Hart notes that the no conflicts thesis, while potentially supporting the idea that international law validates state legal systems, is intended by Kelsen to be independent of the unity thesis. Hart, *Essays in Jurisprudence and Philosophy* (n 65), 331.

[93] Hart, *Essays in Jurisprudence and Philosophy* (n 65), 324.

[94] 'The unity of the supraordinated and the sub-ordinated systems however, proves itself in the impossibly of a contradiction between the content of the norms of the two systems.' Hans Kelsen, Problem der *Souveränität*, 113, cited in von Bernstorff (n 12), 96.

[95] Hart, *Essays in Jurisprudence and Philosophy* (n 65), 333.

the passing of the statute by the state makes that state liable to punishment or sanction under international law. For Kelsen, the absence of conflicts does not relate to the power to deprive the passing of valid norms and render them without legal effect, it relates to the ability of international law to determine whether an act such as the passing of a statute constitutes a breach of the norms of international law and therefore makes the state liable to sanction for this breach.[96] Whereas Hart notes that the argument is 'ingenious'[97] it doesn't provide evidence of the absence of conflicts in fact between international law and state law. Rather it merely 'locates such a conflict at a different point'.[98] Rather than constituting a conflict between a norm of international law and a norm of the state legal system, the conflict, Hart argues, is one of a rule *prohibiting* (international law) and *permitting* (state law) the same action.[99] This is the type of conflict at stake in such conflicts and its existence serves to undermine support for Kelsen's unity thesis.

4.2 The Stronger Version of the Validation Thesis

The stronger version of the validation thesis is that state law and international law necessarily form part of the same legal system from the viewpoint of logic, and that it is not merely the case that they do in the light of the particular features and principles of international law. Hart argues that the support for this conclusion comes from Kelsen's endorsement of an 'epistemological postulate'[100] of juristic knowledge which requires that jurists who accept the validity of different norms (such as the norms of international law and state law) must 'comprehend them as part of one harmonious system'.[101] For Kelsen 'it is logically not possible to assume that simultaneously valid norms belong to different mutually independent systems'.[102] This view was part and parcel of Kelsen's larger project of establishing a general science of law.[103] As such, the

96 Hans Kelsen, *Reine Rechtslehre* (Deuticke, 1960) 331 cited in von Bernstorff (n 12).
97 Hart, *Essays in Jurisprudence and Philosophy* (n 65), 333.
98 ibid.
99 ibid.
100 ibid 373.
101 Kelsen, *General Theory of Law and State* (n 25), 363.
102 ibid.
103 As his disciple, Verdross, saw it: '"If we take a closer look," writes Planck, "the old system of physics did not at all resemble a single picture, but rather a collection of paintings, as there was a separate picture for every class of natural phenomena. And these various paintings were not hanging together; one could remove one without detracting from the others. This will not be possible in the future physical picture of the world. Not a single one of its features will be able to be left out as unessential; rather, each is an indispensable element of the whole and possesses as such a definite meaning for observed nature; conversely, every observed physical manifestation will have to find its precise place within the

unity thesis was the product of the necessary epistemological postulate which was a feature of the scientific quality of law. Hart does not dwell on this feature of the stronger version of the unity thesis, dismissing the idea that we must view all valid law as a unity as a *non-sequitur*.[104]

Like the weaker version of the validation thesis, the stronger version of the validation thesis is also supported by a no conflicts thesis involving a more ambitious claim than the 'weaker' version considered earlier.[105] Leaving aside for now what it means, precisely, for two rules to conflict,[106] Kelsen argues that it is a *logical*, not merely contingent, impossibility for two conflicting valid norms to coexist, whether as part of the same system or between different systems.[107] This is explained by the fact that it is impossible for valid norms to prescribe both that '*A* ought to be' and '*A* ought not to be' which is just as meaningless, Kelsen argues, that *A* is and at the same time it is not.[108]

On the matter of the illogical nature of norm conflicts in support of his unity thesis, Hart argues that Kelsen's arguments 'raise a host of difficulties'.[109] With respect to the logical impossibility of norm conflicts, Hart points out that this is significantly underdetermined.[110] However, the primary reason for the failure of the stronger version of the validation thesis based on the no conflicts thesis is that it is incoherent on Kelsen's own terms. Kelsen himself has observed that when descriptive ought statements (such as *A* both ought and ought not be) are true, they are always only true *relative to the system they describe* (whether that be law or morality).[111] Thus, in making descriptive ought statements about the content of valid norms, they are always made relative to a particular legal system. In the light of this system-relative account of descriptive ought statements, there is no logical contradiction, therefore, between

picture." These words apply also to positive legal scholarship, both historically and programmatically.' Alfred Verdross, *Die Einheit des rechtlichen Weltbildes auf Grundlage der Völkerrechtsverfassung* (Tübingen: JCB Mohr, 1923), Preface, cited in von Bernstorff (n 12), 80.

[104] For a more considered sceptical view on the logical necessity of the unity thesis, see Joseph Raz, *The Authority of Law* (2nd edn, Oxford University Press 2009) ch16, 'The Purity of the Pure Theory'.

[105] A contradiction between valid norms is 'impossible for the cognition of norms'. Kelsen, *General Theory of Law and State* (n 25), 408.

[106] See Hart, *Essays in Jurisprudence and Philosophy* (n 65), 324–32. For further consideration see Nick W Barber, 'Legal Pluralism and the European Union' (2006) 12 European Law Journal 306 329. See further Chapter 4 of this volume.

[107] Hart, *Essays in Jurisprudence and Philosophy* (n 65), 327.

[108] Kelsen, *Introduction to the Problems of Legal Theory: A Translation of the First Edition of the Reine Rechtslehre, or, Pure Theory of Law* (n 92), 206.

[109] Hart, *Essays in Jurisprudence and Philosophy* (n 65), 330.

[110] Partly depending on how 'ought' is defined the statement could be true but there are other possibilities. Moreover, logicians have allowed for the possibility of conflicting obligations. Hart, *Essays in Jurisprudence and Philosophy* (n 65), 331.

[111] Hart, 'Kelsen's Doctrine of the Unity of Law' (n 110), 331, 329.

statements that 'according to state law A ought to be' and 'according to international law A ought not to be'.[112] It would be impossible to jointly conform to both of these norms (assuming that conflicts imply the impossibility of joint conformity), but their coexistence as valid rules would be 'logically possible'.[113] For this reason, then, it is perfectly logical for international law to prescribe that 'A ought to be' and for state law to prescribe that 'A ought not to be'.[114] Thus, Hart concludes, Kelsen's stronger version of the no conflicts thesis fails and, as a corollary, the validation thesis is not proven.

4.3 The Methodology for Establishing the Basic Norm of International Law

Hart also critiques the second stage of Kelsen's argument for the systemic nature of international law: the establishment of a basic norm of international law. He surveys the various classic objections to the status of international law based on the 'world state gap', concluding that none of these factors, by themselves, negate a conclusion that international law is law.[115] Furthermore, Hart argues in a similar way that the absence of a unifying basic norm similarly doesn't mean that the norms of international law are not legally binding norms. As he demonstrated with reference to what he called 'primitive' legal systems, it is possible for binding norms to exist without them necessarily being part of a legal system.[116] In the light of the fact that binding legal norms can exist without their necessarily being part of a legal system, on the question of how we should establish the ultimate grounds of validity of an international legal system to shore up the legal quality of international norms, then, Hart basically doesn't see the point. In order to consider the norms of international law as binding norms, they do not need to be part of an overarching legal system and therefore we do not need to identify a basic norm in relation to it. 'Primitive' law functions with binding norms without an ultimate source, and international law does too.[117] Secondary rules or ultimate sources of authority, while a 'luxury'[118] for some societies, and a necessary condition for the existence of a legal system, are not a necessary condition

[112] ibid 332.
[113] ibid 326.
[114] See discussion at ibid 325–26.
[115] See sections 2 and 3 of Chapter 4.
[116] Hart, *The Concept of Law* (n 34), chIV, 'Sovereign and Subject'.
[117] ibid 235.
[118] ibid 235.

for the existence of binding legal norms. Thus, for Hart, the key question for theorizing international law is not how we can identify a basic norm of an international legal system but what reasons might we have for believing that such a thing exists. Given that the bindingness of international legal norms does not rest on the existence of a unifying basic norm of the international legal system, the only reason we would have to identify a basic norm of international law would be if the evidence of the 'actual character'[119] of international law suggested that such a norm existed.[120] In short, the question of the systemic status of international law and the identification of an international legal basic norm becomes one of 'fact'.[121]

On this particular score, he notes that theorists 'have found very great difficulties in formulating the "basic norm" of international law'.[122] Reflecting on *pacta sunt servanda* as a candidate for this status, he notes that most theorists have 'abandoned' this norm as a basic norm for the international legal system on the grounds that not all obligations that arise under international law (such as customary international legal norms) rise from a '*pacta*', 'however widely that term is construed'.[123] This has led to it being replaced by the formulation 'States should behave as they customarily behave'[124] based on the idea that the basic norm of international law must be a norm which 'countenances custom as a norm-creating fact'.[125] However, even here he considers the idea of a basic norm of an international legal system couched in this customary language as artificial, comical even.[126] The (in Hart's view unnecessary) attempts to establish the basic norm of an international legal system in the face of evidence to the contrary has led to the 'empty repetition of the mere fact that the society concerned ... observes certain standards of conduct as obligatory rules'.[127] Kelsen's formulation of the basic rule of the international legal order is one such example which does nothing more than state, redundantly, that 'those who accept certain rules must also observe a rule that the rules ought to be observed';[128] a mere

[119] ibid 234.
[120] 'Here the first and perhaps the last question to ask is: why should we make [the a priori assumption of a basic norm] and so prejudge the *actual character of the rules of International law*?', ibid, emphasis added.
[121] ibid 236.
[122] ibid 233.
[123] ibid 234.
[124] Albeit that he does not attribute the phrase directly to Kelsen, it is a direct citation of Kelsen—see earlier: ibid. See also Kelsen, *General Theory of Law and State* (n 25), 369.
[125] Kelsen, *General Theory of Law and State* (n 25), 369.
[126] Hart, *The Concept of Law* (n 34), 236.
[127] ibid.
[128] ibid.

'useless reduplication'[129] of the fact that certain rules are accepted by states as binding rules.[130]

5. Raz Joins In

Raz focuses on a circularity in Kelsen's methodology for establishing the basic norm which adds to Hart's refutation of the systemic nature of international law in Kelsen's account. Raz attributes two 'axioms'[131] to Kelsen's theory of the basic norm as establishing the identity of legal systems, the most relevant for current purposes being that 'all the laws of a legal system are authorised, directly or indirectly, by one law'.[132] From this, Raz argues, it follows that two laws, neither of which authorizes the creation of the other, do not belong to the same system if there is no law authorizing the creation of both.[133] Thus, for a putative international legal system, the various forms of law practiced by a legal community such as customary law and treaty law form part of a single legal system by virtue of the presupposition of the basic norm which validates both.[134] However, problems emerge with this explanation of the unity of norms into a legal system when we try to identify the basic norm which unifies these two norms into a single legal system. If we try to understand whether, for example, international customary law and international treaty law are part of a single legal system, Kelsen advises us to look at the facts through which the order is 'created and applied'.[135] At the international level, for example, we must 'start from the lowest norm within international law, that is, from the decision of an

[129] ibid.

[130] For a critique of this feature of Hart's rebuttal, see Giudice (n 27), 159.

[131] Lars Vinx, *Hans Kelsen's Pure Theory of Law: Legality and Legitimacy* (Oxford University Press 2007) 184.

[132] Raz, *The Authority of Law* (n 104), 123. The other axiom is that 'two laws, one of which directly or indirectly authorizes the creation of the other, necessarily belong to the same legal system' (ibid). Like Hart, Raz argues that the mere fact that a norm purports to validate another legal system does not give us sufficient reasons to conclude that it belongs to the same legal system. Such an approach fails to capture the significant other reasons why we should conclude that it is not the case, including historical and sociological reasons (ibid 127). For example, on Kelsen's account, where a society previously under colonial rule breaks away from the metropole and establishes its own legal order, and the metropole passes a norm effecting such independence, on Kelsen's account we should continue to conclude that the legal system of the newly independent society and the legal system of the former colonial society are part of the same legal system given that the colonial legal system still claims to validate the legal system of the independent former colony. On this view, the legal system of the United States could be said to be part of the same legal system as the United Kingdom. For Raz, like for Hart, what matters more than validating purport is the attitude of the officials and norm-subjects of a legal system to individuate legal systems; not (or not only) the fact that one legal system purports to validate another (ibid 128).

[133] ibid.

[134] ibid 128.

[135] Kelsen, *General Theory of Law and State* (n 25), 120.

international court'[136] and work our way up the 'chain of validity' to the basic norm. Thus, to establish the basic norm of the international legal system we must start with the decision of an international tribunal and then look to the treaty which established the tribunal to a general norm which obliges states 'to behave in conformity with the treaties they have concluded'[137] and ultimately to the basic norm of international law which provides that 'states ought to behave as they have customarily behaved'.[138]

However, as Raz notes, this method is circular.[139] We can only identify the basic norm of a legal system by looking at the positive norms of the legal system which feature in court decisions and treaties. However, we can only identify the positive norms of the legal system as norms belonging to the same legal system *by identifying the basic norm*. As Raz puts it, we can 'only identify the legal system with the help of the basic norm whereas the basic norm can be identified only after the identity of the legal system has been established'.[140] This means that the role of the basic norm in establishing the systemic nature of norms and law more generally cannot discharge the function attributed to it by Kelsen.

6. Doth Kelsen Protest (International Legal Validity) Too Much?

A comprehensive defence of Kelsen's idea of the basic norm will not be provided here. However, there are two things that can be said in response to the challenges by Hart and Raz to Kelsen's view of the systemic nature of international law on the circularity of establishing the basic norm and the problems of using the idea of validating purport as the basis of the identity of a legal system.

With regard to the circularity critique of Kelsen's idea of the basic norm, the point is well taken.[141] On Kelsen's account, to identify the basic norm we need to look at the 'lowest norms' and work our way up the chain of validity to identify the basic norm. However, we cannot work our way up the chain of validity without being sure of which 'links' constitute the 'chain'. Only the basic norm can serve as a guide to do this. However, if we know the basic norm, we have no

136 ibid 369.
137 ibid.
138 ibid.
139 Joseph Raz, *The Concept of a Legal System: An Introduction to the Theory of a Legal System* (Oxford University Press 1980) 102.
140 Raz, *The Authority of Law* (n 104), 129.
141 Although see Vinx (n 131).

need to work our way up the 'chain' to identify it. So, it is clear that this method is circular.

As noted earlier, Hart's (but also Raz's) solution to this problem is to focus, instead, on the 'mode of recognition',[142] especially by courts, of the sources of the validity of the legal system. However, as has been well documented, Hart's own account of recognition as the basis of the sources of validity of legal systems is *also* beset by circularity.[143] For Hart, the existence of a legal system involves the union of primary and secondary rules, including a rule of recognition specifying 'some feature or features possession of which by a suggested rule is taken as conclusive affirmative indication that it is a rule of the group'.[144] Moreover this rule 'must be effectively accepted as common public standards of official [behaviour] by its officials'.[145] Thus, in order to establish whether legal norms belong to a given legal system, we must look to the grounds of validity of those norms as contained in the rule of recognition of the system as actually recognized by the officials of the system. The question then is how we can identify the relevant officials whose acceptance of the rule of recognition is crucial for the existence a legal system. We are left with two unsatisfactory choices. We can look to alternative grounds to establish who the officials of the legal system are in order to identify the rule of recognition which places in doubt the role of the rule of recognition as the ultimate criteria of validity of the system, as Hart maintains. This is due to the fact that *these* criteria for determining the identity of the officials for the purposes of the rule of recognition would then become the ultimate criteria of validity of the legal system. Alternatively, and more pertinent to the issue at hand, however, is the alternative method: looking to the rule of recognition itself. In order to determine the criteria of validity of the norms of a legal system we look to the criteria of recognition recognized by the officials of the system, but in order to determine which officials count for the purposes of the rule of recognition, we must look to the rule of recognition.[146] The result is a circularity similar to that affecting Kelsen's methodology for establishing the basic norm.

Secondly, as Vinx argues, with regard to the relationship of validating purport, while it is true that the relationship of validating purport will not always

142 Hart, *Essays in Jurisprudence and Philosophy* (n 65), 321.

143 For a list see Michael Giudice and Keith Culver, *Legality's Borders: An Essay in General Jurisprudence* (Oxford University Press 2010) 6. For other circularities in Hart's concept of law, see Matthew Kramer, 'The Rule of Misrecognition in the Hart of Jurisprudence' (1988) 8 Oxford Journal of Legal Studies 401.

144 Hart, *The Concept of Law* (n 34), 94.

145 ibid 116.

146 Some have attempted to resolve this problem by reference to the conventional recognition of the officials of a legal system. See Giudice and Culver (n 143), 15.

provide a good account of the grounds of validity of legal systems in the examples provided by Hart such as his hypothetical Soviet Laws Validity Act,[147] Kelsen's specific use of the idea of validating purport is constrained by the idea of the principle of effectiveness. It is not the case that Kelsen assumes that any attempt whatsoever at validating purport necessarily leads to the conclusion that two norms are part of the same legal system.[148] Rather, the relationship of validating purport is subject to the condition of effectiveness.[149] With respect to the relationship between international law and state law, the question of the effectiveness of the validating purport of international law in relation to state law is, it can be argued, ambiguous. Whereas it seems reasonably clear that an attempted validating purport between state legal systems is problematic—such that the claim by the legal system of one state to validate the legal system of another is likely to be on the whole implausible—it is less clear that the validating purport of state law by *international* law suffers the same fate. Given that international law is effective,[150] and makes claims to establish the validity of state legal systems,[151] we cannot immediately dismiss out of hand the perspective of international law on the validity of state legal systems even when subject to the condition of the principle of effectiveness.[152] As Vinx argues:[153]

> the relations between states are stuck in a transitory stage between an international state of nature that would clearly fail to support the internationalist hypothesis on the one hand and a state of undeniable subjection of states to a binding international legal regulation (that would make a nationalist monism) unavailable on the other. Constraints of efficiency, as a result, do not fully determine the jurisprudential perspective on international law.

Thus, it is not beyond the realms of possibility that Kelsen's claims regarding the validity of state legal orders, and ultimately of the basic norm of the international legal system, is, in fact, plausible.[154] Given that Kelsen recognized that

[147] Hart, *Essays in Jurisprudence and Philosophy* (n 65), 319.

[148] Vinx (n 131), 186.

[149] ibid.

[150] In Henkin's well-known formulation, 'almost all nations observe almost all principles of international law and almost all of their obligations almost all of the time'. Louis Henkin, *How Nations Behave: Law and Foreign Policy* (2nd edn, Columbia University Press 1979) 47.

[151] For a classic account, see Hersch Lauterpacht, *Recognition in International Law* (Cambridge University Press 2012).

[152] 'Kelsen appears to assume ... that [the principle of effectiveness] has no straightforward application when it comes to the relationship between national and international law.' Vinx (n 131), 186.

[153] ibid.

[154] For a similar view see Pierre-Marie Dupuy, 'International Law and Domestic (Municipal) Law', *Max Planck Encyclopedia of Public International Law [MPEPIL]* (2011).

the unity thesis was capable of being approached from alternative perspectives, from the perspective of the state legal system or from the perspective of the international legal system, then the validity of state legal systems and the systemic nature of international law is compatible, on a Kelsenian account, with the principle of effectiveness and coherent from the perspective of his pure theory of law.

Thus, in dismissing the unity thesis according to a general axiom of validating purport, both Hart and Raz arguably fail to acknowledge the constraints imposed by the principle of effectiveness as well as the fact that with respect at least to the relationship between state law and international law, the axiom relating to validating purport has some plausibility.[155] As such, we can read Kelsen, Vinx argues, as endorsing not the general axiom relating to validating purport but rather the application of the axiom at least to the specific case of the relationship between international law and state law subject to the condition of effectiveness.[156] With regard to the current state of international law, 'a number of different choices will live up to the threshold requirements of effectiveness' (including the question of the validity of state legal systems) and are therefore 'jurisprudentially viable'.[157]

In sum, none of this is to assert a categorical conclusion that Kelsen's account is correct or even a more plausible one than Hart's, all things considered. Responding to the circularity in Kelsen's methodology for establishing the basic norm by pointing out the circularity in the method for identifying the rule of recognition is a *tu quoque* argument which does not cure the circularity in the former. However, what it does show is that we have one fewer reason to reject Kelsen's account of the systemic nature of international law from a Hartian or Razian perspective. Moreover, given the emphasis on the principle of effectiveness, it also suggests that we may still have good reasons to accept the systemic nature of international law based on Kelsen's account, in the light of the contemporary practices of international law.[158]

155 Vinx (n 131), 187.

156 It is worth re-emphasizing that Hart acknowledged that this could be a plausible scenario although he doubted that it provided an adequate of the actual practices and behaviours of states. See (n 90) above and Hart, *The Concept of Law* (n 34), 236–37. It could therefore be argued that Hart and Kelsen are not as far apart as would seem on this point.

157 Vinx (n 131), 187.

158 For a similar conclusion, see Giudice (n 27). There is another response we could have to Hart's rebuttal of the use of the no-conflicts theory to support the unity thesis of international law and state law. As will be recalled earlier, Hart rebuts this on the ground that conflicting rules can exist as a matter of logic both within and between systems, not least because statements about normative orders are always system relative. (Hart, 'Kelsen's Doctrine of the Unity of Law' (n 110), 332). However, were one minded to defend Kelsen further, one could reply that conflicts in law are only apparent given the that they are always resolved in practice according to conflicts rules applied by courts such as *lex superiori*, *lex specialis*, or *lex posteriori*. Even in supposed 'conflicts' between state legal systems and international

7. The Evolution of International Law

Views on the 'current state of international law' have also loomed large in rebuttals of Hart's assertion that while constituting law, international law was a 'set' of norms rather than a legal system of the type associated with municipal law.[159] International lawyers and legal theorists have adopted a variety of strategies to use Hart's own account of law against him, at least with respect to his conclusions about international law.[160] As Koskiniemmi and Leino note:

> H.L.A. Hart's famous description of international law in terms of 'rules that constitute not a system but a simple set' prompted generations of international lawyers to argue that a position which associated international law with 'primitive law,' denied its grandeur and was thus mistaken.[161]

The main strategy of international lawyers in the face of Hart's challenges to the systemic nature of international law on its own terms has been to either argue that he misunderstood how international law worked (especially with regard to customary international law),[162] or argue, in a 'near consensus',[163] that his view

legal systems, it is, in practice, rarely the case that courts decide that norm-subjects must both undertake and not undertake a particular action. (Hart describes one such rare instance of the 'pathology' of legal systems with an example from South Africa, Hart, *The Concept of Law* (n 34), chVI, 'The Foundations of a Legal System'). The conflicts are always resolved, which may result in the application of the international norm, or the state-based norm and it is this fact of conflict resolution, rather than the existence of potential conflicts, which makes the no conflicts thesis true. Given that Kelsen argued that the relationship between the two could be viewed from either perspective, the fact that conflicts are resolved in a particular way (eg whether according to the state or international norm) does not undermine the no conflicts thesis. For discussion see Ralf Michaels and Joost Pauwelyn, 'Conflict of Norms or Conflict of Laws? Different Techniques in the Fragmentation of Public International Law' (2012) 22 Duke Journal of Comparative & International Law 349; Valentin Jeutner, *Irresolvable Norm Conflicts in International Law: The Concept of a Legal Dilemma* (Oxford University Press 2017).

159 Hart, *The Concept of Law* (n 34), 236.

160 Waldron's critical comments have already been noted in Chapter 2. Waldron (n 13).

161 Koskenniemi and Leino (n 37), 558; Payandeh (n 33), 978.

162 Ian Brownlie, *The Rule of Law in International Affairs: International Law at the Fiftieth Anniversary of the United Nations* (Martinus Nijhoff 1998). In particular, Murphy notes that there *are* criteria for the recognition of international custom which are not embedded in individual rules of customary law themselves around the criteria for what constitutes state practice as well as *opinio juris* as well as the relationship between them which provide evidence of the existence of a rule of customary international law. In the light of these considerations, he argues, Hart is wrong to conclude that there are no general criteria for the validity of rules of international law; at least with respect to norms of customary international law there are. If these are used to sustain the binding nature of treaties (such as *pacta sunt servanda*), then they can be extended to treaties too. Liam Murphy, *What Makes Law: An Introduction to the Philosophy of Law* (Cambridge University Press 2014) 148–49.

163 Michael Giudice, 'Sources and the Systematicity of International Law' in Samantha Besson and Jean d'Aspremont (eds), *The Oxford Handbook of the Sources of International Law: A Philosophical Perspective* (Oxford University Press 2018). See also Pavel (n 13), 319.

is radically outdated in the light of the development of international law in the intervening sixty plus years since he first penned his account of international law.[164] As such, his conclusions are flawed either in general because he misunderstood international law,[165] or are flawed in relation to the contemporary state of international law sixty years after he made his arguments, or both.[166]

With regard to the latter strategy, Payandeh argues that if what distinguishes a primitive form of law (to which, Hart maintains, international law is analogous) from a modern municipal system are the inefficiencies of the former due to a lack of secondary rules of change, adjudication, and recognition, then in thinking about international law from the perspective of municipal law, as Hart did, we should not look at the *form* of international law in terms of institutions and the lack of a global legislature, police force or court with compulsory jurisdiction but rather at whether the three *functions* associated with these secondary rules are replicated in the practices of international law.[167] Whereas international law may be different in structure and form as compared with municipal systems, provided it achieves the same functions of municipal legal systems in terms of the efficiencies of secondary rules, then it is no less of a legal system than municipal legal systems are on Hart's account.[168] Thus Payandeh argues:[169]

> [r]ather than asking whether international law encompasses legislative, judicative, and executive structures comparable to the municipal system in form, it is more convincing to ask whether the international order comprises structures which effectively fulfil legislative, judicature and executive functions which overcome the defects of a primitive social system.

Adopting a functional approach, he argues, leads to the conclusion that in its current form, the international legal system replicates, to a considerable degree, the functions of secondary rules in municipal legal systems, permitting

[164] For a sympathetic view of Hart's general view of international law based on the realities of the time he was writing (the early 1960s), see Payandeh (n 33), 979. For a partial endorsement of Hart's conclusions, see Pavel (n 13).

[165] 'International law is a legal system. Its rules and principles (i.e. its norms) act in relation to and should be interpreted against the background of other rules and principles. As a legal system, international law is not a random collection of such norms. There are meaningful relationships between them. Norms may thus exist at higher and lower hierarchical levels, their formulation may involve greater or lesser generality and specificity and their validity may date back to earlier or later moments in time'—Steering Group on Fragmentation cited in Murphy (n 162), 146.

[166] See Besson (n 13).

[167] Payandeh (n 33), 981.

[168] ibid.

[169] ibid.

the conclusion that international law is indeed systemic on a Hartian conception of legal system.[170]

With regard to rules of change, whereas the classic understanding of the creation of rules of international law resemble contracting between parties in the form of international treaties, as opposed to rules created for those parties by an authoritative law-maker, Payandeh argues that law-making at the international level has been 'professionalized and institutionalized'[171] in a way which does not fit the classic contract model of the creation of rules of international law.[172] Even the supposedly 'legislation-free' form of customary law has evolved in terms of what constitutes state practice and *opinio juris* which, in part, draws on the voting practices of states in international forums and the resolutions of international organizations.[173] To this can be added the significant law-making powers of international organizations which have developed in the ensuing decades since Hart was writing, including the 'quasi-legislative' functions of the UN Security Council and the legislatures of supranational organizations such as the European Union,[174] as well as the 'legislative' development of peremptory norms of international law.[175]

With respect to rules of adjudication, he notes that whereas international law has not developed to the extent to which there exists an international court of compulsory jurisdiction, the rise of international courts and tribunals which have jurisdiction to determine the law on the matter, as well as the fact that both municipal legal systems and the international legal system both frequently elicit a plurality of adjudicatory structures, mean that there is sufficient analogy between municipal and international legal systems to warrant the conclusion that they both contain rules of adjudication.[176]

Finally, with respect to the question of the validity of international law, and the grounds for envisaging a rule of recognition of international law, Payandeh challenges Hart's conclusions surrounding the non-existence of an international rule of recognition and his rejection of *pacta sunt servanda* as the rule of recognition for international law based on the fact that many obligations under international law do not explicitly stem from international treaties.[177] With respect to the lack of an obvious candidate rule of recognition for a

[170] ibid.
[171] ibid 982.
[172] For example, in the context of the Law of the Sea see James Harrison, *Making the Law of the Sea: A Study in the Development of International Law* (Cambridge University Press 2011).
[173] Payandeh (n 33), 983. See also Murphy (n 162).
[174] Payandeh (n 33), 984.
[175] ibid.
[176] ibid 986.
[177] ibid 989.

putative international legal system, Payandeh observes that Hart is tellingly reticent to specify the precise content of the rule of recognition of *municipal* legal systems. Legal scholars have encountered problems identifying a single rule of recognition of municipal systems in a manner similar to international lawyers doing the same for international law.[178] Moreover, if the function of the rule of recognition is to specify the criteria of validity of the norms of the international legal system, then Article 38(1) of the Statute of the International Court of Justice does a pretty good job of discharging this function.[179] Also, the ambiguities and gaps in different sources of international law (particularly customary international law) are no worse than those that afflict parts of municipal legal systems[180] and the lack of a formal hierarchy of norms does not preclude the systemic resolution of conflicts according to norm-based criteria.[181]

> Thus, he concludes: 'Following Hart's general concept of law, only a characterisation of international law as a legal system, consisting of secondary rules of recognition, change and adjudication, does justice to international law as it presents itself as a normative order in practice and scholarship.'[182]

8. Conclusion

What the preceding discussion illustrates is that when it comes to thinking about constitutional plurality in the suprastate context, there is more than one way to think of a collection of suprastate norms constituting a legal system.[183] It is not implausible to suggest that the current state of international legal practice betrays systemic qualities, whether by reference to a Kelsenian 'principle of effectiveness' or by adopting a 'functional' approach to Hart's account of 'developed' legal systems as the union of primary and secondary rules. Furthermore, even if we assume, *ex hypothesi*, that international law is not a system on a Hartian model of legal validity or reject the conclusion that a basic norm of international law exists, international law could, potentially, be considered systemic in other ways. Even a set of rules of direct validity, as Hart characterized the rules of international law, can be connected in different ways; for example,

178 ibid. See generally Matthew D Adler and Kenneth Einar Himma (eds), *The Rule of Recognition and the U.S. Constitution* (Oxford University Press 2009).
179 Payandeh (n 33), 990; Murphy (n 162), 147.
180 Payandeh (n 33), 991. For discussion in the US context see Adler and Himma (n 178).
181 Payandeh (n 33), 992.
182 ibid 994.
183 Murphy (n 162), 150.

by referring to each other or developing against the background of the existence of other norms.[184] In this way the international legal system could be considered a system of 'interlocking norms', even if not a system on Hart's terms.[185] These norms can serve a variety of functions including providing the basis for the resolution of conflicts between different norms of international law.[186]

Murphy argues that the extent to which we determine whether international law constitutes a system or not depends on which sense of 'system' is 'worth worrying about',[187] leading us back to the questions we considered at the beginning of the chapter. If it is the case that there are different ways of thinking about legal systems and about international law, then our examination of the extent to which international law does or does not constitute a system will depend on what our particular concerns are. If they relate to the question of the fragmentation of international law, we will look for conceptions of legal system which respond to those concerns.[188] If we wish to promote world peace or identify the foundations of a global state or global government, then our conception of system may take a more normative 'Kelsenian' cosmopolitan flavour.[189] On the question of fragmentation, Murphy himself concludes, in a manner similar to Vinx, that international law neither consists in a single overarching legal system with a foreseeable answer to every question which can arise, nor distinct isolated legal systems or regimes but is 'somewhere in the middle'[190] of these two poles. Ultimately, the question of whether an international legal system exists will depend on where our attention lies, and on which practices we focus. With respect to *our* particular concerns, then, the preceding discussion allows us to conclude that we have good reasons to believe that collections of norms beyond the state *can* constitute legal systems *without* the shadow of the state, provided that the 'principle of effectiveness' or the 'attitude of legal officials' conforms with a plausible account of the particular practice in question. In such cases, the 'world state gap' is not a significant impediment to viewing international law, and by extrapolation other forms of suprastate normative ordering at least in principle, in systemic terms, which was our main object of concern. Thus, the possibilities of transnational constitutional plurality remain wide open. Whereas there is more work to be done on the precise shape of *an* overarching international legal system,[191] as well as the types of suprastate

[184] ibid.
[185] ibid.
[186] ibid. See also Michaels and Pauwelyn (n 158).
[187] Murphy (n 162), 152.
[188] Which, as Murphy notes, Raz's looser idea of 'interlocking norms' may suffice here. ibid 150.
[189] See Vinx (n 131), ch6, 'Kelsen's Legal Cosmopolitanism'.
[190] Murphy (n 162), 154.
[191] Vinx (n 131).

normative ordering which can be theorized in systemic terms once the potential obstacle of the 'world state gap' has been removed,[192] we will leave this matter here for now.[193] Rather, based on the conclusions of this chapter, we will, in Chapter 4, examine the question of the identity of legal systems which is our final step towards theorizing the—particularly legal—circumstances of transnational constitutional pluralism.

[192] Terence C Halliday and Gregory Shaffer, *Transnational Legal Orders* (Cambridge University Press 2015); Schultz (n 11).

[193] See Halliday and Shaffer, ibid.

4

Moving Beyond the Monist Manner in Theorizing Constitutional Plurality

1. Introduction

In Chapter 3, we considered the possibilities of understanding international law in systemic terms notwithstanding the existence of the 'world state gap'. This was an important step in theorizing transnational constitutional plurality. However, the circumstances of constitutional pluralism also present us with the fact that not only do multiple legal systems coexist at different levels but that they also overlap, interact, and potentially conflict. This feature of the circumstances of constitutional pluralism raises a further puzzle for our pluralist constitutional theory: in what way do legal systems 'interact' and how do we theorize this interaction? That is, how should we understand the increasingly common phenomenon under the circumstances of constitutional pluralism whereby the courts of one legal system self-consciously recognize and apply the norms of another 'external' system such as, for example, when the courts of a state apply the norms of a transnational legal system, or when the courts of a transnational legal system apply the norms of general public international law? One way to theorize this situation is to conclude that the norms in question all belong to the same legal system such that when the courts of one legal system, say that of a state, apply the norms of another legal system such as international law, those norms are incorporated into, and therefore form part of, the applying legal system. This view is essentially a form of the weaker version of Kelsen's monistic unity thesis considered in Chapter 3. We noted, moreover, in Chapter 3 that if we invoke the principle of effectiveness, this is not an entirely implausible jurisprudential account of the 'ambiguous' current state of the relationship between international law and state law and that Hart conceded that it could, potentially, constitute a good account of this relationship even in terms of account of a legal system which focuses on the attitude of legal officials.[1] However, the extent to which this provides a good account of the relationship

[1] HLA Hart, *Essays in Jurisprudence and Philosophy* (Oxford University Press 1983) 320.

New Constitutional Horizons. Cormac S. Mac Amhlaigh, Oxford University Press. © Cormac Mac Amhlaigh 2022.
DOI: 10.1093/oso/9780198852339.003.0004

between legal systems will, as noted in Chapter 3, be contingent upon the legal practices of different legal systems. The legal practices of the interactions between different legal systems under the circumstances of constitutional pluralism are, as we would expect, diverse, and we need to entertain the possibility that this type of monism does not in *every case* provide a good account of the interactions between different legal systems under the circumstances of constitutional pluralism. Indeed, it is arguable that in many, if not most, cases of the interactions between legal systems under the circumstances of transnational constitutional pluralism that this particular form of monism does *not* provide a good account of the interactions between, say, state and transnational legal systems, or transnational legal systems among themselves.[2] Moreover, in the cases of other instances of legal plurality such as the application of foreign law by state courts, or the application of state norms by indigenous or religious legal systems or vice versa, it will frequently be the case that such norms are not incorporated into the legal system through their recognition and application.

Therefore, whereas we can leave open the possibility that the weaker version of Kelsen's monistic unity thesis provides a good account of certain types of legal interactions—possibly even beyond the case of international law and the law of states—it seems clear that it cannot account for *all* cases of interactions between legal systems under the circumstances of constitutional pluralism. Therefore, alongside a monistic account of interactions between legal systems, in theorizing the circumstances of constitutional pluralism we require an account of interacting legal systems which is, itself, pluralistic.

This aspect of constitutional plurality brings us to the area of the identity of legal systems and in particular, the ways in which we tell different legal systems apart. The identity of legal systems necessarily involves criteria of individuation: a method of determining whether a norm belongs to one or another legal system. It is the question of the identity of legal systems and satisfactory criteria

[2] Indeed, much of the area of constitutional pluralism, especially in the way in which it has been theorized in the context of the relationship between the legal systems of the European Union and its Member States involve an explicit rejection of a characterization of this relationship in terms of monism. For a theorization of the pluralistic nature of this relationship see Cormac Mac Amhlaigh, 'The Anatomy of Constitutional Pluralism in the European Union' in Gareth Davies and Matej Avbelj (eds), *Research Handbook on Legal Pluralism and EU Law* (Elgar 2018). A minority have endorsed the theorization of this relationship in monistic terms which includes MacCormick himself who ultimately opted for a monistic form of 'pluralism under international law' to resolve potential conflicts between EU law and the law of its Member States. Neil MacCormick, *Questioning Sovereignty: Law, State and Nation in the European Commonwealth* (Oxford University Press 1999) ch7, 'Juridical Pluralism and the Risk of Constitutional Conflict'. Other examples include Catherine Richmond, 'Preserving the Identity Crisis: Autonomy, System and Sovereignty in European Law' (1997) 16 Law and Philosophy 377; Alexander Somek, 'Monism: A Tale of the Undead' in Matej Avbelj and Jan Komárek (eds), *Constitutional Pluralism in the European Union and Beyond* (Bloomsbury Publishing 2012).

of individuation which preserves constitutional plurality where it is relevant under the circumstances of constitutional pluralism and helps us move beyond what we identify later in the chapter as a 'monist manner' in theorizing constitutional plurality.

In this chapter we will examine some of the common approaches to identity and individuation based on validity, the nature of particular norms, as well as purposes-based approaches, arguing that the latter approaches provide the most promising basis for identifying satisfactory criteria of the individuation of legal systems for an account of transnational constitutional plurality. However, it argues that current purposes-based approaches such as Raz's are under-inclusive in that the set of reasons dictating how we should individuate norms as 'internal' or 'external' to the system of the applying court is too limited. It therefore develops and defends a broader purposes-based approach to individuation which is linked to the political importance of legal systems. This approach identifies the reasons why we may wish to classify norms as 'internal' and 'external' as *political* reasons which are connected to the supremacy and openness of legal systems. This approach allows us to capture a more diverse array of reasons for classifying a norm as internal and external according to the core characteristics of legal systems, which reflects the many instances of legal interactions under the circumstances of constitutional pluralism in a better way. Moreover, if we consider the characteristics of legal systems in terms of supremacy and openness as implicating moral considerations such as those entailed in interpretivist approaches to law, the approach also fulfils what we argue is a necessary condition of Dworkin's integrity-based account of law, notwithstanding his claims to the contrary.

2. Individuating Individuation

Perhaps the clearest account of the problem of the individuation of legal systems can be found in Raz's account of the identity of legal systems.[3] Following Raz, we can consider the problem of the identity of legal systems as involving two distinct questions: the aspect of the continuity of legal systems and the aspect of the scope of legal systems.[4] The aspect of continuity relates to the question of how we can distinguish between the existence of a legal system over

[3] The problem of the identity of legal systems involves the 'criterion or set of criteria that determines which laws are part of the systems and which are not'. Joseph Raz, *The Authority of Law* (2nd edn, Oxford University Press 2009) 79.

[4] ibid 81.

particular norm-subjects and its replacement by a new one over the same norm-subjects after a period of substantive reform or upheaval such as revolution.[5] It involves a dynamic conception of a legal system which looks at the identity of a legal system over time.[6] The question of scope, on the other hand, relates to a complete description of the legal system in terms of identifying all of the norms which belong to it.[7] The problem of scope, therefore, involves the conceptualization of a legal system at a given moment in time, a 'snapshot' of a legal system including a full account of all of its laws.[8] A momentary legal system is necessarily part of the question of continuity, however. This is because the problem of continuity requires a method of determining whether two momentary legal systems are part of one continuous legal system.[9]

Of the two questions implicated in the identity of legal systems, it is the question of *scope* which is most relevant to the individuation of legal systems in the context of constitutional plurality.[10] Moreover, as the question of scope relates to the extent of legal systems in attempting to provide a 'snapshot' or overview of *all* the norms of the legal system, it entails both the question of when and how legal systems apply norms of external legal systems which are not incorporated into the legal system, as well as the question of whether and how non-positive standards, such as moral standards, can or should be considered part of legal systems when they are referred to by the positive norms of the system.[11] Thus, the question of the identity of legal systems raises two questions for the criteria of individuation of legal systems. The first relates to the question of the criteria we use to distinguish between *positive* laws of a legal system and *positive* laws applied by a legal system but deemed to belong to another legal system.[12] The second relates to the particular concern of debates between inclusive and exclusive legal positivists regarding the relationship between legal systems and moral standards.

[5] ibid; John Finnis, *Philosophy of Law: Collected Essays: Volume IV* (Oxford University Press 2011) ch21, 'Revolutions and Continuity of Law'.

[6] Raz, *The Authority of Law* (n 3), 81.

[7] ibid.

[8] ibid.

[9] ibid.

[10] References to 'identity' or the 'identity of legal systems' will, for this reason, refer to the problem of scope for the remainder of this chapter.

[11] Contrast Raz, *The Authority of Law* (n 3) and Joseph Raz, *Between Authority and Interpretation: On the Theory of Law and Practical Reason* (Oxford University Press 2009) ch7, 'Incorporation by Law', with Matthew Kramer, 'How Moral Principles Can Enter Into the Law' (2000) 6 Legal Theory 83; Matthew Kramer, 'On Morality as a Necessary or Sufficient Condition for Legality' (2003) 48 The American Journal of Jurisprudence 53; Danny Priel, 'Free-Floating from Reality Discussion' (2008) 21 Canadian Journal of Law and Jurisprudence 429.

[12] In which we can include non-state forms of law such as international law, supranational law, and others such as religious and indigenous laws. See Chapter 1.

3. The Monist Manner

Whereas approaches to law based on the attitude of legal officials have expressed scepticism about Kelsen's unity thesis as we have seen in Chapter 3, they have struggled to account for interactions between legal systems which avoid collapsing into the weaker version of his unity thesis. Writing over fifty years ago, Hart identified the problem of the identity of legal systems as part of the 'unfinished business of analytical jurisprudence'.[13] Raz, writing a couple of decades later, also noted that questions of the problems of identity had been neglected by legal philosophers as interest had moved elsewhere.[14] Thus, the question of the identity of legal systems still grapples with a 'monist manner' in respect of interactions between legal systems. This is primarily to do with the role of validity in providing criteria for the individuation of legal systems.

The monist manner is a typical feature of recognition-based accounts of legal systems. This approach includes all norms which fulfil the officially recognized criteria of validity of the legal system within the identity of that system. Hart's account of legal validity provides a particularly clear and well-known example of this monist manner. In his account of the rule of recognition, he included criteria of individuation of norms in that it designated rules betraying 'some feature or features' as 'conclusive affirmative indication that it is a *rule of the group*'.[15] Perhaps more clearly, Hart asserted that '[t]o say that a given rule is valid is to recognize it as passing all the tests provided by the rule of recognition and so as a *rule of the system*'.[16] Thus, on a Hartian account, the rule of recognition contains the criteria for identifying all the laws which the officials of the systems ought to apply,[17] and therefore entails criteria for the individuation of legal systems. The fact that the rule of recognition may be vague and open-textured as well as the fact that it could be incomplete does not undermine its individuating function.[18]

Validity appears, initially, to be a natural and useful way of thinking about the identity of legal systems. It is a necessary condition for considering whether norms belong to a legal system in relation to the question of scope. Of the many potential candidates for the norms of the legal system,

[13] Hart (n 1), 335.

[14] Joseph Raz, 'Two Views of the Nature of the Theory of Law: A Partial Comparison' in Jules Coleman (ed), *Hart's Postscript: Essays on the Postscript to 'The Concept of Law'* (Oxford University Press 2001) 11.

[15] HLA Hart, *The Concept of Law* (Joseph Raz and Penelope Bulloch eds, 2nd edn, Clarendon Press 1994) 92, emphasis added.

[16] ibid 100, emphasis added.

[17] Raz, *The Authority of Law* (n 3) 93.

[18] ibid.

it is only those that the officials of the system ought to recognize and apply that qualify as norms of the legal system.[19] Thus, for accounts of law which emphasize the attitudes of legal officials in legal practice, responding to the question of scope requires, at a minimum, that all the norms that are valid according to the criteria of validity of the system and which the officials of the system ought to apply, are candidate norms for inclusions within in the identity of the legal system.[20]

However, the problem with using validity exclusively as the criteria for the individuation of legal systems is its monist manner. Where the rule of recognition includes criteria of validity for, for example, certain norms of international law, then the norms of international law become part of the state legal system. This is essentially a weak version of Kelsen's unity thesis where the perspective of the unity of international law and state law is viewed from the perspective of state legal officials subject to the principle of effectiveness.[21] This monist manner based on validity as the criteria for the individuation of legal systems therefore transforms the law, as Shapiro colourfully puts it, 'into a vortex that sucks the rules of other normative systems into its voracious maw'.[22]

Therefore, whereas validity does have a role to play in the individuation of legal systems—only those norms which officials ought to recognize and apply according to the criteria of the recognition of the system are part of the identity of the system—it is, by itself, insufficient as an account of constitutional plurality. For this reason, validity is best considered as a necessary, but not sufficient, condition for the criteria of individuation of legal systems.[23]

[19] This remains the case even if, as Raz argues, the rule of recognition itself does not necessarily contain all the criteria of validity of the norms of the system and that legal systems can contain more than one rule of recognition. ibid 94–95.

[20] That we include the norms that officials ought to apply, rather than actually do apply, is explained by our focus on the question of scope relating to a static conception of a legal system at a given moment in time. As Raz notes, given that criteria of validity such as a rule of recognition can be incomplete, indeterminate, and subject to change as a customary rule, courts can and do modify the rule of recognition when they resolve problems of ambiguity or incompleteness in the rule of recognition (ibid). Therefore, when looking at the question of scope, we refer to all the norms a court *ought* to apply based on the available information regarding the criteria of validity at a given moment in time—when the 'snapshot' of the legal system is taken.

[21] Hans Kelsen, *General Theory of Law and State* (Anders Wedberg tr, Harvard University Press 1945) 121.

[22] Scott Shapiro, 'What Is the Rule of Recognition (And Does It Exist)?' in Matthew D Adler and Kenneth Einar Himma (eds), *The Rule of Recognition and the U.S. Constitution* (Oxford University Press 2009) 246–47. Hart was aware of the problem and advanced inchoate criteria based on 'original' and 'derivative' recognition. Hart (n 1), 342.

[23] Raz, *The Authority of Law* (n 3).

4. Beyond the Monist Manner: The Nature of Norms as Criteria of Individuation

It is in part due to the over-inclusiveness of criteria of individuation involving simple recognition-based validity that exclusive legal positivists have argued for the exclusion of moral standards from the identity of legal systems. Raz, for example, argues for an approach to the criteria of individuation based on the *nature* of particular norms which has the effect, on his account, of excluding moral standards recognized and applied by courts from the identity of legal systems. For Raz, the mere fact that the law refers to a standard—validating it and making it applicable within a legal system—cannot mean that that standard then becomes part of the legal system.[24] Otherwise anything and everything normative can be considered part of the legal system including 'the edicts of the Pope or the writings of Kant' where they are referred to by a legal system.[25] Thus, to avoid the over-inclusiveness of a simple criterion of validity, that is the 'monist manner' in theorizing plurality, we need additional conditions to delimit the identity of a legal system. We can, Raz argues, exclude certain norms applied by a legal system from its identity where they are, in Kramer's words 'acceptance-independent'.[26] That is, their validity and applicability to individuals does not depend on their recognition by the law. Moral standards are one such example of 'acceptance-independent' norms. As moral standards apply to individuals anyway, the law cannot 'turn'[27] moral standards into legal standards nor 'empower'[28] morality by referring to it. Even if the law did not refer to the moral duty to keep our promises, for example, the moral duty to keep our promises would still apply to us.[29] From this fact, Raz goes on to argue that when legal systems refer to moral standards, such as the moral standards contained in constitutional bills of rights for example, we should not consider those moral standards as forming part of the identity of the legal system; that is, that our criteria of individuation should designate such norms as 'external' norms.

He offers a primary reason and a subsidiary reason for this conclusion. The primary reason is based on his view of the relationship between valid law and morality. As valid law is itself based on moral principles, when legal provisions

[24] A position he calls the 'simple-minded view' which he attributes to inclusive legal positivism. Raz, *Between Authority and Interpretation: On the Theory of Law and Practical Reason* (n 11), 200.

[25] ibid 194.

[26] Kramer, 'On Morality as a Necessary or Sufficient Condition for Legality' (n 11) , 73

[27] Raz, *Between Authority and Interpretation: On the Theory of Law and Practical Reason* (n 11), 201.

[28] ibid 190.

[29] ibid 184.

refer to moral standards such as the freedom of expression in constitutional bills of rights, the law does not, Raz argues, *incorporate* the moral norm (such that we should consider it as part of the law). Rather, the law *changes the ways in which morality applies to people* by, for example, setting limits to the ways that law-makers can exclude morality, empowering courts to modify moral considerations or considering the impact of certain norms on moral considerations.[30]

The subsidiary reason[31] for excluding morality from the identity of legal systems is based on the political relevance of legal systems. Whereas Raz notes that the reasons for distinguishing between internal and external norms such as moral norms often make 'no practical difference',[32] it does matter for other reasons. The law, Raz argues:[33]

> [is] not merely a set of guides for court decisions. It is a political institution of great importance to the working of societies and to their members. From this point of view a British person cannot say 'Polish law is my law' just because it will be followed by British courts when their conflict-of-law rules direct them to do so. The distinction between standards that the courts have to apply and those that are the law of the land is vital to our ability to identify the law as the political institution it is.

Thus, there are important political reasons for excluding certain norms from the identity of legal systems based on the idea that what is considered 'the law of the land' is important politically.

However, it is not easy to parse precisely the reasons why we should consider the fact that moral norms are directly applicable to subjects, whereas other norms such as those of international law or the law of other state legal systems are not, as significant from the viewpoint of identity. As Kramer has argued, it is not clear that the criteria of acceptance-dependence or independence succeed as criteria of individuation of legal systems on this score. The norms of other legal systems, as well as customary norms, are both acceptance-dependent, yet as Kramer notes, Raz himself acknowledges that customary law *can* form part of the identity of legal systems while the norms of other legal systems cannot.[34] Thus, in Raz's account, there are clear cases of acceptance-dependent norms

30 ibid 196–97.

31 We call this a subsidiary reason as it is not given the extensive discussion and justification as the justification of the primary reason based on Raz's views on the relationship between normatively valid law and morality. See further at section 5.

32 Raz, *Between Authority and Interpretation: On the Theory of Law and Practical Reason* (n 11), 199.

33 ibid.

34 Kramer, 'On Morality as a Necessary or Sufficient Condition for Legality' (n 11), 71, 75.

which we *should* consider part of a legal system which applies its norms, such as customary law, and there are clear cases of acceptance-dependent norms which *should not* properly be considered part of a legal system applying its norms, such as the norms of foreign legal systems. Therefore, simple criteria of acceptance-dependence or independence cannot do the individuating work required to distinguish between norms which are included and excluded from the identity of a legal system.

More generally, it is not clear why the fact that morality applies to us anyway should exclude moral standards from the identity of legal systems when referred to by positive legal norms. How, Raz asks, can a reference to a moral standard by the law turn that moral standard into law?[35] The inclusion of moral standards referred to by the law as part of the identity of legal systems results, he argues, in a lack of resources 'to distinguish between law directing us and the courts to follow some foreign law or to obey the rules of some associations, and so on, and the incorporation of morality'.[36] His worry seems to be that considering moral references in the law as part of the law will result in people thinking that moral standards apply to them only if they are referred to in the law.[37] But why should this be the case? We can coherently view moral standards as binding regardless of their relationship to the law as well as consider moral standards part of the legal system where referred to by that legal system. This remains the case even if we adopt the view that when the law refers to moral standards, it *modifies* how morality applies to us rather than creating fresh moral obligations for us.[38] We will still be able to recognize moral standards that apply to us anyway as well as moral standards whose application has been modified by the law.

Indeed, it seems that the fact that the law has determined that particular moral norms which apply to us anyway should be applied to us in a particular

[35] Raz, *Between Authority and Interpretation: On the Theory of Law and Practical Reason* (n 11), 201.
[36] ibid.
[37] '[The incorporation thesis] has a special difficulty with [the incorporation of morality], for morality applies anyway, and the incorporation thesis suggests that it applies only if incorporated.' ibid 202.
[38] Dworkin picks up and rejects two other reasons Raz advances for the exclusion of moral norms from the identity of legal systems: the fact that law can fail to exist but moral norms cannot and that legal communities can have moral rights and duties that are not legal rights and duties. For these reasons, Raz argues, moral norms should be excluded from the identity of legal systems when applied. Dworkin makes relatively short shrift of these arguments noting that the contingency of the existence of law has no bearing on the question of whether moral norms form part of the law when applied by courts and the fact that there can be moral norms in a legal community which are not part of the law is tantamount to saying that '[w]hen we say that John Donne made certain words part of his poetry we do not deny that there are words he did not make part of his poetry or that there is a difference between the concept of Donne's poetry and the concept of a word'. Ronald Dworkin, *Justice in Robes* (Belknap Press 2006) 240.

way is an analytically relevant fact of interest to our 'general conception of what a legal system is'.[39] The fact that a legal system modifies our moral obligations in a particular way as compared with another legal system which modifies them in a *different* way seems like something which we might want to include in our account of the identity of those legal systems. It is therefore an analytically relevant fact that a legal system chooses to enforce moral standards that already apply to the population in a particular way because just as a population can fail to have law,[40] it can also fail to have law which enforces (already applicable) moral standards in a particular way.

The distinctive way or ways in which legal systems modify moral norms which apply to us seem also to matter for the purposes of identity on the subsidiary ground of Raz's justification: namely, the political import of legal systems and what counts as 'the law of the land'.[41] It would seem that the ways in which a legal system modifies the way that morality applies to us is of considerable 'political importance' (as well as being analytically relevant) in the way Raz describes. This is particularly the case in light of the fact that Raz acknowledges that 'different claims about [the relationship between law and morality] will imply different demarcations of the boundary of law'[42] in different systems. Thus, for example, the (particularly libertarian) way in which the US Constitution modifies our moral obligations not to inhibit freedom of expression is a characteristic feature of the US legal system *qua* political institution such that we should include the way in which such morality is modified as contributing (potentially significantly) to the identity of the US legal system.

Therefore, we have reasons to doubt that Raz's arguments regarding the relationship between law and morality, and in particular the idea that references to moral standards by legal systems modify how morality applies to us rather than create moral obligations for us, can justify the exclusion of moral references to the law from our account of the identity of legal systems. It is at least arguable that our criteria of individuation should catch moral standards referred to by the system even on Raz's view of the relationship between normatively valid law and morality.

39 Raz, *Between Authority and Interpretation: On the Theory of Law and Practical Reason* (n 11), 195.

40 Raz argues that the fact that a population can fail to have law but not morality is a reason for excluding moral references from the identity of the legal system law. ibid 200.

41 ibid 199.

42 ibid.

4.1 'Free-Floatingness' as Determining Identity

Kramer offers alternative criteria of individuation based on the nature of norms in response to Raz's attempts to exclude moral norms. He argues for the inclusion of norms which are 'free-floating' in the sense that they are 'not the products of formally authoritative institutions'[43] within the identity of a legal system that refers to them.[44] Examples of 'free-floating norms' according to Kramer include customary norms as well as, significantly, moral norms.[45] The quality of being free-floating, Kramer argues, makes such norms 'available for incorporation' into 'this or that legal system as one of its laws',[46] leading to the conclusion that they should be properly considered part of the identity of a legal system when referred to by the legal system.

Kramer's approach to the question of individuation, and in particular his criteria of 'free-floatingness', resulting in the inclusion of moral standards referred to by the law as part of the identity of the referring legal system, also, however, leaves room for doubt as to whether this provides satisfactory criteria of individuation. It is not clear why the mere fact of being 'free-floating' has a bearing on whether a norm should be considered as incorporated within a legal system or not.[47] Kramer doesn't explain how the supposed availability of such norms for incorporation into a legal system is distinct from the availability of the positive norms of other legal systems which Kramer argues *should not* be included in the identity of legal systems when referred to, on the grounds that they are the product of some 'contemporaneous system of authority' to which they 'distinctively belong'.[48]

Kramer argues for the inclusion of 'free-floating' norms in the identity of legal systems by contrasting the purposes behind their application to the purposes for recognizing the positive norms of other systems. He argues:[49]

[43] Kramer, 'On Morality as a Necessary or Sufficient Condition for Legality' (n 11), 70.

[44] This is part of a 'disjunctive test' of individuation developed by Kramer which includes a validity-based criteria based on the 'authoritative law-generating organs of the system', ibid. This validity-based criteria suffers from the same problems as general validity-based accounts considered earlier in this chapter and so will not be considered further here.

[45] ibid 72.

[46] ibid.

[47] He notes that '[a]lthough they are not engendered by authoritative law-creating organs of the legal system within which they are operative, they are free-floating and are thus available for incorporation into that system. In this pregnant respect they are distinguishable from foreign laws and from the rules of sporting associations, which are neither free-floating nor created by authoritative organs of the legal system within which they are invoked.' ibid 71.

[48] ibid 72.

[49] ibid.

> When legal officials treat [free-floating norms such as customary norms] as a binding standard within their regime, they are not doing so in order to give due acknowledgment to a co-existent institutional scheme in which the norm has emerged through some process of formal enactment. Instead, the officials are incorporating the norm into their matrix of laws as something that can belong integrally thereto precisely because it does not owe its existence and applicability to its having been formally adopted by some alternative jurisdiction or organisation.

The thought here, then, is that when courts apply positive norms of other legal systems, they do so to give 'due acknowledgement' to a 'co-existent institutional scheme'. As neither customary norms nor moral standards are dependent on an institutional scheme for their existence—they are 'free-floating'[50]—no such motivation of 'due acknowledgement' can be attributed to their application by courts. For this reason, they should properly be considered as forming part of the identity of the applying legal system.

However, it is not clear that the quality of 'free-floatingness' can do the individuating work that Kramer attributes to it. Consider, for example, the norms of other positive legal systems which themselves refer to moral standards such as *contra bonos mores* doctrines in contract law or the moral standards contained in fundamental rights norms such as those contained in the European Convention of Human Rights (ECHR). Where such norms are recognized and applied by another system of authority—such as the UK's implementation of the ECHR in its Human Rights Act 1998—such norms simultaneously enjoy the quality of being both 'free-floating' as well as the 'product of some contemporaneous system of authority'. According to Kramer's criteria, this fact could result in the recognized norm or set of norms both being and not being considered part of the recognizing legal system on the grounds that the norms are both free-floating as well as fulfilling the 'due acknowledgment' condition of his criteria of individuation.

Moreover, there are cases where such 'free-floating' norms are recognized and applied with a specific *reciprocal* regulatory intent; that is, to give 'due acknowledgment to a coexistent institutional scheme' which also recognizes those 'free-floating' norms. Again, this is a common feature of much state behaviour in relation to international human rights law. States often incorporate international human rights law into their legal systems in order to regulate

[50] ibid, noting that both customary norms and moral norms satisfy the criteria of being 'free-floating' based on his 'disjunctive test' of individuation which includes validity-based criteria.

certain matters in a way that others have done (in this case the international community) in order to boost their reputation with the international community; for example, where (moral) human rights norms are recognized and applied by a state legal system to signal a state's status as a legitimate member of the international community.[51] It also occurs between transnational and state legal systems where a transnational legal system wishes to signal to a state legal system its credentials as a legitimate legal system. For example, the judicial development of fundamental rights within the EU's legal system occurred as part of an effort to assuage the fears of Member State courts regarding its human rights *bona fides* in response to criticism from those courts.[52]

In light of the different reasons we may have for considering whether specific norms contribute to the identity of legal systems or not, we can conclude, *pace* Raz and Kramer, that the *nature* of the norm in question *cannot be determinative of questions of identity*. That is, that whether a norm is created by an autochthonous system of authority or an external system of authority, or is acceptance-dependent or acceptance-*in*dependent, or even 'free-floating' cannot, by itself, provide us with satisfactory criteria for the individuation of legal systems. We may have a variety of cross-cutting purposes and reasons to include, as well as exclude, both positive norms of other legal systems as well as moral norms referred to by legal systems within the criteria of the identity of a legal system.

4.2 The Reasons for the Application of a Norm as Criteria of Individuation

We have already seen how the purpose of giving 'due acknowledgement' to alternative systems of authority features in Kramer's criteria. In a similar way, Raz offers two supplementary conditions to his criteria of individuation. He argues that valid norms are to be considered part of the identity of the applying system unless they are applied, 'because the system intends to respect the way that [another] community regulates its activities, regardless of whether the same regulation would have been otherwise adopted' or they are norms made

[51] See, for example, Dana Zartner and Jennifer Ramos, 'Human Rights as Reputation Builder: Compliance with the Convention Against Torture' (2011) 12 Human Rights Review 71.

[52] See, for example, *Internationale Handelsgesellschaft mbH v Einfuhr—und Vorratsstelle für Getreide und Futtermittel*. ECLI:EU:C:1970:114. See generally Gráinne de Búrca, 'The Road Not Taken: The European Union as a Global Human Rights Actor' (2011) 105 The American Journal of International Law 649, 667–68.

by norm-subjects pursuant to powers conferred by the legal system 'in order to enable individuals to arrange their own affairs as they desire'.[53] Where either of these conditions apply to the norms which are valid according to the legal system, we can conclude that the norms are recognized by the system but not part of it.[54]

Each of these 'regulatory intent' conditions supplement validity to make more comprehensive criteria of individuation moving beyond the monist manner. The first, capturing, for example, the application of foreign law under private international law rules,[55] involves a 'co-regulation' condition whereby the application of a norm by a legal system due to an intention to 'co-regulate' an activity in the manner regulated by another system should not mean that the norm is considered to be an internal norm of the applying system. The second captures a 'regulatory autonomy' condition whereby legal systems can be said to facilitate the regulatory autonomy of norm-subjects in particular circumstances. In such cases, the norms applied pursuant to this regulatory autonomy condition should be considered to be external norms applied by the system.

There are a number of questions which these additional 'regulatory intent' criteria of individuation raise. Raz is not particularly forthcoming as to how we might determine regulatory intent in legal systems nor why this should count as part of the criteria for the individuation of legal systems. From his rather terse statement of the criteria, we can glean two motivations relating to each condition. The co-regulation condition seems to stem from a desire or intention on behalf of a legal system to 'respect' the way in which another community regulates its activities. The question then is: what might this desire or intention to respect entail? Should such recognition emerge from some sort of moral compulsion to 'do justice' based on particular 'fact patterns' or according to a particular consequential 'comparative impairment' or some 'governmental interest' or other functional considerations which justify the application of foreign law under private international law rules?[56] Must it conform to ideals of comity, for example, under private international law more generally,[57] or out

[53] Raz, *The Authority of Law* (n 3), 120.

[54] ibid.

[55] ibid.

[56] Ralf Michaels and Joost Pauwelyn, 'Conflict of Norms or Conflict of Laws? Different Techniques in the Fragmentation of Public International Law' (2012) 22 Duke Journal of Comparative & International Law 349, 358–59.

[57] However conceived: as an expression of a moral obligation, expedience, courtesy, reciprocity, utility, or diplomacy. Joel R Paul, 'The Transformation of International Comity' (2008) 71 Law and Contemporary Problems 21; Elisa D'Alterio, 'From Judicial Comity to Legal Comity: A Judicial Solution to Global Disorder?' (2011) 9 International Journal of Constitutional Law 394 <https://doi.org/10.1093/icon/mor036> accessed 18 June 2021.

of some normative ideal of mutual recognition and respect between legal systems? If the latter, what might the limits of such mutual recognition and respect be? Moreover, there is a sense in which the co-regulation condition involves an element of recognition on the part of the external system.[58] Does it matter if the target community is aware of or acknowledges such respect or recognition? Must they acquiesce in this recognition? Can a co-regulatory intent be unilateral?

The condition of regulatory autonomy is similarly ambiguous. It seems to involve a desire or intent on behalf a legal system to 'enable individuals to arrange their own affairs as they desire'.[59] The question then is whether moral criteria of autonomy pursuant, say, to a substantive liberal political philosophy can be attributed to this condition. If so, is it the case that this is a general feature of legal systems or something which only applies to legal systems which can be said to embody or pursue politically liberal ends? What does this then say about the relationship between the moral standards of liberalism and legal systems?

Without clear answers to these questions, it is not clear that regulatory intent is sufficient to determine whether a norm belongs to a legal system or not. If we focus on Raz's first condition, a norm, or a set of norms valid according to the legal system should not be included within the identity of the legal system where they are applied in order to respect or defer to the way an external system regulates a particular matter for whatever reason. However, there may be circumstances where the criteria of validity of a legal system validate a norm or series of norms for reasons which conform with the regulatory intent condition but which should still be excluded from the identity of a legal system on *other* grounds. For example, where a legal system unilaterally 'borrows' norms or even a complete regulatory regime on a particular matter for reasons of efficiency or to solve particular problems internal to the legal system which have nothing to do with the fact that such recognition is acknowledged by the external legal system, it is not clear that such norms should be considered external norms. In such circumstances we may wish to impose a unilaterality exception to the co-regulation condition.

Furthermore, the reasons why a legal system may validate external norms can be more complex than mere regulatory intent. For example, a legal system may have reasons of regulatory continuity for deferring to another legal system on the regulation of particular matters. However, such reasons of regulatory

[58] Particularly in the light of the last line of Raz's criteria: 'regardless of whether the same regulation would have been otherwise adopted', Raz, *The Authority of Law* (n 3), 120.
[59] ibid.

continuity may be superseded by other considerations relating to the autonomy of the legal system when it comes to criteria of individuation. One example of this is the UK parliament's EU (Withdrawal) Act 2018. This is one of the measures taken by the UK legislature to give effect to the 2016 referendum to leave the European Union (including its legal system and the jurisdiction of its courts) while minimizing the economic and social disruption from the act of leaving a political and legal system with which the UK's legal systems have been integrating for the best part of five decades.[60] On its face, the Act fulfils the first condition of Raz's test. It is an explicit intention by the UK legislature to 'respect the way that the [EU] regulates its activities' in a broad array of policy areas after it leaves the organization. As such, when courts in the United Kingdom apply the norms of EU law pursuant to this Act, the norms of EU law should, under Raz's regulatory intent condition, be considered as norms external to the UK's legal systems; that is that they should not be considered part of the identity of the UK's legal systems. However, taking into account the broader political context within which this law was passed, the purpose of this law is to (re)assert the autonomy of the UK's legal systems precisely by incorporating its norms into those legal systems.[61] Thus, whereas Raz's condition of regulatory intent may give us reasons to consider the EU norms as external norms, the purpose of the Act, and the political context within which it was passed, arguably give us stronger reasons for including them within the identity of the UK's legal systems. This latter interpretation arguably better reflects the political purposes of the Act as part of the UK's withdrawal from the European Union, including the freedom to diverge from its regulatory sphere when considered desirable while minimizing the social and economic disruption of departure, than Raz's simpler regulatory intent condition.[62]

What this example shows is not that Raz's criteria are incorrect but rather that they are incomplete. There is a sense in which the question of the criteria

[60] Cormac Mac Amhlaigh, 'Back to a Sovereign Future?: Constitutional Pluralism after Brexit' (2019) 21 Cambridge Yearbook of European Legal Studies 41, 41–48.

[61] ibid 51. See European Union (Withdrawal) Act 2018 Explanatory Notes available at: https://www.legislation.gov.uk/ukpga/2018/16/notes which speaks of 'converting EU law into domestic law', p 5.

[62] Of course, the precise status of EU law in Member State legal systems has been the subject much attention from legal theorists in recent years. For a particularly clear illustration of the issues see Julie Dickson, 'How Many Legal Systems?: Some Puzzles Regarding the Identity Conditions of, and Relations Between, Legal Systems in the European Union' (2008) 1 Problema. Anuario de Filosofía y Teoría del Derecho 9; Julie Dickson, 'Towards a Theory of European Union Legal Systems' in Julie Dickson and Pavlos Eleftheriadis (eds), *Philosophical Foundation of European Union Law* (Oxford University Press 2012); Richmond (n 2); Gareth Davies and Matej Avbelj (eds), *Research Handbook on Legal Pluralism and EU Law* (Edward Elgar 2018). The issue was clarified somewhat by the UK Supreme Court for the purposes of the UK's legal systems in its '*Miller I*' decision: *Miller v Secretary of State for Exiting the European Union* [2017] UKSC 5. See Mark Elliott, 'The Supreme Court's Judgment in Miller: In Search of Constitutional Principle' (2017) 76 The Cambridge Law Journal 257; Mac Amhlaigh (n 60).

of individuation of legal systems is more complex, involving a series of broader and more diverse reasons for concluding that a norm is an internal one of the system or an external one than the 'co-regulation' or 'regulatory autonomy' conditions of Raz's regulatory intent criteria.

5. Does the Monist Manner Matter?

Dworkin's account of law offers a potential alternative which implicitly endorses the monist manner, arguing that the question of identity is not really a problem worth addressing at all. While he notes that what we take to be relevant to determine what legal rights and duties people and officials have is important,[63] little turns on the taxonomic exercise of sifting out these considerations as distinctly legal considerations or belonging to one or another legal system. We may, for linguistic reasons or reasons of clarity talk of what is 'special to law'[64] in general in order to exclude, for example, mathematical formulae from statements about the law. In a similar way we may prefer to exclude foreign law or customary law from a discussion about the law of a particular state and include moral principles in our definition of law when describing the particular practices of courts.[65] However, such a way of talking about the law diverts our attention from what law and legal practice is really about, and runs the risk of committing the mistake of supposing that the 'law' of a community consists of a 'finite body of rules, principles, and other standards that might in theory be listed and counted'.[66] For Dworkin the law is not a fixed set of standards 'of any sort',[67] thereby making the entire taxonomic enterprise of marginal relevance. For Dworkin, as the determination of what the law requires in a given case is ultimately about the 'correct resolution of a moral issue',[68] when judges decide cases, what matters is that they correctly resolve the moral questions raised by the particular dispute.[69] For this reason, when courts adjudicate on what the law requires it matters little whether they consider themselves to be reasoning about the law (thereby distinguishing between legal norms and moral norms) or reasoning according to the law (determining what the law requires when referring to moral standards); they involve considerations of

63 Dworkin, *Justice in Robes* (n 38) 238.
64 ibid.
65 ibid 238–39.
66 ibid 239.
67 ibid 234.
68 ibid 237.
69 ibid 236.

political morality 'all the way down'.[70] The question of the individuation of legal systems has little or nothing to do with this exercise in moral reasoning. In the light of the centrality of the morality to his account of adjudication, it would appear that Dworkin's approach to identity would be entirely comfortable with some sort of unity thesis where here the unity relates not to positive law, as in Kelsen's account, but the resolution of disputes according to universal moral standards. On this reading, then, the monist manner is not the 'sting' of a monistic 'bug' but a central feature of an interpretivist account of law.

However, it is not clear that this monistic reading of Dworkin's views on individuation coheres with his account of law as integrity more generally. As is well known, Dworkin's account of law as integrity involves the interpretation of the 'brute facts of history'[71] in their best light by reference to an underlying scheme of principle.[72] Moreover, the underlying scheme of principle is made up of 'associative obligations'[73] assumed by members of a 'community of principle'[74] which involves bonds of fraternity and an equal concern for members of the community.[75] However, as Dworkin explicitly acknowledges, the associative obligations generated by communities of principle are *not* universal moral standards emanating from a universal morality or natural law which might support a monistic reading of this interpretive account of law.[76] They are autochthonous principles generated by the distinctive social practices of distinctive communities of principle.[77] He makes very clear that the associative obligations of a given community of principle 'may be different from those of other communities',[78] and that the bonds of fraternity and equal concern that they entail are *not* extended to non-members of the group.[79] In this way,

[70] ibid.

[71] ibid 255.

[72] In earlier work, Dworkin saw the relevance of integrity to law as having two dimensions: the dimension of fit—relating to the 'brute facts of legal history' and providing a 'rough threshold requirement that an interpretation of some part of the law must meet if it is to be eligible at all'—and the dimension of justification—requiring an interpretation of the historical record informed by the scheme of principles of political morality upheld by the community of principle which shows the historical record in its best light. Ronald Dworkin, *Law's Empire* (Belknap Press 1986) 255. However, in later work he rejected this 'two-systems picture' on the grounds that it simultaneously endorses two incompatible views of law: an analytical positivist one implied in the dimension of fit, and an interpretivist one based on the dimension of justification; and endorsed a single system view whereby the determination of the relevant historical record implicated the underpinning justificatory principles' which treats law as 'part of political morality'. Ronald Dworkin, *Justice for Hedgehogs* (Belknap Press 2011) 403.

[73] Dworkin, *Law's Empire* (n 72), 196.

[74] ibid 227.

[75] ibid 213.

[76] ibid 263, 397.

[77] ibid 263. Moreover, these will, in part, be determined by the size and shape of the particular community: ibid 197.

[78] Dworkin, *Law's Empire* (n 72), 213.

[79] For Dworkin, these associative obligations are 'special' in that the yield 'distinctly within the group, rather than as general duties its members owe equally to persons outside it', ibid 199.

Dworkin's associative obligations serve to define—individuate even—a particular community of principle and its law from other communities of principle. In short, the nature of associative obligations imbues a community of principle and its law with a distinctive moral, political, and legal *identity*.

Given the way in which these obligations of political morality feature in Dworkin's concept of law—justifying judicial decision-making and legitimating coercion more generally[80]—then recognition of the particular moral identity of the community of principle is central to his account of law as integrity. As Dworkin makes clear, if judicial decisions are based on considerations which do not involve those principles, such as the personal convictions of individual judges, then the decision cannot be legitimate. Integrity requires, in the terms of Dworkin's memorable metaphor, that judges decide cases based not on unconstrained personal conviction, but rather as multiple authors of a 'chain novel' who are therefore 'constrained' by the development of the 'novel' by previous 'authors'.[81] By the same token, we can conclude that if a judicial decision is based on the law (including the principles of political morality) of a *different* community of principle, such as another state, or a supranational community such as the European Union, then such a decision could not be legitimate under Dworkin's scheme in that it would not keep with the 'spirit' of the previous 'chapters' of the 'chain novel'. Therefore, Dworkin's account of law as integrity arguably presupposes the individuation of different communities of principle, their associative obligations, and their *law* in order to allow judges to make decisions which conform with the requirements of integrity. It therefore is not compatible with a monist manner in thinking about the identity of legal systems.

The fact that the principles of integrity necessarily include considerations of the individuation of communities of principle does not mean that a judge deciding on the basis of the law of another political community or system can *never* be justified. It may be the case that a judicial decision based on the law of another community can serve to legitimate coercion. Rather, integrity must require that where the courts in a community of principle apply the law of another community of principle, the *relevant laws of the different communities be appropriately individuated.*

This point is developed somewhat by Dworkin himself in his posthumously published paper on international law.[82] Here Dworkin provides a way of

[80] ibid 188.

[81] Dworkin, *Law's Empire* (n 72), ch6, 'Integrity'. See also Ronald Dworkin, *Freedom's Law: The Moral Reading of the American Constitution* (Oxford University Press 1996).

[82] Ronald Dworkin, 'A New Philosophy for International Law' (2013) 41 Philosophy and Public Affairs 2.

understanding the legitimacy of applying the norms of other communities (in this case primarily the norms of the international community) within a distinct state-based community of principle in the form of a principle of 'salience'.[83] The justification of coercive political power, for Dworkin, arises not just within states but with regard to the system of international law as a whole.[84] Thus, the principles that legitimate the (external) international legal system are not independent 'but are actually part of the coercive system each of those states imposes on its citizens'.[85] From this, Dworkin argues, it follows that:

> [t]he general obligation of each state to improve its political legitimacy includes an obligation to try to improve the overall international system. If a state can help to facilitate an international order in a way that would improve the legitimacy of its own coercive government, then it has a political obligation to do what it can in that direction.[86]

According to the principle of salience, then, states are under an obligation to subscribe to an international regulatory scheme developed by the international community where it has the effect of enhancing its own legitimacy as well as the legitimacy of the international system as a whole.[87] Furthermore, the domestic relevance of the principle of salience requires that the constitutional courts of states should be 'drawn to notice and attempt to achieve some integrity with the constitutional principles of other nations'.[88] The principle of salience, therefore, grounds the moral obligation on communities of principle to apply the norms of other communities of principle such as the international community, or other states, in certain circumstances.

However, lest it be construed that Dworkin is here arguing for some sort of transcendental or universal moral standard of legitimacy along the lines of a monist manner which would undermine the role and relevance of identity to his conception of law as integrity, he continues that this obligation demands 'only what, in the circumstances, is feasible'.[89] 'It does not require any state', Dworkin argues, 'to ignore the division of the world into distinct states *and suppose that it has the same responsibilities to citizens of other nations as it has to its own*.'[90] Thus, the obligations stemming from the principle of salience as

[83] ibid 19.
[84] ibid 16.
[85] ibid 17.
[86] ibid, emphasis added.
[87] ibid.
[88] ibid 21.
[89] ibid 17.
[90] ibid, emphasis added.

legitimating the coercion of states through the application of the law of other communities are subject to a key distinction between different communities of principle. This distinction holds even if, as Dworkin argues, one of the principles which supports the legitimacy of the international system—the principle of salience—requires that courts apply the law of other (state) communities of principle.[91]

This demand need not rule out expressions of solidarity and coherence of purpose with other legal systems such as those prescribed by the principle of salience. What it does require, however, is that law is *individuated*, as a preliminary matter, into distinct communities of principle so as to ensure that coercion is properly legitimated.

6. Individuation as (Political) Reasons

At this juncture, it is worth taking stock of our argument. Establishing the identity of a legal system through some sort of criteria of individuation is necessary to avoid the 'monist manner' in analytical approaches to legal systems and give a fuller account of constitutional plurality in the contemporary world. Simple validity is a necessary but insufficient condition for determining the identity of legal systems as it exemplifies the monist manner. The nature of the norm in terms of its acceptance-dependence, independence, or 'free-floatingness' is itself contingent upon other reasons we might have for including or excluding norms from the identity of a legal system. Finally, regulatory intent, particularly as elaborated by Raz, is under-inclusive.

In this section, a reasons-based approach to the identity of legal systems will be defended, drawing upon but broadening Raz's reasons-based approach. The reasons for individuating norms in a particular way in this account are reasons that relate to the *political importance of legal systems*. As we noted in our discussion of Raz's reasons for excluding morality from the identity of legal systems in section 4, legal systems are *political* institutions which are important to the societies over which they govern.[92] The criteria of individuation between what features as part of the 'law of the land' and what standards a court merely has to apply are central to the political importance of legal systems.[93] Moreover, the political importance of legal systems stems from the particularly intimate

[91] ibid 21.
[92] Raz, *Between Authority and Interpretation: On the Theory of Law and Practical Reason* (n 11), 199.
[93] ibid.

relationship between legal systems and political systems. Revising and updating to a constitutional pluralist context Raz's comments on the relationship between law and the state,[94] we can argue that every political system and social system has a legal system that constitutes the law of that system.[95] The identity of the legal system is, moreover, 'bound up'[96] with the political system. We can conclude from this, paraphrasing Raz, that a theory of law must be based at least partly on a theory of a political and social system and that a theory of a political and social system is partly based on a theory of law.[97] We can therefore see that the relationship between normative political and social systems and legal systems of whichever type are important for the identity of legal systems and therefore for criteria of individuation.

Furthermore, we can identify two general ways in which legal systems are politically important. One relates to the identificatory function of legal systems which Raz emphasizes when he speaks of the political importance of legal systems in terms of constituting the 'law of the land'.[98] In this regard, legal systems contain 'political laws'[99] which are a 'function'[100] of the identity of the political system. Legal systems contribute to the definition and identity of a political community through these 'political laws' which protect particular values of the political and social system. For this reason, with respect to the relationship between the political and legal systems of *states* in particular, constitutional and administrative laws are more relevant to the identity of the legal system than the law of contract or torts.[101]

A second way in which legal systems are politically important is the way they facilitate interactions between a political system and other systems. As Raz notes, political systems interact with other political systems.[102] Legal systems contribute to these interactions by applying norms of other political systems through private international law rules, giving effect to international law and so on. Political systems, furthermore, interact with other *social* systems including the society which they organize politically.[103] A legal system again

[94] Raz's own contribution to a 'pluralist jurisprudence' including the claim that a jurisprudential focus on state legal systems is not justified has already been considered in Chapter 2. Joseph Raz, 'Why the State?' in Nicole Roughan and Andrew Halpin (eds), *In Pursuit of Pluralist Jurisprudence* (Cambridge University Press 2017).
[95] Raz, *The Authority of Law* (n 3), 98–99.
[96] ibid 99.
[97] ibid.
[98] Raz, *Between Authority and Interpretation: On the Theory of Law and Practical Reason* (n 11), 193.
[99] ibid 100.
[100] ibid.
[101] ibid.
[102] ibid.
[103] ibid.

can facilitate these interactions by recognizing and applying norms of social sub-systems, for example, the norms of private associations or other social groupings, and thereby support the politically important interactions between a political system and a social system. In all of these ways, then, legal systems can be politically important.

Moreover, viewing the identity of legal systems through the prism of the political importance of legal systems helps us better understand the core features of legal systems as institutional systems identified by Raz. Legal systems, Raz argues, have three characteristic features: comprehensiveness, supremacy, and openness.[104] It is these features that distinguish legal systems from other normative systems. Comprehensiveness involves the idea that legal systems claim authority to regulate any type of behaviour.[105] Supremacy, an entailment of comprehensiveness, involves the idea that legal systems claim authority 'to regulate the setting up and application of other institutionalized systems by its subject-community'.[106] With regard to the question of openness, Raz says that a normative system is an open one 'to the extent that it contains norms the purpose of which is to give binding force within the system to norms which do not belong to it'.[107] The reasons why legal systems recognize these norms stem from a desire to 'maintain and support'[108] other forms of social grouping such as private associations as well as from a desire to have relations and interact with other legal (and therefore also political) systems.

If we treat comprehensiveness and supremacy as a single feature of legal systems given the entailment of the latter by the former, we can see how the core features of legal systems map on to the ways in which legal systems are politically and socially important. The politically important identificatory function of legal systems is expressed in the claims to supremacy of legal systems over other institutionalized systems of the subject community. It is this claim to supremacy of the legal system which supports the political identity of the political system by giving clear definition to what the subjects of the legal system have in common: the legal and political system.[109] Moreover, the openness of legal

[104] ibid 116.
[105] ibid.
[106] ibid 118.
[107] ibid 119.
[108] ibid.
[109] We can, in this regard, invoke Kelsen's remarks on the way in which law gives expression to political unity. Hans Kelsen, 'On the Essence and Value of Democracy' [1927] in Arthur Jacobson and Bernhard Schlink (eds), *Weimar: A Jurisprudence of Crisis* (University of California Press 2000) 90. We don't need to go as far as Kelsen in assuming that a political system can *only* exist through the legal system, though, to argue that law and legal systems have a role in institutionalizing and shaping the political unity of political systems. Moreover, given this important identificatory role, the legal system gives expression to this political identity by claiming supremacy over other institutional systems of the norm-subjects

systems somewhat self-explanatorily expresses the interactions between the political system and other political systems and between the political system and social systems.

The basis for the criteria of the individuation of legal systems defended here, therefore, lies in the ways in which a particular norm applied by a legal system serves one of these two politically important features of legal systems in a better way. If, in a given context, a valid legal norm can be said to express the supremacy of a legal system (and therefore its broader political identificatory function), then it is best considered an internal norm of the system. On the other hand, if a valid legal norm can be said to express the politically important function of the openness of legal systems, it is best designated as an 'external' norm of the system, adopted but not incorporated into the system. We can formulate our criteria of individuation based on these political reasons in the following terms: a norm is an internal norm of a legal system if, and only if, it is valid according to that system and supports the supremacy of that legal system; a norm is adopted but not incorporated into a legal system if, and only if, it is valid according to that system and supports the openness of that system.

According to this approach, therefore, the method of creation of the norm is relatively unimportant. The fact that a norm was produced by the 'authoritative law-creating organs'[110] of the *applying* legal system will only contribute to its being considered an internal norm of the system by virtue of its relationship to the supremacy of that system. By the same token, the fact that a norm applied was originally created by an 'alternative system of authority'[111] will only contribute to its designation as an external norm to the extent that its application is related to the openness of the legal system. The nature of the norm in terms of being acceptance-dependent, acceptance-independent, or free-floating will, in a similar way, only matter to the extent to which it helps us establish whether the norm in question relates to one of these two conditions. However, none of these characteristics of norms can be determinative of the question of whether the norm is to count as an 'internal' or an 'external' norm. We may have reasons to designate a norm as internal even if it was produced by

of the system. For a good example of the way in which the supremacy claims of a legal system shore up the identity of the political system, see the German Federal Constitutional Court's deployment of a 'constitutional identity' doctrine in respect of potential conflicts with EU law. See Christian Calliess, 'Constitutional Identity in Germany: One for Three or Three in One?' in Christian Calliess and Gerhard van der Schyff (eds), *Constitutional Identity in a Europe of Multilevel Constitutionalism* (Cambridge University Press 2019).

[110] Kramer, 'On Morality as a Necessary or Sufficient Condition for Legality' (n 11), 71.
[111] ibid.

an alternative system of authority on the grounds that its validity relates more closely to the supremacy of the applying legal system. Arguably, the UK's EU Withdrawal Act 2018 which refers to the corpus of EU law on the date of the UK's withdrawal is an instance of this. Similarly, notwithstanding the 'free-floating' nature of a norm such as a moral norm, we may have reasons to conclude, *pace* Kramer, that the norm is better understood as an external norm where the bindingness of the norm is more closely related to the openness of a legal system, such as where human rights norms are recognized by a legal system for reputational reasons. Alternatively, we may, *pace* Raz, have reasons to designate an acceptance-independent norm such as a moral norm as an *internal* norm where the reasons conform more closely with the supremacy condition of individuation. This could occur where a legal system recognizes and applies a moral standard as part of its 'constitutional identity'[112] and therefore conforms in a more apt way to the supremacy condition, or the particular way in which a legal system modifies or modulates the ways in which moral reasons apply to individuals.

These two overarching criteria provide a better account of the reasons we have to individuate norms than the alternatives considered earlier in a way which moves beyond the monist manner. First of all, they add that important missing condition to validity. Furthermore, they help us make sense of the ways in which the type of norm involved, such as its method of production or its 'free-floating' nature, relates to the question of identity. They also broaden the number of reasons we may have for considering a norm as an external or internal one based on the political importance of legal systems beyond those contained in Raz's 'regulatory intent' condition.

Approaching the question of individuation in terms of the dual criteria of supremacy and openness-related reasons for designating norms as internal or external norms also sheds light on the nature of putative conflicts between legal systems. The rise in the number of legal systems over the past number of decades, particularly at the transnational level, has resulted in the increased threat of conflicts between the norms of each system.[113] These are often characterized as *inter*-systemic conflicts[114] and a wide variety of solutions have been

[112] See, for example, the role of fundamental rights in the 'constitutional identity' doctrine of the German Federal Constitutional Court. Calliess (n 109).

[113] Neil MacCormick, 'Risking Constitutional Collision in Europe?' (1998) 18 Oxford Journal of Legal Studies 517; Erich Vranes, 'The Definition of "Norm Conflict" in International Law and Legal Theory' (2006) 17 European Journal of International Law 395; Valentin Jeutner, *Irresolvable Norm Conflicts in International Law: The Concept of a Legal Dilemma* (Oxford University Press 2017); Michaels and Pauwelyn (n 56).

[114] Michaels and Pauwelyn (n 56), 375.

advanced to resolve these conflicts.[115] However, characterizing such conflicts as conflicts *between* legal systems presupposes an Archimedean vantage point from which such conflicts can be approached. However, as noted in Chapter 3, Kelsen's 'no-conflicts' justification for his unity thesis is based on statements about what norms require ('descriptive ought statements'),[116] which set up the possibility that two norms could require conflicting things are always made *relative* to the systems that they describe.[117] Moreover, this can only make sense if we eschew the monist manner in thinking about the identity of legal systems. Thus, a putative conflict say, between a state constitutional norm and a norm of the EU legal system,[118] is not a true conflict between the norms of each system as the requirements of their norms, even if they require contrary things, are relative to each system. Rather, in the many cases, particularly involving EU law, which are adduced as evidence of conflicts between legal systems,[119] the criteria of individuation defended here show us how such putative inter-systemic conflicts are better understood as conflicts *within* a legal system involving norms designated as 'internal' and 'external' according to the supremacy and openness of the legal system. The fact that such conflicts emerge internally in a legal system as opposed to between two different systems does not result in the reintroduction of the monist manner by the back door, however. The reasons for this are similar to the reasons why Hart and Raz rejected the stronger version of Kelsen's monism in Chapter 3; namely, the attitude of legal officials. For Hart and Raz, it was the fact that state legal officials did not in fact recognize the unity of state legal systems and international law that led to their rejection of monism in all cases. In a similar way, it is the fact that courts do not accept, for example, that the norms of EU law and state legal systems form part of one big legal system which precludes a monist view of their interactions and potential conflicts. This is clearly evidenced by their individuation of norms into 'internal' (domestic) and 'external' (EU) norms in their invocation of constitutional identity.[120]

Such conflicts therefore involve a norm which relates to the supremacy of the legal system and a norm which relates to the openness of a legal system. Ultimately, therefore, these conflicts involve a putative conflict between the

[115] See Matej Avbelj and Jan Komárek, *Constitutional Pluralism in the European Union and Beyond* (Hart 2012); Davies and Avbelj (n 62).

[116] Hart (n 1), 333.

[117] ibid 331.

[118] MacCormick (n 113).

[119] Calliess (n 109).

[120] ibid, *passim*. For a nuanced account of debates on constitutional identity in the EU context, see Julian Scholtes, 'Abusing Constitutional Identity' (2021) 22 German Law Journal 534–56.

political ends of the supremacy of a legal system and the political ends of the openness of a legal system to be resolved internally by the organs of the legal system itself according to these ends. Of course, the way in which such conflicts are managed and resolved will have an impact on external legal systems, particularly a system which may 'claim' the norm deemed to be 'external' in the conflict as 'internal' to its system. Moreover, how the officials of the external legal system view the way in which the conflict is resolved may influence the resolution of the conflict within the applying system, potentially resulting in, for example, a preference for the political ends of openness over the political ends of supremacy in a given case. However, this does not change the fact that the conflict remains internal to the applying legal system.

As the designation of a norm as internal or external is based on political reasons on the view defended here, each designation will be dependent upon the political context in which the norm is applied. This means that this approach to individuation does not provide a particularly sharp test to determine the identity of legal systems.[121] After all, Raz does recognize that the question of individuation is 'particularly vague'.[122] However, approaching the question in terms of political reasons for designating the norms one way or another does, it is submitted, serve a useful goal of at least clarifying some of the vagueness surrounding the question by acknowledging the diversity of reasons we will have for making the designation, classifying them according to the binary criteria of supremacy or openness, and recognizing that they relate to political reasons stemming from the fact that legal systems are politically important, and ultimately, provides an account of the identity of legal systems beyond the 'monist manner' of other accounts which is more conducive to constitutional plurality and the circumstances of pluralism more generally.

7. The Political Importance of Law as Integrity

This approach also supports the individuation of law necessary for law as integrity. As noted earlier, notwithstanding Dworkin's claims to the contrary, we have good reasons to believe that integrity also requires criteria of individuation to justify coercion in the manner Dworkin proposes. The moral norms which support law as integrity are the autochthonous principles which emerge from the associative obligations of communities of principle. Applying the law

[121] Raz, *The Authority of Law* (n 3), 84.
[122] Raz, *Between Authority and Interpretation: On the Theory of Law and Practical Reason* (n 11), 195.

according to the personal convictions of judges or applying principles which do not stem from the associative obligations of the relevant community of principle, would, without more, fail to justify coercion in this way. The one exception to this is the principle of salience, where supporting and applying the law of other communities of principle such as other states or the international community can also serve to legitimate coercion.

The approach outlined here based on the politically important reasons of supremacy and openness can therefore support Dworkinian integrity too. If we understand the supremacy of legal systems as supporting the application of the scheme of principle stemming from the associative obligations of communities of principle, and the political importance of openness as supporting the principle of salience, we can see that they can also be supported by moral considerations which support law as integrity. If the moral principles of the relevant community of principle justify coercion in that community, supremacy serves the important moral purpose of identifying the principles of that community which legitimate that coercion. Similarly, if the principle of salience plays a role in justifying coercion within the community through the application of 'external' law, then openness serves the purpose of legitimating coercion according to these external norms. Furthermore, on a Dworkinian account, the reasons which are included within the criteria of supremacy or openness can themselves be thoroughgoing moral reasons of the relevant community of principle. For example, we can easily envisage moral reasons relating to democracy, self-determination, or a more general 'constitutional identity' for considering the principles emerging from the associative obligations of a community as internal norms of the system. In the same way, substantive moral considerations can support the designation of norms of the law of a community of principle as external norms according to the principle of salience. One striking example of this is provided by Dworkin himself where he argues that coercion can be legitimated through the application of (external) laws whose ends are a stable international order which 'protects political communities from external aggression, protects citizens of those communities from domestic barbarism, facilitates coordination when this is essential, and provides some measure of participation by people in their own governance across the world'.[123] Moreover, we can see how the ends of justice can be said to be served through the facilitation of interactions by the legal system between political and social systems whether in terms of distributive justice, corrective justice, or otherwise.[124]

[123] Dworkin, 'A New Philosophy for International Law' (n 82), 22.

[124] See, for example, Anthony T Kronman, 'Contract Law and Distributive Justice' (1980) 89 Yale Law Journal 472.

However, notwithstanding the fact that the question of individuation can be moral 'all the way down' for Dworkin's account of law as integrity, the determining criteria of individuation will be morally relevant reasons relating to the supremacy and openness of the law of the relevant community of principle.

8. Conclusion

The issue of the identity of legal systems and establishing criteria of individuation of norms is central to avoiding the monist manner and providing a better account of constitutional plurality under the circumstances of constitutional pluralism. This is particularly the case where identity becomes central to the resolution of potential conflicts between 'internal' and 'external' norms which is becoming increasingly common in certain contexts such as the application of EU law in the legal systems of its Member States.[125]

If the 'vagueness' which characterized the distinction could be excused by the infrequency with which we need to rely on it,[126] then, under our contemporary circumstances of constitutional pluralism, this is arguably no longer the case. In this regard, it is argued that criteria of supremacy and openness based on the political importance of legal systems provide an improvement on extant approaches to the question of individuation which moves beyond the monist manner in conventional approaches to identity and provides a better account of constitutional plurality for our contemporary circumstances of constitutional pluralism.

[125] Avbelj and Komárek (n 115).

[126] Raz notes that the 'vagueness' between 'what is part of the law and what are standards binding according to the law' is unsurprising because 'we do not often need to rely on it'. Raz, *Between Authority and Interpretation: On the Theory of Law and Practical Reason* (n 11), 195.

PART II
LEGITIMACY

5
Constitutional Dualisms

1. Introduction: Constitutional Dualisms

Having examined the descriptive idea of 'constitution' as an account of legal systems in Part I, we now move on to look at the value of 'constitutionalism' as a normative account of legitimate political authority. In this opening chapter of Part II, we examine in more detail the different ways in which constitutionalism has been interpreted as a political value in terms of a schematic overview of the dominant trends which have emerged in thinking about constitutionalism as a normative political theory of legitimate authority. Our analysis will therefore address the variety of meanings associated with the idea of constitutionalism as a series of constitutional 'dualisms'. Approaching the concept of constitutionalism in terms of these dualisms helps improve our understanding of the conceptions at stake in the critiques of constitutionalism considered in Chapters 6 and 7 and establish the groundwork for a normative account of transnational constitutional pluralism developed and defended in Chapter 8.

2. What is Constitutionalism?

When Thomas Paine asked, 'what makes a good constitution?' and answered that it is one which is novel, republican, and guarantees equality and freedom,[1] he was referring to a constitution not merely in our descriptive sense as an account of a legal system but to a *particular type* of governing regime: one which is *legitimate*. What Paine was doing in his account of a 'good' constitution was advancing the idea of a constitution as a normative theory of legitimate government; that is, an account of constitutional*ism*. 'The last two syllables of "constitutionalisM'—the "-ism" suffix', Waldron advises, 'should alert us to the possibility of *additional* meanings' to the descriptive meaning considered in Part I of our volume which 'involve a theory or a set of normative claims.'[2]

[1] John J Meng, 'The Constitutional Theories of Thomas Paine' (1946) 8 The Review of Politics 283.
[2] Jeremy Waldron, *Political Theory: Essays on Institutions* (Harvard University Press 2016) 24.

New Constitutional Horizons. Cormac S. Mac Amhlaigh, Oxford University Press.
DOI: 10.1093/oso/9780198852339.003.0005

Thus, Waldron argues, '[c]onstitutional*ism*, is like 'liberal*ism*, social*ism*, or scient*ism*';[3] a 'sort of ideology'[4] entailing an attitude that constitutions are important and that deviation from them should elicit an attitude of disapprobation. In this sense, constitutionalism is a form of normative political theory which contains norms and standards which, the theory claims, serve to legitimate a particular governing regime.[5]

Constitutionalism, then, marks a shift in register from a concept which describes and explains the idea of fundamental law and legal system contained in our discussion of constitution in the first part of the book to a normative theory which entails a set of normative standards of good government which support a 'right to rule'.[6] An arrangement set up by a constitution which practices or inculcates the virtues of constitutionalism can therefore claim to be a legitimate arrangement from the viewpoint of normative political theory.[7]

Normative theories of constitutionalism betray a diversity of approaches as to what, precisely, makes government legitimate in constitutional terms, bringing us to the first of our dualisms reflecting two general approaches to the idea in constitutional discourse: regulative constitutionalism and constitutive constitutionalism.[8] The first connotes the idea of *limited government* such that the limitations placed on governing power by theories of constitutionalism serve to legitimate the exercise of that power.[9] The second involves the idea that constitutionalism facilitates the activity of governing or provides it with legitimate foundations and to this extent has an affinity with the etymological root '*constitūere*'[10] which, Kalyvas argues, involves a portmanteau of '*con-*' whose

[3] ibid 24.

[4] ibid 25.

[5] Cormac Mac Amhlaigh, 'Harmonising Global Constitutionalism' (2016) 5 Global Constitutionalism 173, 184.

[6] ibid. Allen Buchanan and Robert O Keohane, 'The Legitimacy of Global Governance Institutions' (2006) 20 Ethics & International Affairs 405, 411.

[7] M Loughlin, 'Constitutional Theory: A 25th Anniversary Essay' (2005) 25 Oxford Journal of Legal Studies 183.55; Mac Amhlaigh (n 5), 183.

[8] Dario Castiglione, 'The Political Theory of the Constitution' (1996) 44 Political Studies 417, 418. These two approaches can also be expressed in terms of a medieval distinction between gubernaculum and jurisdiction; between 'government' and 'law' as highlighted by McIlwain. See Charles McIlwain, *Constitutionalism: Ancient and Modern* (Liberty Fund 1947) 71. For discussion of this distinction in the context of the rule of law, see Gianluigi Palombella, 'The Rule of Law and Its Core' in Gianluigi Palombella and Neil Walker (eds), *Relocating the Rule of Law* (Bloomsbury 2009).

[9] Giovanni Sartori, 'Constitutionalism: A Preliminary Discussion' (1962) 56 The American Political Science Review 853, 864. In this sense, the constraints on governing are instrumental in that they serve to enhance the legitimacy, and therefore the capacity, of public power. Martin Loughlin, *The Idea of Public Law* (Oxford University Press 2004) 86.

[10] Andreas Kalyvas, 'The Basic Norm and Democracy in Hans Kelsen's Legal and Political Theory' (2006) 32 Philosophy & Social Criticism 573, 588.

meanings include 'with' or 'together' with '*statuo*' meaning to 'cause to stand, to set up, to construct, to put, to place, to erect'.[11] Thus, according to Kalyvas, the word 'literally denotes the act of founding together, founding in concert, or creating jointly'[12] where that which is being 'established' or 'founded' is a legitimate authority.[13]

3. Regulative Constitutionalism

The core idea of regulative constitutionalism as normative theory involves the idea of *limited* government, what Sartori has called *guarantisme* constitutionalism.[14] As Sartori notes, however, what precisely is being guaranteed receives 'different complex and changing answers'.[15] Within the idea of regulative constitutionalism, then, we encounter our next dualism in that the regulative constitutionalism prescribes two forms of limiting government: legal and institutional.

3.1 Legal Constraints

Legal constraints on the exercise of political power may be the older of the two in chronological terms. McIlwain, for example, makes the claim that '[i]n all its successive phases … constitutionalism has one essential quality: it is a legal limitation on government'[16] and that 'the most ancient, the most persistent, and the most lasting of the essentials of true constitutionalism still remains what it has been almost from the beginning, the limitation of government by law'.[17] In contemporary constitutional thought this form of *guarantisme* constitutionalism is reflected in viewing the constitution as 'supreme' or 'higher law'.[18] Thus, constitutionalism denotes a form of law which is superior and supreme over ordinary law to which even the governing authority must

[11] Andreas Kalyvas, 'Popular Sovereignty, Democracy, and the Constituent Power' (2005) 12 Constellations 223, 235.
[12] ibid 236.
[13] ibid.
[14] Sartori (n 9); Martin Loughlin, *Foundations of Public Law* (Oxford University Press 2010); Castiglione (n 8).
[15] Sartori (n 9), 855.
[16] McIlwain (n 8), 24.
[17] ibid 24.
[18] Dieter Grimm, 'Types of Constitutions' in Michel Rosenfeld and András Sajó (eds), *The Oxford Handbook of Comparative Constitutional Law* (Oxford University Press 2012) 109.

conform,[19] thereby limiting its freedom of action. In practical terms, the idea of constitutionalism as limitation on government through its status as higher law cashes out primarily in terms of the issue of constitutional amendment. If the constitution is to function as a restraint on government, it must be a form of law which is hierarchically superior to the ordinary law created by government and therefore binding not only on citizens but on governing authorities themselves.[20] Fundamental laws which can be amended by government in the manner of ordinary legislation would provide little restraint and fail to conform to the ideals of constitutionalism as higher law.[21] Thus, whereas the limiting function of constitutional law pursuant to constitutionalism's ideals of limited government do not necessarily require that the constitution be immutable, it usually requires that the hurdles to amendment are higher than those for ordinary laws.[22] Therefore, one key prescription of regulative constitutionalism as a legal limitation on government is the *entrenchment* of constitutional law, at least to some degree.

Another key prescription commonly associated with constitutionalism as a legal limitation on government is the role of the judiciary in the interpretation and enforcement of constitutional norms. Given the fact that constitutionalism as limited government has often meant legal limitations, it is unsurprising that courts have been increasingly associated with *guarantiste* accounts of constitutionalism, as the ultimate arbiters of the constitutionality of governmental action, and ultimately, therefore, the guarantors of the protections and limits entailed in the idea of constitutionalism. The 'year zero' of this development in modernity[23] can be identified as 1803, the year in which US Chief Justice John Marshall enunciated his view that 'it is emphatically the province and duty of the judicial department to say what the law is'[24] in the celebrated *Marbury v Madison* decision of the fledgling Supreme Court of the United States.[25] The

[19] In this respect constitutionalism as 'higher law' guarantisme constitutionalism is the antithesis of '*legibus solitus*' accounts of governing authority. See Juan Linz, *Totalitarian and Authoritarian Regimes* (Lynne Rienner 2000) 51.

[20] Grimm (n 18), 109.

[21] ibid 110.

[22] See Bruce Ackerman, 'Constitutional Politics/Constitutional Law' (1989) 99 The Yale Law Journal 453.

[23] Ancient Athens also had recourse to the law to resolve political disputes albeit that their courts were forms of popular assembly rather than the types of professionalized judicial bodies we recognize today. See Paul Cartledge, *Democracy: A Life* (Oxford University Press 2016) ch10, 'Athenian Democracy in Court: The Trials of Demos, Socrates, and Ctesiphon'.

[24] 5 US (1 Cranch) 137, 177 (1803).

[25] Even if the tracing of judicial supremacy back to this decision is arguably largely tenuous and judicial supremacy has as much to do with post-war constitutional politics in both the United States and Europe. See Keith E Whittington, *Political Foundations of Judicial Supremacy: The Presidency, the Supreme Court, and Constitutional Leadership in U.S. History* (Princeton University Press 2009); Akhil Reed Amar, 'Foreword: The Document and the Doctrine' (2000) 114 Harvard Law Review 26.

positioning of courts—and particularly apex courts such as supreme or constitutional courts—as the ultimate interpreter of constitutional values slowly spread throughout the globe and undertook a particularly rapid acceleration in the mid-twentieth century.[26] In the light of this trend, then, 'constitutionalism' as a legal restraint on the exercise of governing power has become increasingly synonymous with judicial supremacy.

The idea of constitutionalism as a normative account of legally limited government draws upon two significant traditions of political thought: the rule of law and the idea of natural or human rights.[27] The ideals of the rule of law as the 'government of laws and not of men' can be traced back to Ancient Greece[28] and its use as a justification for constitutional entrenchment and judicial supremacy is easy to understand. If a key virtue of government is one which follows the law, then it is entirely legitimate in the pursuit of this ideal for constitutional systems to ensure that all branches of government conform to the law. This can include mechanisms to disarm the government from acting contrary to law through ordinary legislative measures by establishing supervisory mechanisms to ensure that unlawful acts are identified and rectified. The obvious candidate institution to undertake this latter task are legal experts—courts—who can review, and where necessary strike down, the acts of the other institutions which are contrary to the law. On this view, there is a clear logical progression from constitutionalism as legal limitation as supported by the ideals of the rule of law, to access to judicial remedies to ensure that cases of breach by governing institutions are identified and resolved, to, ultimately, judicial supremacy.

The idea of rights as providing the justification for legal limitations on government can be traced back to the social contract tradition and particularly Locke's account thereof.[29] If individuals are endowed with natural rights and import these rights from the state of nature to civil order, then any mechanism through which these rights are protected, including disbarring government from infringing these rights through judicial control if necessary, is entirely

[26] Mainly following the arrangements established in the Austrian constitution of 1920 influenced by See Tom Ginsburg, 'The Global Spread of Constitutional Review' in Keith Whittington, R Daniel Kelemen, and Gregory Caldeira (eds), *The Oxford Handbook of Law and Politics* (2008) 82. Goldoni argues that the intellectual origins of constitutional review can be found in the writings of de Sieyès, see Marco Goldoni, 'At the Origins of Constitutional Review: Sieyès' Constitutional Jury and the Taming of Constituent Power' (2012) 32 Oxford Journal of Legal Studies 211.

[27] Ginsberg adds a need to adjudicate jurisdictional disputes between different levels of government as another important motivation for judicial review. Ginsburg (n 26), 85

[28] Jeremy Waldron, 'The Rule of Law' (2020) *Stanford Encyclopedia of Philosophy* <https://plato.stanford.edu/archives/sum2020/entries/rule-of-law> accessed 21 June 2021; Brian Z Tamanaha, *On the Rule of Law: History, Politics, Theory* (Cambridge University Press 2004) ch1, 'Introduction'.

[29] See Tamanaha (n 28), ch4, 'Locke, Montesquieu, the Federalist Papers'.

legitimate. In contemporary constitutional thought this ideal is reflected in liberal theories which justify the exclusion of particular values from governmental interference based on the fact that they emerge from an 'original position,'[30] 'overlapping consensus,'[31] or are based on the 'sovereign virtues' of a particular constitutional settlement.[32] Given that these values are most basic or fundamental, then, they can and should be shielded from quotidian political processes through legal means such as their codification in a bill of rights or some other form of 'higher law' beyond the reach of daily politics.[33]

3.2 Structural Regulation

The second form of limited government which has informed understandings of constitutionalism draws on one particular tradition of republicanism.[34] This structural form of regulative constitutionalism, which is based primarily on Roman as opposed to Greek ideals of government, and particularly Roman republican ideals of mixed government,[35] as resurrected in the city-states of the Italian peninsula and subsequently adopted and endorsed further north in France, England, and the United States[36] posit constitutionalism as a legitimate form of government based on the existence not of a single ruler or single ruling institution but rather a plurality of ruling institutions, which will keep each other in check. This idea was perfected in the idea of the 'separation of powers' promoted by Montesquieu and the French and American revolutionaries.

The key justification for this structural form of limiting government is clear in Montesquieu's *Spirit of the Laws* where he argued that '[c]onstant experience shows us that every man invested with power is apt to abuse it' such that '[it is] necessary from the very nature of things that *power should be a check to power*'.[37] This idea was prominent in the French Declaration of the Rights of Man and the Citizen where it stated in no uncertain terms that a society where

[30] John Rawls, *A Theory of Justice* (Harvard University Press 1973).

[31] John Rawls, *Political Liberalism* (Columbia University Press 1993).

[32] Ronald Dworkin, *Taking Rights Seriously* (Duckworth 1977).

[33] Rawls (n 31), 218.

[34] That is the 'instrumental turn' in republican thought as opposed to the 'civic humanist' interpretation of republican thought. See generally Frank Lovett, 'Republicanism' (2018) *Stanford Encyclopedia of Philosophy* <https://plato.stanford.edu/archives/sum2018/entries/republicanism> accessed 21 June 2021.

[35] John Thornton, 'La Costituzione Mista in Polibio' (2011) 3 Montesquieu.it 1.

[36] JGA Pocock, *The Machiavellian Moment: Florentine Political Thought and the Atlantic Republican Tradition* (Princeton University Press 2009).

[37] Charles de Montesquieu, *Montesquieu: The Spirit of the Laws* (Anne M Cohler, Basia Carolyn Miller, and Harold Samuel Stone eds, Cambridge University Press 1989) 214.

the separation of powers is not secured '*has no constitution at all*'.[38] However, it is, perhaps, in the thinking which influenced the drafting of the US constitution where Montesquieu's ideas were perfected by the American federalists. For example, James Madison in *Federalist* No 47 argued that 'the great security against a gradual concentration of the several powers in the same department, consists in giving to those who administer each department the necessary constitutional means and *personal motives* to resist the encroachments of the others', concluding with perhaps the most aphoristic statement of the purpose of the separation of powers: 'Ambition must be made to counteract ambition.'[39] In a similar vein John Adams argued that legitimate government required that '[p]ower must be opposed to power, force to force, strength to strength, interest to interest, as well as reason to reason, eloquence to eloquence, and passion to passion'.[40]

Part of the reason for the insistence by the US founding fathers on *structural*, rather than mere *legal* limitation on government was based on the experiences of the constitutions of the thirteen states of the confederation. It was the failure of legal limitations in the state constitutions which preceded the US federal constitution of 1787 which led them to believe that an institutional separation of powers was required to deliver the ideals of this particular form of *guarantisme* constitutionalism. For example, Hamilton noted:[41]

> The propensity of the legislative department to intrude upon the rights, and to absorb the powers, of the other departments ... *the insufficiency of a mere parchment delineation of the boundaries of each* ...; and the necessity of furnishing each with constitutional arms for its own defence, has been inferred and proved.

Madison, in a similar manner asked:[42]

> [w]ill it be sufficient to mark, with precision, the boundaries of these departments in the constitution of the government, and to trust to these *parchment barriers* against the enriching spirit of power? This is the security which

[38] Art 16.

[39] Alexander Hamilton, James Madison, and John Jay, *The Federalist: With Letters of Brutus* (Terence Ball ed, Cambridge University Press 2003) No 47

[40] Loughlin, *Foundations of Public Law* (n 14), 57; Zsolt Haraszti, John Adams and the Prophets of Progress (Harvard University Press, 1952) 219, cited in Hannah Arendt, *On Revolution* (Penguin 1973) 152.

[41] Hamilton, Madison, and Jay (n 39); *Federalist* 73, emphasis added.

[42] ibid; *Federalist* No 48.

> appears to have been principally relied on by the compilers of most of the American constitutions. But experience assures us, that the efficacy of the provision has been greatly overheated; and that some more adequate defence is indispensably necessary for the more feeble, against the more powerful, members of the government.

The precise method of checks and balances to which this particular mode of regulative constitutionalism relates can take a variety of forms. It is, perhaps, more perfectly achieved in presidential systems with a sharp separation between the executive and the legislature, and in systems with bi-cameral legislatures such as in the United States, and less perfectly achieved in parliamentary executives with unicameral legislatures such as in Scotland. However, at the very least, checks and balances constitutionalism as a form of regulative constitutionalism involves a structural separation between the executive, legislative, and judicial branches of government.[43]

The most common justification for the separation of powers is to avoid 'abuse of power' or 'tyranny'; tyranny here often equated with absence of liberty.[44] Notwithstanding the fact that liberty and the avoidance of tyranny has become a commonplace justification for this particular type of regulative constitutionalism, the relationship between separating powers and preventing tyranny and securing liberty has, Waldron argues, traditionally been underspecified.[45] He argues that Montesquieu's justifications, in particular, are 'mostly tautologies'[46] and that modern constitutionalism takes for granted that the separation of powers is necessary to avoid tyranny but doesn't explain why.[47] For Waldron, a better, albeit non-exhaustive, justification of the separation of powers, at least between the executive and legislature, lies in Locke's admonition that those who make the law should not execute them given the temptation for leniency with respect to one's own actions.[48] Furthermore, Locke's arguments for legislation by representative assembly contains a similar justification: that allowing

[43] Jenny S Martinez, 'Horizontal Structuring' in Michel Rosenfeld and András Sajó (eds), *The Oxford Handbook of Comparative Constitutional Law* (Oxford University Press 2012). Waldron identifies five distinctive (albeit close-knit) principles in the separation of powers; Waldron (n 2), 49.

[44] In Montesquieu's words: 'When the legislative and executive powers are united in the same person, or in the same body or magistracy, there can be then no liberty.' Montesquieu (n 37), 216. Madison in *Federalist* No 51 argued that the separation of powers was 'essential to the preservation of liberty'. Hamilton, Madison, and Jay (n 39). See also MJC Vile, *Constitutionalism and the Separation of Powers* (Liberty Fund 2012) 14.

[45] Waldron (n 2), 45.

[46] ibid 45.

[47] ibid 44. 'Much of what [Montesquieu] said consists of simple assertions' (ibid 60). More generally he argues that there is a distinct 'lack of argument in the canonical sources' (ibid 62).

[48] ibid 54.

non-privileged actors (ie ordinary citizens) to make the law means that they will be mindful that they will be subject to those self-same laws resulting in law-making which will be more conducive to the public good than private interests.[49]

A much more substantive and robust justification for the structural regulation of governing power beyond 'Montesquieu's tautologies' has been developed in neo-republican theories of freedom, as exemplified in the work of Philip Pettit.[50] This particular conception of freedom is distinguished from freedom as non-frustration and freedom as non-interference[51] by highlighting 'the absence of a power of interference on the part of another'; in short, non-domination.[52] Thus, freedom on this view is inconsistent with the relative freedom of the slave of a benign master, or the relative freedom of a neglected colony given that the risk always remains of the benign master or the colonial power interfering with the choices of the slave or the colony. This republican view of freedom takes the contingency out of interferences with individual freedom through structural means by ensuring that individuals are free by removing the capacity of other actors to arbitrarily interfere with their choices.[53] From this basis, a relatively simple argument can be constructed for structural constraints on governing power. To the extent that individual power-wielding institutions are inhibited from arbitrarily interfering in the choices of its citizens due to the existence and capacity of other governing institutions to provide a check and balance to their power in a form of 'mixed constitution' or a separation of powers mechanism, then republican freedom is secured.[54]

[49] ibid 54.

[50] Philip Pettit, *Republicanism: A Theory of Freedom and Government* (Clarendon Press 1997). Philip Pettit, *On the People's Terms: A Republican Theory and Model of Democracy* (Cambridge University Press 2012).

[51] Variously associated with Hobbes and Berlin. See Pettit, *On the People's Terms: A Republican Theory and Model of Democracy* (n 50), ch1, 'Freedom as Non-domination'.

[52] ibid 64.

[53] ibid.

[54] ibid 220–24. This equation of republican freedom and structural regulation shouldn't mask considerable disagreement about what role courts should have in such a 'mixed constitution.' For example, Pettit argues that the aims of structural regulation types of constitutionalism should include 'editorial' non-electoral institutions such as courts to correct 'electoral shortfalls' (ibid 233–34). In the light of this endorsement of courts in particular as legitimate institutions to correct the deficiencies of representative institutions in ensuring republican freedom, Richard Bellamy—notably a fellow republican—argues that Pettit's own prescriptions in terms of institutional design end up violating the republican ideal of freedom. Richard Bellamy, *Political Constitutionalism: A Republican Defence of the Constitutionality of Democracy* (Cambridge University Press 2007) 175–79. For discussion on this point and a republican defence of judicial supremacy, see Tom Hickey, 'The Republican Core of the Case for Judicial Review' (2019) 17 International Journal of Constitutional Law 288.

4. Constitutive Constitutionalism

As with regulative constitutionalism, we encounter a further constitutional dualism in the idea of constitutive constitutionalism. We can think of the idea of 'constitutive' constitutionalism in two senses: as facilitating the (normative) ends of government and as providing or establishing the basis of legitimate political power. In the former, thinner, sense the existence of the constitution itself—that is the rules, structures, and institutions set up by the constitution which provide the basic order of governing authority—take on a normative significance. A normative theory of constitutive constitutionalism in this thinner sense sees the existence of basic rules and institutions as instrumental, facilitating the achievement of values of coordination and guidance.[55] Again, as Waldron notes, constitutions 'empower'.[56] Through the establishment of basic norms and institutions which regulate how other norms can be created and through which governing institutions can be established, constitutions create the conditions for achieving the benefits of coordination which produces the conditions for what we might abstractly call 'the goods of the political'.[57] 'Constitutions do not merely limit power', Holmes argues, they can also 'create and organize power as well as give it direct[ion]'.[58] 'When a constituent assembly establishes a decision procedure', he continues 'it actually *creates a framework* in which the nation for the first time, [can] have a will.'[59] Constitutionalism is therefore associated with the activity of government and all its associated benefits.[60]

Constitutions can, moreover, also facilitate the achievement of other normative values associated with governing authority, such as democracy. From a democratic point of view, constitutive constitutionalism can establish the conditions which make democracy possible. These goods of constitutive constitutionalism are nicely captured by Waldron:

> The constitution ... provides housing for the political activity of a society, establishing an in-between of furniture and formality so that public

[55] Joseph Raz, *Ethics in the Public Domain: Essays in the Morality of Law and Politics* (Clarendon 1995) ch10, 'Authority, Law, and Morality'.

[56] Waldron (n 2), 34.

[57] Frank Michelman, 'Ida's Way: Constructing the Respect-Worthy Governmental System' (2003) 72 Fordham Law Review 345.

[58] Stephen Holmes, *Passions and Constraint: On the Theory of Liberal Democracy* (University of Chicago Press 1997) 163–64, emphasis added.

[59] ibid 175.

[60] As expressed in the idea of 'gubernaculum'. See Graham Maddox, 'A Note on the Meaning of "Constitution"' (1982) 76 The American Political Science Review 805 809.

> deliberation becomes a structured enterprise, allowing the views of one person to be brought articulately into relation with the views of others and facilitating the formation of well-thought-through, responsible, and politically effective opinions. This is not primarily a matter of constraint; it is a matter of what a constitution affirmatively makes possible out of what would otherwise be the loose, lurching and dangerous politics of the street.[61]

In this sense, then, constitutions provide the structures or the 'grammar and syntax' of democracy and politics more generally.[62]

The second, thicker sense of constitutive constitutionalism relates to what Paine had in mind when he stated that a constitution is a 'thing antecedent to the government'.[63] On this view all constitutions are established 'on the authority of a people' or the 'nation'.[64] On this thicker sense of constitutive constitutionalism, it is not enough that mere fundamental laws exist bestowing powers on governing institutions to achieve the goods of the political, but the fundamental laws must be established by the *correct agent* with the *correct will* in order for the institutions and the law they produce to be legitimate. This influential understanding of constitutive constitutionalism reflects the tradition of thinking about constituent power.[65] The idea of a constituent power has, itself, taken the form of a variety of dualisms.[66] It has been used to both support and resist royal power,[67] to capture the distant historical foundations as well as the living embodiment of constitutional government,[68] as the expression, as well as the antithesis of constitutional democratic ideals, as well as an expression of political mobilization which is not constrained by institutional or legal structures and therefore can be mobilized against established constitutional arrangements.[69] As a result, the invocation of a constituent power to support particular values, such as democracy, is not particularly straightforward. It could be argued that the constituent power gains expression in a democratically

[61] Waldron (n 2), 36.

[62] ibid 294. As Waldron notes, this idea of a constitution as a necessary condition for politics and freedom is a core theme in the writings of Hannah Arendt (n 2), ch12, 'The Constitutional Politics of Hannah Arendt'.

[63] Thomas Paine, *Paine: Political Writings* (Bruce Kuklick ed, Cambridge University Press 1989) 81.

[64] ibid.

[65] See generally Martin Loughlin and Neil Walker (eds), *The Paradox of Constitutionalism: Constituent Power and Constitutional Form* (Oxford University Press 2008).

[66] On the uses and abuses of historical genealogies of the idea of constituent power see Lucia Rubinelli, *Constituent Power: A History* (Cambridge University Press 2020) 'Introduction'.

[67] ibid.

[68] ibid 20. On constituent power as the embodiment of contemporary government, see Loughlin's 'relational' account, Loughlin, *The Idea of Public Law* (n 9), ch6, 'Constituent Power'.

[69] Carl Schmitt, *Political Theology: Four Chapters on the Concept of Sovereignty* (George Schwab tr, University of Chicago Press 2010).

elected deliberative legislative chamber,[70] which militates against other organs of government—notably the judiciary—interfering in the acts of the legislature. In this sense it could be invoked as a bulwark against judicial supremacy.[71] However, the idea of constituent power can and has been used to *support* judicial supremacy where the judiciary is cast as the true custodian of the will of the constituent power as against the more prosaic legislative power of transient political representatives.[72] Indeed, it can be used to support a particularly strong form of judicial supremacy which applies even to attempts to amend the constitution itself, potentially undoing or interfering with the acts of the original constituent power in the recognition of 'unconstitutional constitutional amendments'.[73] As Rubinelli notes, however, notwithstanding their diversity, all these discourses of constituent power share a desire to 'translate the abstract principle of popular power into concrete political and institutional realities'[74] which involve distinctive moments in the process of 'negotiation, reassessment and redefinition of the meaning and extension of popular power'.[75]

5. Constitutionalization

Given that the term has gained increasing currency, and for the sake of completeness, it is worth also looking at the different meanings that can be attributed to the term 'constitutionalization'. As the suffix '-ation' suggests, denoting a noun of action,[76] 'constitutionalization' captures the idea of *becoming constitutional*.[77] As it describes a process of becoming 'constitutional'

[70] Such as the attempt, for example, to equate the UK doctrine of parliamentary sovereignty with the expression of a constituent power. Dicey, for example, noted that Parliament's unlimited law-making power to change 'fundamental or so-called constitutional laws ... in the same manner as other laws' is nothing more than what some call 'constituent power'. Albert Venn Dicey, *Introduction to the Study of the Law of the Constitution* (3rd edn, Macmillan & Co. 1889) 37. Similarly, de Tocqueville remarked how the UK parliament is at once a 'legislative and constituent assembly'. Alexis de Tocqueville, *Democracy in America* (David Campbell 1994). See generally, Joel I Colon-Rios, *Constituent Power and the Law* (Oxford University Press 2020).

[71] In a similar manner to the way in which the doctrine of parliamentary sovereignty operates to disbar the judiciary from ever questioning the constitutionality of the legislation of the UK parliament. See generally Paul Reid, *Public Law* (4th edn, Green 2020) ch3, 'Foundations'.

[72] Waldron (n 2), 39; Ackerman (n 22); Grimm (n 18).

[73] Yaniv Roznai, *Unconstitutional Constitutional Amendments: The Limits of Amendment Powers* (Oxford University Press 2017). Richard Albert, *Constitutional Amendments: Making, Breaking, and Changing Constitutions* (Oxford University Press 2019); Silvia Suteu, *Eternity Clauses in Democratic Constitutionalism* (Oxford University Press 2021).

[74] Rubinelli (n 66), 32.

[75] ibid 31.

[76] See OED online '-ation' suffix. https://www-oed-com.ezproxy.is.ed.ac.uk/view/Entry/12523?rskey=dm4Rsp&result=1&isAdvanced=false#eid.

[77] Martin Loughlin, 'What Is Constitutionalisation?' in Petra Dobner and M Loughlin (eds), *The Twilight of Constitutionalism* (2010).

or 'constitution-like', our understanding of constitutionalization will therefore depend on how we understand 'constitution'. The diversity of meanings of constitution and constitutionalism in a descriptive as well as a normative register considered here and in Chapter 2 means that we can understand constitutionalization similarly to refer to a descriptive or a normative process of becoming 'constitution-like'. At a descriptive level constitutionalization can simply mean formalization, and particularly legal formalization. Thus, a set of informal practices could be said to be 'constitutionalized' when they are put into more formal terms such as through their codification or through the establishment of formal constitutions. In this sense, constitutionalization can simply mean 'legalization'[78] or 'juridification';[79] that is, the putting into formal legal measures practices which were previously informal.

A second sense of constitutionalization, a particularly jurisprudential one, involves the evolution of what Hart and Kelsen called 'primitive' legal orders to 'municipal' or 'developed' legal orders.[80] As noted in Chapter 2, 'primitive' legal orders are primarily customary legal systems which may lack formal institutions of enforcement.[81] For Kelsen, 'primitive' legal systems are decentralized in that the enforcement of their norms in cases of violation are left to the interested parties to the case. More 'developed' legal systems, such as state legal systems, have centralized enforcement mechanisms with bureaucracies and specialized organs and agencies to determine cases of breach and determine and apply the consequences of violations of the norms of the system.[82] A similar distinction was drawn by Hart in his account of primitive and municipal legal systems. Hart noted that it was possible to imagine 'primitive' societies lacking formal institutions of government made up almost entirely of 'primary rules of obligation'.[83] The rules of such societies would lack the certainty of identifying the valid applicable rules, they would be static in terms of the lack of an efficient method of amending the rules to address new circumstances, and they would also be inefficient in terms of their interpretation and application.[84] For Hart, these defects can be remedied through the introduction of 'secondary rules'

[78] See generally Judith Goldstein and others, 'Introduction: Legalization and World Politics' (2000) 54 International Organization 385, 399.

[79] At least in the cognate sense to legalization involving the institutionalization of social practices in law or the expansion of legal forms of interaction. See Lars C Blichner and Anders Molander, 'Mapping Juridification' (2008) 14 European Law Journal 36.

[80] Hans Kelsen, *General Theory of Law and State* (Anders Wedberg tr, Harvard University Press 1945) 160; HLA Hart, *The Concept of Law* (Joseph Raz and Penelope Bulloch eds, 2nd edn, Clarendon Press 1994) chV, 'Law as the Union of Primary and Secondary Rules'.

[81] Kelsen (n 80), 160.

[82] ibid.

[83] Hart (n 80), 91.

[84] ibid 92–93.

which regulate the identification of valid rules, the procedures for their production and amendment, as well as the method of interpretation and application. Such rules are enjoyed by 'developed' legal systems[85] and it is the presence or absence of such secondary rules which distinguished 'developed' municipal legal systems from 'primitive' legal systems. Thus, in this jurisprudential sense, then, constitutionalization can refer to the process through which the norm-based practices of a society of primary rules of obligation evolves into a 'developed' legal system through more centralized enforcement or the gradual evolution or introduction of secondary rules. It is unsurprising, then, that this meaning of constitutionalization has been particularly popular as a means of capturing the 'constitutionalization' of international law as considered in Chapter 3.[86]

With regard to a process of becoming constitutional in a normative register, this captures the process through which governmental practices increasingly conform to the normative ideals of constitutionalism through, for example, the promotion of the rule of law, the development of the judicial review of governing actions, or the increased protection of fundamental rights. This notion has been frequently adopted in recent times to capture the transformation of authoritarian regimes into liberal democracies in Iberia, the former Soviet empire and, more latterly, the 'Arab Spring'.[87] It has also been used to describe changes in transnational governance towards, for example, the enhanced protection of fundamental rights in the development of transnational law and policy[88] or the increased transparency or responsiveness of global governance organizations.[89] In some cases 'constitutionalization' has been used in a pejorative sense, as involving the spread of a particular neoliberal ideology involving the attempt to 'subject the exercise of all types of public power, whatever the medium of its exercise' to the discipline of constitutional procedures and norms',[90] a critique we will explore in more detail in Chapter 6.

[85] ibid 95.

[86] Jan Klabbers, Anne Peters, and Geir Ulfstein, *The Constitutionalization of International Law* (Oxford University Press 2009) ch1, 'Setting the Scene'.

[87] See generally Nimer Sultany, *Law and Revolution: Legitimacy and Constitutionalism After the Arab Spring* (Oxford University Press 2017).

[88] An exemplary form of which is the development of fundamental rights protection within the European Union. See Gráinne de Búrca, 'The Road Not Taken: The European Union as a Global Human Rights Actor' (2011) 105 The American journal of international law 649.

[89] Anne Peters, 'Compensatory Constitutionalism: The Function and Potential of Fundamental International Norms and Structures' (2006) 19 Leiden Journal of International Law 579; Benedict Kingsbury, Nico Krisch, and Richard B Stewart, 'The Emergence of Global Administrative Law' (2005) 68 Law & Contemporary Problems 16.

[90] This, for example, is Loughlin's interpretation of constitutionalization. Loughlin, 'What Is Constitutionalisation?' (n 77), 47. See also Kanishka Jayasuriya, 'Globalization, Sovereignty, and the Rule of Law: From Political to Economic Constitutionalism?' (2001) 8 Constellations 442.

6. Conclusion

Our focus for the remainder of this book will be on the concept of 'constitutionalism' in particular as a normative theory of legitimacy. We will therefore leave the cognate concept of 'constitutionalization' to one side for now. However, even limiting our discussion to the concept of constitutionalism leaves much work to be done in understanding how it can provide a normative theory of transnational constitutional pluralism. In Chapters 6 and 7, we will consider various challenges to the idea of constitutionalism as a form of normative theory, with a particular focus on the challenges posed to constitutionalism at the transnational level. The schematic overview of the concept of constitutionalism undertaken here helps us identify the different conceptions of constitutionalism at stake in these critiques of the idea of constitutionalism.

6

What's Wrong with Constitutionalism? Between Cacophony and Coercion

1. Introduction: Critiquing Constitutionalism

As we have seen in Chapter 5, constitutionalism is a normative ideal which can trace its roots back to the ancients and has been subjected to a variety of different meanings in different times and places. As a result, the long history of the concept can support a variety of different definitions in contemporary constitutional discourse, employing a range of subsidiary values. The problem with the variety in defining these terms for contemporary constitutional discourse is that it can make progress on pinning down its core features or values difficult. Our seeming inability to advance a clear and uncontested definition of the term, as evidenced by the various 'dualisms' considered in Chapter 5, can render constitutional discourse cacophonic.[1] These persistent 'definitional conundrums'[2] potentially question the utility of the concept as a way of understanding or endorsing normative positions in respect of governing authority at the *state* level, let alone in the 'foreign climate' of transnational law and governance.

The variety of meanings of constitutionalism in constitutional discourse is related to a second problem identified with constitutionalism as a normative theory of political legitimacy. As we have seen, a key assumption of much constitutional discourse is the idea that the concept relates to a form of legitimacy and that following its prescriptions will enhance the legitimacy of an authority.[3] However, the (implicit) claims to legitimacy of constitutionalism as a normative theory have been criticized on other, particularly democratic, grounds. This alerts us to the fact that constitutionalism could, potentially, achieve the

[1] Cormac Mac Amhlaigh, 'Harmonising Global Constitutionalism' (2016) 5 Global Constitutionalism 173.

[2] Jeffrey L Dunoff and Joel P Trachtman (eds), *Ruling the World?: Constitutionalism, International Law, and Global Governance* (Cambridge University Press 2009), 9.

[3] John Rawls, *Political Liberalism* (Columbia University Press 1993). 41. Jeremy Waldron, *Political Political Theory: Essays on Institutions* (Harvard University Press 2016), 24.

New Constitutional Horizons. Cormac S. Mac Amhlaigh, Oxford University Press. © Cormac Mac Amhlaigh 2022.
DOI: 10.1093/oso/9780198852339.003.0006

precise opposite of what many of its proponents endorse: that is that it serves to *delegitimize* rather than *legitimize* governing authority.

In this chapter we will explore these two problems, which we call the 'cacophony' and 'illegitimacy' critique of constitutionalism respectively, in more detail. With respect to constitutionalism's 'definitional conundrums' we will examine the problems these pose for the development of a normative theory of constitutionalism (and also transnational constitutionalism). We will then go on to consider in more detail the problems associated with constitutionalism's claims to legitimate political authority both within its statist domicile as well as particular critiques that have been levelled at the claims of *transnational* constitutionalism in the form of a critique of 'new constitutionalism'.

2. Of Semantic Stings and Other Things

In a perhaps overwrought allegory on language and meaning, the protagonist, Alice, in Lewis Carroll's *Through the Looking-Glass*, finds herself in conversation with a character from a popular Anglophone children's nursery rhyme, Humpty Dumpty. In the course of their discussion, Humpty Dumpty speaks of glory:[4]

> 'I don't know what you mean by "glory",' Alice said.
>
> Humpty Dumpty smiled contemptuously. 'Of course you don't—till I tell you. I meant "there's a nice knock-down argument for you!" '
>
> 'But "glory" doesn't mean "a nice knock-down argument",' Alice objected.
>
> 'When *I* use a word,' Humpty Dumpty said, in rather a scornful tone, 'it means just what I choose it to mean—neither more nor less.'
>
> 'The question is' said Alice, 'whether you *can* make words mean so many different things.'
>
> 'The question is' said Humpty Dumpty, 'which is to be master—that's all.'

We do not require too much imagination to see a similar type of conversation playing out with regard to the concept of constitutionalism in light of the variety of meanings in the form of the various dualisms considered in Chapter 5. Even if we do not need to adopt the cynicism with regard to language and meaning

[4] Lewis Carroll, *Alice's Adventures in Wonderland and Through the Looking Glass* (Penguin Classics 1998), 186.

betrayed by Humpty Dumpty in Carroll's book, there is a sense that when discussing the concept of constitutionalism, contestation about whether it means legal or structural constraints or a particular foundational justification for political authority could, reasonably quickly, descend into the sort of nonsense conversation imagined by Carroll. This disagreement surrounding the concept of constitutionalism lies at the root of a 'cacophony' objection to constitutionalism as a form of normative theory.

Of course, the fact that a word or a concept, not least one expressing a particular political value, is subject to disagreement as to its meaning is not necessarily problematic, even from the viewpoint of normative theory. As Gallie argued in his idea of an essentially contested concept, disagreement around concepts and values can have 'very desirable' consequences by providing 'permanent potential critical value' to our 'use or interpretation of the concept in question'.[5] As such, thinking about a concept such as constitutionalism as an essentially contested one can result in a 'marked raising of the level of quality of arguments in the disputes of the contested parties'.[6] This can occur when, in disagreeing and contesting the meaning or value of a particular concept, we revise our understanding or position on the issue, which makes it sharper and clearer. However, the 'cacophony objection' to the concept of constitutionalism focuses on the potentially negative features of disagreement around the use of language and linguistic concepts, particularly concepts of political value; on what we might call 'mere' as opposed to 'essential' contestability. This form of disagreement, rather than enhancing and clarifying our meaning serves to obfuscate or undermine it, including for potentially malign ends.

The first problem highlighted by the 'cacophony' objection to constitutionalism based on the series of 'dualisms' considered in Chapter 5 is that it fails, as aptly illustrated by the conversation between Alice and Humpty Dumpty, to result in successful communication. That is, that in attempting to engage in meaningful debate about the meaning and value of constitutionalism within the context of broader debates about the legitimacy of political authority, either we assume that disagreement doesn't exist or we end up simply talking past each other. A version of this problem is exemplified by Dworkin's idea of the 'semantic sting'.[7] As is well known, Dworkin accuses particular theories of law such as Hart's as suffering from a 'semantic sting' which involves the elision of actual disagreement about concepts such as law or constitutionalism as well

[5] WB Gallie, 'Essentially Contested Concepts' (1955) 56 Proceedings of the Aristotelian society 167.
[6] ibid.
[7] Ronald Dworkin, *Law's Empire* (Belknap Press 1986), ch2.

as, potentially, disagreement about the conventional linguistic rules for using particular words or concepts in a particular way as opposed to substantive theoretical disagreement.[8] This results from an approach to conceptual analysis which assumes that concepts are borne of 'plain facts'[9] shored up by necessary and sufficient conditions.[10] Dworkin argues that certain accounts of law—particularly, but not limited to positivist accounts such as HLA Hart's—assume, counterfactually, agreement on those necessary and sufficient conditions of particular concepts or envisage a different 'empirical'[11] type of disagreement to substantive theoretical disagreement. This leads to a series of unsatisfactory conclusions. First, the counterfactual assumption of agreement in these accounts of law means that they fail to explain particular phenomena such as legal discourse as it actually exists in society which, as Dworkin shows through a series of sample cases, is rife with disagreement, up to and including the deliberations of judges of the most superior courts of legal systems.[12] Moreover, because it assumes agreement on concepts based on 'plain' historical facts, any disagreement about concepts must be rejected as hypothetical—that is what should be the case rather than what is the case—as lacking good faith, a form of ironic or strategic discourse, or as espousing 'self-contradictory nonsense'.[13] More generally, the 'plain fact' approach to concepts can lead to semantic rather than substantive disagreement; that is that it necessarily leads to the view that actual disagreement relating to particular concepts, such as those considered in our previous survey of the meanings of 'constitutionalism', must relate to the correct linguistic usage of terms such as 'law' or 'constitutionalism', hence the 'semantic sting'.[14]

[8] ibid 31. Somewhat ironically, the precise meaning of the 'semantic sting' and its role in theoretical disagreement is, itself, contested. For a clear and informative discussion on the matter see Scott J Shapiro, 'The "Hart–Dworkin" Debate: A Short Guide for the Perplexed' in A Ripstein (ed), *Ronald Dworkin* (Cambridge University Press 2007); Dale Smith, 'Theoretical Disagreement and the Semantic Sting' (2010) 30 Oxford Journal of Legal Studies 635.

[9] Dworkin (n 7), 33.

[10] What Dworkin later referred to as 'criterial concepts'. R Dworkin, *Justice in Robes* (Belknap Press 2006), 9. For an extended discussion, see Chapter 8.

[11] Dworkin (n 7), 33.

[12] ibid 15–30. In Shapiro's formulation, 'legal positivists are unable to account for a certain type of disagreements that legal participants frequently have, namely, those that concern the proper method for interpreting the law'. Shapiro (n 8), 35. For an examination of the relationship between judicial disagreement and deliberative democracy see Conrado Mendes, *Constitutional Courts and Deliberative Democracy* (Oxford University Press 2013).

[13] Dworkin (n 7), 31. On the idea of strategic discourse more generally see Habermas's distinction between 'strategic' and 'communicative' action. Jürgen Habermas, *The Theory of Communicative Action/Vol. 1, Reason and the Rationalization of Society*. (T McCarthy tr, Heinemann 1984); Jürgen Habermas, *The Theory of Communicative Action/Vol. 2, Lifeworld and System: A Critique of Functionalist Reason*. (T McCarthy tr, Polity Press 1987).

[14] Shapiro (n 8), at note 57.

It we try to reinterpret the 'semantic sting' in terms of theoretical disagreement, our disagreement becomes pseudo disagreement resulting in interlocutors talking past each other rather than engaging in substantive theoretical disagreement. In this respect, then, the only way that this approach can account for actual disagreement about concepts such as constitutionalism is to characterize it as a cacophony; we are claiming to interpret the same object such as propositions of law or a concept of constitutionalism when in fact we are interpreting different things determined by the defining conditions of our concepts, which is the result of approaching political concepts in terms of 'plain historical fact[s]'.[15]

Thus, the problem from our viewpoint as constitutional theorists is that if we suffer from the 'semantic sting', we fail utterly as constitutional theorists. Taking this approach, we must assume, counterfactually, that there is no disagreement about the concept of constitutionalism because any disagreement can be resolved through the identification of the relevant historical facts, and that anyone who persists with their disagreement in the face of such facts is either foolish, stupid, or not acting in good faith. Taking a view of the disagreement from one remove, moreover, presents actual contestation of concepts such as constitutionalism as disagreement about the correct use of a particular word or concept based on rules of linguistic usage; that is not substantive disagreement about value but disagreement about semantics, or, alternatively, a form of pseudo disagreement as we are not talking about the same thing. A fundamental prerequisite for any type of normative theorizing such as our current enterprise has to be successful communication.[16] In this regard, the 'constitutional cacophony' threatens to undermine our enterprise before it even gets off the ground.

A related problem with the disagreement surrounding the concept of constitutionalism is that such disagreement has the potential to undermine the utility of particular terms and concepts in practical reasoning. Constitutionalism, on this view, can become a 'debased conceptual currency'.[17] As Waldron notes: '[a]s political philosophers, we like to keep our armoury of concepts in good shape; that's why we devote so much energy to the analysis and clarification of terms like "liberty", "justice" and "law"'.[18] Moreover, he highlights the importance of a reasonable correspondence between an analytical account of a concept and

[15] Dworkin (n 7), 31.
[16] ibid 44. Smith (n 8), 646.
[17] Neil Walker, 'The Idea of Constitutional Pluralism' (2002) 65 The Modern Law Review 317, 333.
[18] J Waldron, 'Is the Rule of Law an Essentially Contested Concept (in Florida)?' (2002) 21 Law and Philosophy 137.

its ordinary usage 'on the streets'.[19] If 'street-level use' is 'completely confused', he argues, we have no alternative but to pronounce the term 'meaningless'.[20] In such cases, concepts become 'empty slogans', which are 'incapable of driving one's argument much further forward than the argument could have driven on its own'.[21] The conclusion of this particular view of the constitutional farrago is that we do better to abandon the concept altogether as it doesn't advance our understanding but rather serves to occlude it further. Thus, the disagreement surrounding the term constitutionalism is not simply an 'intellectual challenge' prompted by the semantic sting but also a practical one; our concepts fail to provide, or at least aid and support, solutions to the practical problems faced by societies.[22] This leaves us with the potentially unhappy conclusion that, given its prevalence as a form of 'object language' in practical discourse, we cannot do without the concept of constitutionalism due to this disagreement, but nor can we 'collectively do anything with it'.[23]

To these woes, we can add, presaging our discussion of the illegitimacy critique later in this chapter, a view of the disagreement surrounding the concept of constitutionalism which invites or promotes forms of coercive domination. The variety of definitions of constitutionalism increases the risk that it can be co-opted strategically for malign ends. It was this risk that Shklar warned of when she spoke of the 'ideological abuse and general over-use' of concepts turning them into "self-congratulatory rhetorical devices that grace ... public utterances"'.[24] In this way, co-opting the term 'constitutional' or 'constitutionalism' to describe or support a particular state of affairs runs the risk of perpetuating or even exacerbating forms of injustice and domination. This problem which emerges from the cacophony is essentially a form of constitutional fraud; it claims the mantle of legitimacy by taking a concept which has traditionally been somewhere in the ballpark of a normative account of legitimacy, for practices, institutions, or structures which are, by any objective measure, wholly illegitimate. Constitutionalism, on this view, by the mere co-option and application of the concept borne of the disagreement as to its meaning serves

19 ibid.
20 ibid.
21 ibid 139
22 Walker (n 17), 333.
23 ibid 333. This particular form of the cacophony objection has an affinity with 'external skepticism' with regard to the question of truth in matters of political value. See further Chapter 8.
24 Judith Shklar, 'Political Theory and the Rule of Law' in AC Hutcheson and P Monahan (eds), *The Rule of Law: Ideal or Ideology* (Carswell 1987) 1.

to sanctify that which ought not to be sanctified,[25] and highlights the sinister overtones of Humpty Dumpty's conclusions about 'which is to be master'.[26]

3. Constitutional Illegitimacy

More generally, the idea of constitutionalism as form of legitimacy has been the subject of a backlash in constitutional theory in the past number of decades. The roll-out of judicial review and ultimately judicial supremacy,[27] including in Westminster parliamentary systems which traditionally eschewed US-style judicial review,[28] the application of liberal constitutionalism to regimes in transition (particularly in post-Soviet states) as well as the transformation of global governance and the establishment of 'higher laws' of transnational governance binding and constraining the activities of states[29] have all been the subject of sustained critique. The basic thrust of these attacks is that rather than *legitimizing* political power and *enhancing* governing authority, constitutionalism actually *delegitimizes* the exercise of political power.[30] For these critical views, discourses of constitutionalism are therefore doubly pernicious from the viewpoint of legitimacy: they make claims to and promote themselves as 'legitimacy-enhancing'[31] when they are actually *il*legitimacy enhancing—that is that the practices of constitutionalism serve to exacerbate, rather than resolve the perennial legitimacy questions associated with governing authority.[32]

Whereas the precise form of these critiques is diverse—some are based firmly in the state and concerned with certain trends in institutional design and particularly the rise of judicial review, others are concerned with the transformation of global governance—they all share a central concern for the role of consent in legitimate government and the ways and extent to which, in their view, constitutionalism as normative theory results in the undermining of

[25] See, for example, Nico Krisch, *Beyond Constitutionalism: The Pluralist Structure of Postnational Law* (Oxford University Press 2010), 57.

[26] Carroll (n 4).

[27] Mark Tushnet, *Taking the Constitution Away from the Courts* (Princeton University Press 2000). Larry D Kramer, *The People Themselves: Popular Constitutionalism and Judicial Review* (Oxford University Press 2004). Marco Goldoni and Christopher McCorkindale, 'The State of the Political Constitution' (2013) 14 German Law Journal 2103.

[28] Janet L Hiebert, *Parliamentary Bills of Rights: The Experiences of New Zealand and the United Kingdom* (University Press 2015). Stephen Gardbaum, *The New Commonwealth Model of Constitutionalism: Theory and Practice* (Cambridge University Press 2013).

[29] See generally Alexander Somek, *The Cosmopolitan Constitution* (Oxford University Press 2014).

[30] Euan MacDonald, 'Counterproductive Constitutionalization' (2018) 16 International Journal of Constitutional Law 1232.

[31] ibid 1236.

[32] ibid.

consent-based democratic procedures and institutions and the suppression of popular power more generally.[33] Thus, the core of the critique of constitutionalism in recent years has been the idea that constitutionalism has anti-democratic tendencies, and that it functions to *dis*empower people and popular movements, rather than *em*power them.[34] Here we will consider democratic critiques of constitutionalism in its legal regulative guise and particularly the association between constitutionalism and legally entrenched 'higher law', judicial supremacy and the 'new constitutionalism' of transnational governance.[35]

4. The Illegitimacy of Constitutional Entrenchment

This critique of constitutionalism attacks the idea of the necessity and legitimacy of the status of the constitution as a 'higher law' of a legal and political system beyond simple democratic control. It disputes the various arguments advanced to support the entrenchment of constitutional law and it is therefore worth briefly reviewing these justifications in more detail. The first justification for entrenchment relates to our '*guarantisme*' sense of constitutionalism outlined in Chapter 5. As noted, the normative value here is the value of limited government and the avoidance of tyranny and/or securing of liberty.[36] In order to achieve these goods of limited government, the fundamental laws of government must be binding on the institutions of government. This is, in turn, achieved by immunizing these fundamental laws from amendment through ordinary law-making procedures, or by immunizing certain provisions of the fundamental laws from amendment *tout court*.[37]

This rationale for entrenchment has been defended on the grounds that entrenchment protects particular core 'constitutional essentials' which secure the legitimacy of government more generally.[38] This is a form of '*guarantisme*'

[33] Jeremy Waldron has been one of the most articulate democratic critics of constitutionalism in its entrenchment and judicial supremacy forms and his work will form a particular focus here. See generally Jeremy Waldron, *Law and Disagreement* (Oxford University Press 1999).

[34] Waldron, *Political Political Theory: Essays on Institutions* (n 3), 37.

[35] Stephen Gill, 'New Constitutionalism, Democratisation and Global Political Economy' (1998) 10 Pacifica Review: Peace, Security & Global Change 23.

[36] Charles de Montesquieu, *Montesquieu: The Spirit of the Laws* (Anne M Cohler, Basia Carolyn Miller, and Harold Samuel Stone eds, Cambridge University Press 1989).

[37] Such as, for example, the so-called eternity clauses such as Art V of the US constitution, the entrenchment of republican form of government in the French and Italian constitutions and the German constitution's famous 'eternity clause', Art 79(3) GG. This is also reflected in the 'basic structure' doctrine of the Indian constitution. *Kesavananda Bharati v State of Kerala* [1973] Supp SCR 1. See generally Silvia Suteu, *Eternity Clauses in Democratic Constitutionalism* (Oxford University Press 2021).

[38] Rawls (n 3), Lecture VI 'The Idea of Public Reason'.

constitutionalism but a form which gives substantive moral content to the values against which guarantees against governmental interference must be secured. This approach, therefore, requires that constitutionalism as higher law satisfies certain particular benchmarks of legitimacy before it can be a legitimate theory of authority and good government.[39] An exemplar of this form of '*guarantisme*' constitutionalism as legitimate government is Rawls's liberal principle of legitimacy which stipulates that '[o]ur exercise of political power is fully proper only when it is exercised in accordance with *a constitution the essentials of which* all citizens as free and equal may reasonably be expected to endorse in the light of those principles and ideals acceptable to their common human reason.'[40]

In attempting to identify what those constitutional essentials might be, we can, Rawls argues, exclude what he calls 'comprehensive doctrines'; that is, conceptions of justice drawn from, for example, religious doctrines, which apply to 'all subjects' and whose virtues cover 'all parts of life.'[41] This is because such worldviews are not shared by all members of the society and they are not, therefore, part of what all citizens 'may reasonably be expected to endorse.' Thus, in a diverse and pluralistic society, it cannot be expected that all citizens can reasonably endorse morality as promulgated by the Roman Catholic church, or it cannot be expected that all citizens can endorse living according to the law and morality of the Koran.

Thus, for Rawls, for an entrenched and higher constitutional law to be legitimate, it must be 'freestanding' in the sense that it is removed from, or independent of, the comprehensive doctrines which citizens may hold.[42] Only such freestanding criteria can meet the approval of all citizens as values which can be legitimately entrenched and made the subject of higher constitutional law. For Rawls, not all citizens need to endorse the entrenched values and higher law for the same reasons. It will necessarily be the product of an 'overlapping consensus': citizens will endorse the norms of the entrenched constitution for distinctive reasons, part of which will overlap with the reasons of other citizens.[43]

Once the constitutional essentials have been identified as the product of an overlapping consensus conforming with the liberal principle of legitimacy, Rawls argues that such values should be *protected* from amendment by the

[39] 'A political conception of justice covers the fundamental question addressed by higher law and sets out the political values in terms of which they can be decided.' ibid 234.

[40] ibid 137.

[41] ibid 4.

[42] ibid 14.

[43] ibid 164.

ordinary law-making processes of government. Given that the substantive political values of the liberal principle of legitimacy are 'are very great values', they should not be easily overridden and 'the ideals they express are not to be lightly abandoned'.[44] In this way a democratic constitution 'is a *principled* expression in *higher law* of the political ideal of a people to govern itself in a certain way' and the aim of public reason is to 'articulate this ideal'.[45]

Entrenchment has also been defended on more procedurally democratic grounds. Ackerman's conception of 'dualist democracy',[46] for example, envisages two levels of decision-making in constitutional systems—a decision of the people and a decision of the government[47]—which place higher standards for amendment of the constitution than ordinary law. A decision by the *people* occurs rarely and under special conditions and it is these special conditions that 'earn the special kind of legitimacy the dualist [democrat] accords to decisions made by the People'.[48] The government also makes decisions under special conditions of democratic representation and constitutional constraints; however, for Ackerman, it is important to keep both types of decision-making separate.[49] This is because the special conditions on decision-making by the government, while onerous to the extent that they require electoral victory, are not as serious and onerous as those for decisions by the people.[50] Thus, dualist democracy establishes a 'two-track law-making system'.[51]

4.1 A Critique of Entrenchment

The core of the critique of constitutionalism as prescribing entrenchment is based on a particular understanding of democracy: what Ackerman has called 'monistic democracy'.[52] For monistic democrats, democracy requires 'the grant of plenary law-making authority to the winners of the last general election—so

[44] ibid 218.
[45] ibid 232. Indeed Kelby argues that Rawls can be read as endorsing the idea of an unconstitutional constitutional amendment to the extent that the 'constitutional essentials' conforming to public reason should not be subject to subsequent amendment. Charles A Kelbley, 'Are There Limits to Constitutional Change? Rawls on Comprehensive Doctrines, Unconstitutional Amendments, and the Basis of Equality' (2004) 72 Fordham law review 1487. See in particular Rawls (n 3), 239.
[46] Bruce Ackerman, 'Constitutional Politics/Constitutional Law' (1989) 99 The Yale Law Journal 453, 461 et seq.
[47] ibid 461.
[48] ibid.
[49] ibid 461.
[50] ibid 462.
[51] ibid 464.
[52] ibid 464, 463.

long, at least, as the election was conducted under free and fair ground rules and the winners do not seek to use their power to prevent the next free and fair election'.[53] For monistic democrats, the most undemocratic form of constitutionalism lies in unamendable constitutional provisions and in the idea of unconstitutional constitutional amendments.[54] However, even if all constitutional norms are amendable in principle, the tendency to put hurdles in the way of amendment such as requirements of supermajorities or elite-controlled referendums are undemocratic in that they fail to respect the equality of citizens expressed through simple majority voting.[55] To the extent that a supermajority is required, for example, the individual votes of citizens are diluted in that a simple majority is not enough to pass an amendment.[56] Thus, on this view, any method of constitutional amendment which requires anything more than a simple majority of representatives voting in a legislature is undemocratic. As such, during the period between elections, '*any* institutional check upon the electoral victors' and particularly those envisaged in the prescriptions of '*guarantisme*' constitutionalism, is 'presumptively anti-democratic'[57] and the 'enfranchisement of ordinary people'[58] is put in jeopardy.[59]

A version of the democratic critique of entrenchment, albeit not necessarily involving conceptions of monistic democracy, can also be said to lie behind more traditional 'dead hand of the past' arguments against constitutional entrenchment. This version of the critique asks why those who laid down the constitution in the past—whether they be founding fathers or those deemed to exercise a historical constituent power—should have any special purchase on the society of today? Why should their will be superior to the will of those who are actually governed? This criticism of constitutionalism was articulated in a particularly clear way by Thomas Jefferson, in his recommendation that a new constitutional convention be convened every twenty years for the US Constitution.[60]

[53] ibid 464, 463.

[54] Yaniv Roznai, *Unconstitutional Constitutional Amendments: The Limits of Amendment Powers* (Oxford University Press 2017), 191–193.

[55] Waldron, *Law and Disagreement* (n 33), 275. See also Stephen Tierney, *Constitutional Referendums: The Theory and Practice of Republican Deliberation* (Oxford University Press 2012).

[56] Waldron argues that constitutionalism in this sense 'takes democracy and the power assigned to ordinary people through elective and representative procedures as its natural enemy.' Waldron, *Political Political Theory: Essays on Institutions* (n 3), 38.

[57] Ackerman (n 46), 463.

[58] Waldron, *Political Political Theory: Essays on Institutions* (n 3), 37.

[59] Moreover, this view holds even if we need some basic ground rules in order to get decision-making off the ground. The fact that we need constitutive rules in politics does not mean that such rules should be immune from revision in the future. Waldron, *Law and Disagreement* (n 33), 275 et seq.

[60] 'No society can make a perpetual constitution, or even a perpetual law. The earth belongs always to the living generation. They may manage it then, and what proceeds from it, as they please, during their

A more specific version of the democratic critique lies behind a rejection of Rawls' recommendation for the entrenchment of 'constitutional essentials' conforming with his ideal of liberal legitimacy. This critique, like the critique of judicial supremacy to be considered below, focuses on the question of disagreement, and in particular the extent to which the disagreement about public values envisaged by Rawls' account can be overcome. It questions whether 'constitutional essentials' can, in fact, be identified, which everyone can 'reasonably be expected to endorse', which are then isolated and entrenched to support the legitimacy of a government which respects those essentials. That Rawls is very cognizant of societal disagreement in questions of legitimacy and authority is clear in his emphasis of the circumstances of justice and his recognition and consideration of comprehensive doctrines in developing his liberal principle of legitimacy.[61] In fact, he traces the basis of societal disagreement on these matters back to the 'burdens of judgement' where different life experiences will lead to the promotion and prioritization of different values.[62] Thus, the critique of a Rawlsian approach to questions of constitutional entrenchment is not that he doesn't take disagreement seriously but that he doesn't take disagreement seriously *enough*. Not only will we disagree about conceptions of the good as evidenced through the diversity of comprehensive doctrines about the good life, but societal disagreement can, and does, also extend to questions of justice, and in particular the extent to which Rawls's liberal principle of legitimacy is, in fact, an acceptable standard of political justice and is, in fact, sufficient for the legitimacy of government.[63] Waldron, for example, argues that

usufruct. They are masters too of their own persons, and consequently may govern them as they please. But persons and property make the same of the objects of government. The constitution and the laws of their predecessors extinguished then in their natural course with those who gave them belong. This could preserve that being till it ceased to be itself, and no longer. Every constitution then, and every law, naturally expires at the end of 19 years. If it be enforced longer, it is an act of force, and not of right.' T Jefferson, Letter to James Madison, 9 September 1789, Papers XV: 392 cited in A Gordon Reed, 'The resonance of minds: Thomas Jefferson and James Madison in the republic of letters' in Frank Shuffelton (ed), *The Cambridge Companion to Thomas Jefferson* (Cambridge University Press 2009) 186.

[61] 'We must remember that political liberalism owes its very origin in great part to the plurality of incompatible comprehensive doctrines and the absence of any moral authority to pronounce one of them as true ... if there are no comprehensive doctrines, this would contradict the obvious fact of pluralism on matters religious, moral and philosophical, which was the original motivation for Rawls's attempt to transform his theory of justice into a freestanding conception.' Charles A Kelbley, 'Are There Limits to Constitutional Change—Rawls on Comprehensive Doctrines, Unconstitutional Amendments, and the Basis of Equality' (2004) 72 Fordham Law Review 1487, 1493

[62] 'Different conceptions of the world can reasonably be elaborated from different standpoints and diversity arises in part from our distinct perspectives. It is unrealistic ... to suppose that all our differences are rooted solely in ignorance and perversity, or else in the rivalries for power, status, or economic gain ... many of our most important judgements are made under conditions where it is not to be expected that conscientious persons with full powers of reason, even after free discussion, will arrive at the same conclusion.' Rawls (n 3), 58.

[63] Waldron, *Law and Disagreement* (n 33), 151.

notwithstanding Rawls's recognition of disagreement and pluralism of value in society, his approach to the liberal principle of legitimacy, and in particular the identification of constitutional essentials, is oriented almost entirely at differing conceptions of the good contained in 'comprehensive doctrines' at the cost of considering disagreement about questions of justice.[64] Moreover, Rawls' insistence that the entrenched constitutional essentials be established to the exclusion of comprehensive doctrines excludes the potentially large number of citizens who are incapable of disentangling their views about justice from their comprehensive doctrines.[65] It has also been argued that Rawls' liberal principle of legitimacy is, itself, a comprehensive doctrine making the exclusion of the comprehensive doctrines, and particularly religion-based comprehensive doctrines, arbitrary.[66]

5. Judicial Supremacy and Democracy

A similar type of democracy-based critique has been levelled by Waldron at the way in which constitutionalism tends towards judicial supremacy in the interpretation and enforcement of constitutional values. This critique relies more on the institutions rather than the values which are interpreted and enforced within constitutional regimes. As we noted in our introduction, and with respect to our additional 'circumstance of constitutional pluralism' Waldron emphasizes political disagreement as the starting point for theorizing political legitimacy.[67] As we saw with respect to our concept of constitutionalism, and especially the question of entrenchment, not only do we disagree about the meaning of the good but we also disagree about the right, and the origins, nature, and meaning of fundamental rights as well as the values which they purport to protect, yet we still require collective action on these matters. As such, and notwithstanding such disagreement, some decision-making authority is necessary which acts by resolving the disagreement about the right and the good without replicating it. However, we also need a decision-making procedure which is worthy of the respect of those over whom decisions are made. Waldron argues that the most legitimate form of decision-making authority

[64] 'Nowhere does [Rawls] infer that for the same reasons [that we cannot expect moral and religious consensus], in a society, reasonable people might be expected to disagree fundamentally about the basic terms and principles of their association.' ibid 152.

[65] ibid 161.

[66] F d'Agostino, Free Public Reason: Making it Up as we Go along (OUP, 1996).

[67] Waldron, *Law and Disagreement* (n 33), 102.

is one which makes decisions according to a procedure which is respectful of all citizens involved in disagreement by treating them equally,[68] and for this reason concludes that in questions of institutional design, and particularly the choice between judicial or legislative supremacy with regard to decision-making in the circumstances of politics, that the latter form best respects the premises of equality in the face of disagreement and is therefore the most legitimate form of institutional design.[69]

More specifically, Waldron identifies two types of reasons for determining the legitimacy of decision-making by courts and legislatures: consequentialist 'outcome-related reasons' and deontological 'process-related reasons'.[70] He examines the reasons for and against courts and legislatures based on both of these types of reasons, concluding that the case for either judicial or legislative supremacy based on outcome-related reasons is inconclusive (or argues in favour of legislatures), due to the fact that empirically courts have proven no better than legislatures in preventing rights violations and that the outcomes-based reasons for favouring courts, such as reason-giving and a focus on particular circumstances among others, apply as much to legislatures or don't apply to either.[71] Process-based reasons, however, Waldron argues, weigh wholly in favour of decision-making by deliberative democratically representative institutions rather than judicial ones.[72] This latter position forms the basis of the 'core'[73] of the case in favour of legislative supremacy. The process-based reasons for legislative supremacy as a more legitimate form of constitutional design are predicated, as noted earlier, on the notion of political equality, and particularly the equality of a citizen's influence in decision-making. The optimal way to secure this, for Waldron, is through 'fair elections to the legislature where [citizens] are treated equally along with their fellow citizens'.[74] Furthermore, majority decision-making within the representative legislature allows for decisions to be made while treating participants equally, giving 'each expressed opinion the greatest weight possible compatible with giving equal weight to all opinions'.[75] Waldron illustrates this idea by reference to a hypothetical citizen C_n. For Waldron, the legitimacy of decision-making turns on giving reasons to this hypothetical citizen, 'who is to be bound or burdened'[76]

[68] ibid 109.
[69] Waldron, *Political Political Theory: Essays on Institutions* (n 3), ch 9.
[70] ibid 214.
[71] ibid 217–226
[72] ibid 231–2.
[73] ibid 197.
[74] ibid 227.
[75] ibid 227.
[76] ibid 226.

by a decision with which she disagrees, as to why she should 'accept, comply or put up with it'.[77] More specifically, legitimacy, for Waldron, involves furnishing adequate responses to two potential questions which C_n could raise about the decision-making process: what makes the decision-makers legitimate and why didn't C_n's opinion on the matter carry greater weight in the decision-making process?[78] This test, according to Waldron, constitutes, '*the*' theory of political legitimacy.[79] For Waldron, legislative supremacy provides a much more convincing account than judicial supremacy as to why C_n should accept the decision due to the fact that majority decision in a legislature—unlike in the courts—'treats participants equally, and gives each expressed opinion the greatest weight possible compatible with giving equal weight to all opinions'.[80]

6. 'New Constitutionalism' and Democracy

These critiques of the tendencies in constitutional thought towards the putative anti-democratic entrenchment of core constitutional values against the reach of quotidian politics as well as the tendency for constitutionalism to prescribe judicial supremacy as the most legitimate form of constitutional government have also carried over specifically to our area of inquiry, transnational constitutional pluralism. These types of critiques of constitutionalism share many of the democratic concerns of constitutionalism as a theory of legitimacy but take their aim at the tendency in transnational regulatory structures and institutions such as the World Bank, the International Monetary Fund (IMF), the World Trade Organization, or the European Union, to solidify or insist upon the solidification of particular political preferences such as those relating to the role of government in the management of the economy, into higher or constitutional law.[81] Nowhere is this clearer than in the promotion of the idea of 'economic constitutionalism' associated with the ordoliberal school of thought,[82] whereby key choices surrounding economic organization—including open markets, free competition, and restrictions on the ways in which

[77] ibid 226.
[78] ibid 226–27.
[79] ibid 226.
[80] ibid 227.
[81] Adam Harmes, 'New Constitutionalism and Multilevel Governance' in A Claire Cutler and Stephen Gill (eds), *New Constitutionalism and World Order* (Cambridge University Press 2014), 148. See also Quinn Slobodian, *Globalists: The End of Empire and the Birth of Neoliberalism* (Harvard University Press 2018).
[82] Slobodian (n 81). See also Kanishka Jayasuriya, 'Globalization, Sovereignty, and the Rule of Law: From Political to Economic Constitutionalism?' (2001) 8 Constellations 442.

public institutions and public wealth can act in the market both as an economic actor as well as through providing financial support to private industries—are separated from the political realm and 'locked in' to legal regimes at a transnational level.[83] These developments, what Gill calls a 'new constitutionalism',[84] promote a 'market-preserving federalism'[85] embedded in international agreements which are implemented and enforced by supranational administrative technocratic bureaucracies and judicial agencies.[86] The objective of this new constitutionalism is to:

> Prevent national policies on issues related to wealth redistribution and market failures and to confine as many of the undesired tax and regulatory powers as possible to the subnational level, where they will be constrained by inter-jurisdictional policy competition and the need of governments to compete for mobile citizens and firms.[87]

Many of these developments, particularly in low-income countries, have taken place at the behest of global governance organizations such as the IMF or the World Bank.[88] The choices surrounding management of the economy which are emphasized by this idea of 'new constitutionalism' can be understood as particular 'comprehensive doctrines' involving particular conceptions of the moral worth of individuals and in particular their freedom and autonomy, particular 'truths' about how markets operate, the morality of 'winners' and 'losers' in economic competition, as well as determining the 'deserving' and 'undeserving' in terms of public financial or regulatory support. As such, they suffer from a form of entrenchment which cannot even meet the (contested) standards of Rawlsian public reason. The critique of new constitutionalism is therefore potentially more trenchant than the democratic critiques outlined earlier. It shares the concerns of the previous critiques surrounding the disenfranchisement of 'ordinary people',[89] in the face of other forms of social power and in particular economic power. However, not only are these developments in the 'new constitutionalism' undemocratic but they are also undemocratic

[83] Harmes (n 81), 143.
[84] Gill (n 35).
[85] Harmes (n 81). The phrase is Weingast's: See. Barry R Weingast, 'The Economic Role of Political Institutions: Market-Preserving Federalism and Economic Development' (1995) 11 Journal of law, economics, & organization 1.
[86] Michael A Wilkinson, 'Authoritarian Liberalism in Europe: A Common Critique of Neoliberalism and Ordoliberalism' (2019) 45 Critical Sociology 1023.
[87] Harmes (n 81), 145.
[88] ibid 145.
[89] Waldron, *Political Political Theory: Essays on Institutions* (n 3), 37.

in a particular way. They not only shield particular economic 'constitutional essentials' from the attention of ordinary democratic politics but also lock-in a particular, and particularly contested, form of 'constitutional essential' encapsulated in doctrines of ordoliberal and neoliberal economic policy reflecting a particular conception of the *good* as well as the right.

Moreover, their enforcement by transnational counter-majoritarian administrators or judicial actors rather than elected representatives also presents a particularly acute form of the problems associated with judicial supremacy. Thus, 'new constitutionalism' suffers from a double illegitimacy: the problems with the particular entrenched values of economic liberalism as well as the problems associated with counter-majoritarian enforcement.

As the object of our inquiry relates to transnational constitutional pluralism particularly, the new constitutional critique is particularly pertinent. We will therefore briefly consider in more detail two examples of this new constitutionalism in the context of the European Union to highlight the form of the 'new constitutionalism' critique of constitutionalism as normative theory: the constitutional entrenchment of sensitive monetary policies in the aftermath of the EU's currency crisis as an example of 'new constitutional' entrenchment and two controversial decisions of the Court of Justice of the European Union (CJEU) as an example of 'new constitutional' judicial supremacy.

7. The Eurozone Financial Crisis and Economic Constitutional Entrenchment

As is well known, the global financial crisis which erupted in 2008 had particularly acute repercussions in the Member States of the EU's common currency, the euro.[90] Like many other states, Eurozone states suffered from both banking and fiscal crises; however, for Eurozone Member States, the policy levers to manage these crises were stretched across national and supranational levels of government. Of particular interest to the current discussion were the entrenched rules of the EU Treaties which placed particular constraints on Member State responses on how to manage the crisis, particularly in terms of public borrowing and expenditure. There are a number of features of the EU economic constitution's rules on fiscal policy which illustrate the link between entrenchment and 'new constitutionalism'.

[90] Not all EU Member States have adopted the EU's common currency. All but eight are members.

First, the pre-crisis rules which established the common currency enshrined in the Maastricht Treaty of 1992 contained a number of provisions which placed restrictions on the capacity of Member States to manage financial crises.[91] The Treaty established a European monetary policy,[92] whose primary objective was price stability,[93] an independent Central Bank—the ECB—which would be immunized from political interference,[94] and left fiscal and more general economic policy to Member States but with an obligation to pursue 'sound public finances'.[95] To safeguard against Member State 'profligacy',[96] the Treaty also contained the notorious 'no bailout clause' which created a strict constitutional prohibition on Member States sharing liability for public finances with other Member States or the EU institutions,[97] as well as supervision and monitoring mechanisms by EU institutions[98] including enforcement action in the form of the 'excessive debt procedure'.[99] All of this, as Tuori and Tuori point out, left Member States lacking key policy competences to manage localized economic shocks and left them at the mercy of the EU institutions, and in particular the ECB.[100] Thus, even before the financial crisis hit, the 'fiscal' constitution of the European Monetary Union entrenched prudential fiscal policy and price stability as features of the EU's economic constitution.

After the crisis, the legitimacy problems with the 'new constitutionalism' of the monetary union were arguably exacerbated. First, specific conditions were placed on individual Eurozone states regarding their domestic fiscal policies to allow them to avail of emergency funding from the 'troika': a conglomerate of two EU institutions—the European Commission and the ECB—and an international financial institution, the IMF. The aims of such emergency measures were to provide aid to the hardest hit EU states, stabilize their economies, and enhance confidence in the common currency more generally.[101]

[91] See generally, Kaarlo Tuori and Klaus Tuori, *The Eurozone Crisis: A Constitutional Analysis* (Cambridge University Press 2015), ch 2.

[92] Art 3(1)(c) TFEU

[93] Arts'. 119(2) and 127(1) TFEU.

[94] Art 130TFEU

[95] Art 119(3) TFEU.

[96] Schuknecht cited in Tuori and Tuori (n 91), 32.

[97] Now Art 125(1) TFEU: The Union shall not be liable for or assume the commitments of central governments, regional, local or other public authorities, other bodies governed by public law, or public undertakings of any Member State, without prejudice to mutual financial guarantees for the joint execution of a specific project. A Member State shall not be liable for or assume the commitments of central governments, regional, local or other public authorities, other bodies governed by public law, or public undertakings of another Member State, without prejudice to mutual financial guarantees for the joint execution of a specific project.

[98] Arts 121 and 126 TFEU.

[99] Art 126 TFEU.

[100] Tuori and Tuori (n 91), 31.

[101] ibid.

These conditions, contained in Memorandums of Understanding between the troika and the indebted states, stipulated not only how much reduction in the public spending of the receiving state was necessary but also dictated the areas in which such reductions in public spending should be applied.[102]

Initially these conditions were the product of negotiations between the 'troika' and the indebted state seeking aid, and to this extent was still a 'political' feature of Eurozone crisis management. However, conditionality on receiving financial aid in cases of crisis was later 'constitutionalized' into EU law with the amendment of Article 136 of the Treaty on the Functioning of the European Union (TFEU) after the crisis, making conditionality a necessary requirement for states receiving financial assistance in order to safeguard the stability of the euro.[103] This codified and constitutionalized the practice of conditionality already taking place with particular states and further restricted the ability of individual Member States to make choices around their own fiscal and economic policies. This 'crisis regulation' was accompanied by efforts to enhance and improve economic governance in the Eurozone more generally. Alongside the suite of legislative measures to bolster the regulation of Eurozone state deficit and debt, further encroachments on the budgetary and policy autonomy of states were introduced.[104] Perhaps the most notable of these from the viewpoint of constitutional entrenchment was Article 3(2) of the Treaty on Stability, Coordination and Governance in the Economic and Monetary Union, which stated that rules regarding deficits and budgetary decisions were to take the form of 'provisions of binding force and permanent character, *preferably constitutional, or otherwise guaranteed to be fully respected and adhered to throughout the national budgetary processes*'.[105] Moreover, the article also implies that courts should be involved in their enforcement to ensure compliance.[106] Furthermore, the CJEU has jurisdiction to hear disputes between contracting parties with regard to adherence to the budgetary rules.[107] These factors add a dollop of judicial supremacy on top of the seemingly problematic constitutional entrenchment of fiscal policy contained in the Treaty.[108]

[102] ibid 99–100.

[103] Art 136 TFEU. 'The granting of any required financial assistance under the [financial assistance mechanisms] will be made subject to strict conditionally.'

[104] Tuori and Tuori (n 91), 107.

[105] Emphasis added.

[106] Tuori and Tuori note that earlier versions of the article explicitly required judicial oversight of compliance with these budgetary rules, something which was dropped in the final version. However, judicial oversight still seems to be implied in the final text. Tuori and Tuori (n 91), 110.

[107] Art 8 TGCS.

[108] It should be noted that the EU's plan to rebuild eurozone economies after the economic impact of the coronavirus pandemic based on an agreement reached in July 2020 soften these arrangements somewhat. The new plan empowers the Commission to provide financial assistance to eurozone

7.1 Judicial Supremacy and 'New Constitutionalism' in the European Union

The 'new constitutional' structures of EU law, as interpreted by the EU courts have, by judicial fiat, turned the EU treaties into the 'higher law' of the constitutional systems of its Member States, particularly through its doctrines of the supremacy and direct effect of EU law.[109] The upshot of these developments is that national laws which conflict with EU law, and in particular its 'constitutional essentials', including the free movement of the four factors of production as enshrined in the Treaties, were to be disapplied.[110] This judicial development of EU law meant that the CJEU has become a particularly powerful actor in determining the constitutional nature of national measures surrounding the management of the economy of Member States. This was made particularly clear in the cases of *Viking* and *Laval*.

In the Viking and Laval cases, the CJEU was faced with a potential conflict between the 'constitutional essentials' of the EU's legal order in the form of the free movement of goods, services, capital, and labour, and Member State measures allowing workers to take collective action.[111] The *Viking* case involved an attempt by a ferry operator to reflag a vessel from Finland to Estonia in order to circumvent existing collective workers agreements. This move was resisted by domestic and international union organizations.[112] The actions by the unions to resist the ferry operator's attempts to reflag the vessel and strike new collective bargaining agreements were challenged in court by the ferry operator, Viking, which led to a series of questions being put to the CJEU as they implicated provisions of the EU 'constitution' on the freedom of establishment. In deciding the case, whereas the Court recognized the right to strike as a 'fundamental right which forms an integral part of the general principles of

economies. It will allow the Commission to raise funds in the financial markets and disburse the funds through both loans with conditionality as per the post-eurozone schemes, however, significantly, a large portion of funds may also be disbursed in the form of grants. See Chih-Mei Luo, 'The COVID-19 Crisis: The EU Recovery Fund and Its Implications for European Integration—a Paradigm Shift' [2021] European Review 1.

[109] See generally, Cormac S Mac Amhlaigh, 'The European Union's Constitutional Mosaic: Big "C" or Small "c", Is That the Question?' in N Walker, J Shaw, and S Tierney (eds), *Europe's Constitutional Mosaic* (Hart 2011).

[110] Matej Avbelj, 'Supremacy or Primacy of EU Law—(Why) Does It Matter?' (2011) 17 European Law Journal 744.; Cormac Mac Amhlaigh, 'Back to a Sovereign Future?: Constitutional Pluralism after Brexit' (2019) 21 Cambridge Yearbook of European Legal Studies 41. See also Chapter 4.

[111] See generally, Mark R Freedland and Jeremias Adams-Prassl (eds), *Viking, Laval and Beyond* (Bloomsbury Publishing 2015).

[112] Case C-438/05 *ITWF and FSU v Viking Line ABP* [2007] ECR I-10779.

[EU] law',[113] it found that such a right could not place undue restrictions on the freedom of establishment of commercial operators under EU law. In this light, the Court concluded that the measures taken by the unions constituted a disproportionate interference with the freedom of establishment of the commercial operator.

The *Laval* case involved an attempt by a Swedish union to force a Latvian construction company operating in Sweden into collective agreements over the employment conditions of Latvian workers employed by the company in Sweden.[114] The company refused, and the Swedish union took action to prevent the Latvian company from undertaking its operations in Sweden. In this case again, the CJEU had to determine whether the actions of the union breached the employer's fundamental economic rights to provide services in another EU Member State protected by the EU's economic constitution. Again, while noting the protection of the right to strike under EU law, the Court found that the attempts by the union to force the employer into agreements covering the employment conditions of the Latvian workers was an undue interference with the company's freedom to provide services under EU law.

Both cases have been the subject of much analysis and scrutiny;[115] however, for current purposes they provide a good example of the judicial supremacy critiques of the 'new constitutionalism', where economically liberal 'constitutional essentials' are given precedence over other values and public goods by powerful judicial actors.

8. Conclusion

In this chapter we have reviewed two of the three prominent critiques of constitutionalism as a form of normative theorizing. These are powerful critiques and the developments in 'new constitutionalism' at the transnational level in recent years merely seem to exacerbate the problematic aspects of constitutionalism as normative theory. They therefore cannot be strategically ignored when developing an account of constitutional pluralism as a normative account of legitimate authority. We will engage with these critiques of constitutionalism—and particularly the new constitutionalism critique of transnational governance—in due course. However, prior to moving on to these we must address

[113] ibid.
[114] Case C-341/04 *Laval un Partneri Ltd v Svenska Byggnadsarbetareförbundets* [2007] ECR-I 11767.
[115] Freedland and Adams-Prassl (n 111).

another significant objection to constitutionalism-talk at our level of inquiry of transnational law and governance: the 'category error' objection. As our historical overview of constitutional dualisms in Chapter 5 starkly reveals, constitutionalism has been historically intertwined with the development of states and particularly the idea of a constituent power or a 'demos'.[116] To take this state-based and demos-infused idea and attempt to apply it to the radically different context of transnational law and governance is, on this view a 'category error'.[117] It is to this critique of transnational constitutionalism in particular to which we now turn.

[116] Dieter Grimm, *Constitutionalism: Past, Present, and Future* (Oxford University Press 2016); Kenneth Dyson, *The State Tradition in Western Europe: A Study of an Idea and Institution* (Roberston 1980).

[117] Neil Walker, 'Taking Constitutionalism beyond the State' (2008) 56 Political Studies 519, 521 citing Andrew Moravcsik, (2005) 'A Category Error', *Prospect*, 22–26 July.

7

What's Wrong with Transnational Constitutionalism? Dealing with the No Demos Thesis

1. Introduction

An entry in a recent *Handbook on Global Constitutionalism* written by a prominent international lawyer begins as follows:

> Constitutionalism-bashing has been *en vogue* for some time in international legal scholarship. International legal scholars have deployed an incredible amount of energy to discredit any pattern of argument, structure of thought, or conceptual framework that comes with constitutional overtones ... [A] quick scan of the literature suffices to note that constitutionalism-bashing scholarship dramatically outweighs literature promoting constitutionalist thinking.[1]

Alongside the critiques of 'new constitutionalism' considered in Chapter 6, a significant part of this constitutionalism bashing involves the idea that transnational constitutionalism is, itself, a 'category error'.[2] Virtually all versions of transnational constitutional scepticism accept that *some* forms of constitutionalism can play a *limited* role in the context of the legitimacy of transnational governance, such as forms of constitutionalism promoting due process or some human rights protections. However, they argue that this form of constitutionalism—'constitutionalism lite'[3]—is not up to the task of tackling the problems of legitimacy associated with transnational governance under the

[1] Jean d'Aspremont, 'International Legal Constitutionalism, Legal Forms and the Need for Villains' in Anthony Lang and Antje Wiener (eds), *Handbook on Global Constitutionalism* (Edward Elgar 2017) 155.

[2] Andrew Moravcsik, (2005) 'A Category Error', Prospect, 22–26 July cited in Neil Walker, 'Taking Constitutionalism beyond the State' (2008) 56 Political Studies 519, 521.

[3] Jan Klabbers, 'Constitutionalism Lite' (2004) 1 International Organizations Law Review 31.

New Constitutional Horizons. Cormac S. Mac Amhlaigh, Oxford University Press.
DOI: 10.1093/oso/9780198852339.003.0007

circumstances of constitutional pluralism. The types of constitutionalism that could, potentially, provide the relevant panacea to this problem—a constitutive 'foundational'[4] constitutionalism establishing the legitimate foundations of governing or public power—can have no part to play in this context primarily due to the radical dissimilarities between state-based law, politics, and society, and its transnational analogue. Thus, the core of this particular sceptical case regarding constitutionalism as a response to the circumstances of constitutional pluralism fixates on one particular understanding of constitutionalism considered in Chapter 5: 'constitutive' constitutionalism and particularly the idea of a constituent power or 'demos'. Marshalling the concept of a demos to their cause, transnational constitutional sceptics argue along the following lines: within the context of the problems of legitimacy under the circumstances of constitutional pluralism, if constitutionalism is to mean anything, it must entail the idea of a demos;[5] it is a fact that the transnational political space, such as it is, whether at regional, international, or global levels, is marked by fragmentation, heterogeneous cultural, linguistic, political, historical, and religious outlooks, power asymmetries, intractable disagreement, and weak institutional structures. In such a context, the notion of a demos, and therefore constitutionalism, makes little sense, given its association with strong commonalities and affinities of language, culture, history, and nationality. Transnational constitutionalism is therefore dismissed as 'radical' or 'wishful thinking'[6] or a 'utopian' project,[7] in favour of other, more modest, 'realistic' alternatives, such as global administrative law,[8] pluralism,[9] or reinvigorated domestic accountability for the exercise of foreign relations powers under state constitutions.[10]

This chapter will interrogate this transnational constitutional scepticism regarding the use of constitutionalism, particularly in its 'heavier' forms, as a potential solution to the legitimacy concerns emerging from our circumstances

[4] Nico Krisch, *Beyond Constitutionalism: The Pluralist Structure of Postnational Law* (Oxford University Press 2010) 47.

[5] Martin Loughlin, 'The Concept of Constituent Power' (2014) 13 European Journal of Political Theory 218.

[6] Nico Krisch, 'Pouvoir Constituant and Pouvoir Irritant in the Postnational Order' (2016) 14 International Journal of Constitutional Law 657, 669.

[7] Krisch (n 4), 57.

[8] See generally, Benedict Kingsbury, Nico Krisch, and Richard B Stewart, 'The Emergence of Global Administrative Law' (2005) 68 Law & Contemporary Problems 16; Nico Krisch, 'Global Administrative Law and the Constitutional Ambition' in Petra Dobner and Martin Loughlin (eds), *The Twilight of Constitutionalism?* (Oxford University Press 2010).

[9] Krisch (n 4).

[10] See, for example, Anne-Marie Slaughter, 'Disaggregated Sovereignty: Towards Public Accountability of Global Government Networks' (2004) 39 Government and Opposition 159.

of constitutional pluralism. It argues that we have reasons to be sceptical of the sceptical charge on two counts. First, if idealism or utopianism in normative theory is a flaw, excavating the normative claims which underpin the idea of a demos and demotic constitutionalism reveals that it, too, is susceptible to counterfactual, idealistic, or utopian tendencies, making the charge self-defeating by its own lights. Second, it argues that it is not even clear that idealism or utopianism is problematic in normative theory. Drawing on recent debates in political philosophy, the chapter argues that within certain parameters even radically idealistic theories can contribute to the types of questions tackled by normative theory, including the legitimacy questions under the circumstances of constitutional pluralism.

2. What's Wrong with Transnational Constitutionalism?

As the extract at the beginning of this chapter makes clear, transnational constitutional scepticism is a thriving business. Indeed, barely had contemporary transnational constitutional discourse got off the ground in terms of conceptualizing transnational law and politics in constitutional terms than the backlash had begun.[11] The scepticism straddles legal fields, with constitutional lawyers and international lawyers alike making common cause on the impossibilities of transnational constitutionalism, based on its lack of realism or its utopian tendencies. A leading constitutional lawyer, and prominent sceptic, Dieter Grimm, for example, has emphasized the unrealistic nature of transnational constitutionalism, noting that the 'aspiration contained in the concept of constitutionalism'[12] cannot even be 'approximately realized'[13] at the transnational

[11] For an overview in the European context see Joseph HH Weiler and Joel P Trachtman, 'European Constitutionalism and its Discontents' (1997) 17 Northwestern Journal of International Law & Business 354. See also Robert Howse and Kalypso Nicolaïdes, 'Legitimacy and Global Governance: Why Constitutionalizing the WTO is a Step Too Far' in Roger B Porter and others (eds), *Efficiency, Equity and Legitimacy: The Multilateral Trading System at the Millennium* (Brookings Institution Press 2001). Of course, these developments relate primarily to post-war transnational constitutional discourse which emerged initially in relation to the development of the European Union. International constitutionalism has a longer pedigree, including, significantly, the Vienna School of international law which includes Kelsen's account of international law considered in detail in Chapter 3 which was also subject to a backlash, notably from the likes of Carl Schmitt. See generally Jochen von Bernstorff, *The Public International Law Theory of Hans Kelsen: Believing in Universal Law* (Cambridge University Press 2010). See also Josef Laurenz Kunz, 'The "Vienna School" and International Law' (1933) 11 New York University Law Quarterly Review 370.

[12] Dieter Grimm, 'The Constitution in the Process of Denationalization' (2005) 12 Constellations 447, 460.

[13] ibid.

level due to a lack of 'social integration'.[14] His conclusion is that the notion of transnational constitutionalism still '*lacks a solid basis in reality*'.[15] Grimm is even pessimistic about the prospect of a transnational constitutionalism *à venir*, arguing that there is no prospect of transnational constitutionalism neither 'for the time being'[16] nor even 'in the long term'.[17] Another prominent constitutional lawyer and leading sceptic, Martin Loughlin, accuses transnational constitutionalism of launching a direct attack on the 'inclusionary–exclusionary dynamic that lies at the core of any political understanding [and] the concept of the political'[18] by questioning the basis of a demos at national level as an obstacle to the idea of transnational constitutionalism. He dismisses such a move as categorically unrealistic and accuses its proponents of deploying 'the tactic of *impossibilism*'.[19]

Among the international legal scholarly community, Nico Krisch has emerged as a prominent voice leading the charge against transnational constitutionalism for its lack of realism and impractical nature. He argues that the transnational sphere is a sphere of 'fate, not of constitution',[20] meaning that attempts to link this sphere to reason-based origins in the exercise of a constituent power or demos 'will ring utopian at best, illusory at worst'.[21] While not wholly dismissive of the idea of transnational constitutionalism, he argues that at least for the time being, we need to 'remain aware'[22] of the absence of satisfactory conditions for constitutionalism at the transnational level at present, including the distinction that 'persists—and will long persist—between ideal and reality'[23] in respect of transnational constitutionalism. As such, he concludes that transnational constitutionalism can only 'find a home'[24] in the contemporary world as a set of 'highly *idealized assumptions* about the institutional structure of global governance—and even then, only with significant limitations'.[25]

[14] Dieter Grimm, 'Integration by Constitution' (2005) 3 International Journal of Constitutional Law 193, 208.
[15] ibid, emphasis added.
[16] Grimm (n 12), 460.
[17] ibid.
[18] Martin Loughlin, 'Constitutional Pluralism: An Oxymoron?' (2014) 3 Global Constitutionalism 9, 28.
[19] ibid, emphasis added.
[20] Krisch (n 6), 668.
[21] ibid.
[22] ibid 677.
[23] ibid.
[24] ibid 671.
[25] ibid, emphasis added.

Whereas it is clear that transnational constitutional scepticism is founded on the perceived unrealistic or utopian nature of the idea, what is less clear in the critical literature is precisely how and why this is so. While we do get some hints, for example, in Loughlin's charge of 'impossibilism', defined by the *Oxford English Dictionary* as a 'belief in ideas, especially on social reform, which cannot be reasonably put into practice',[26] for a clearer sense of the problems which a lack of realism in transnational constitutional theory pose, we need to turn to methodological questions in political philosophy, where the problems with idealism in normative theory have been examined in more detail.

3. What's Wrong with Idealism in Normative Theory?

In order to understand the charge of idealism in normative theory, and particularly the reasons why it might be considered to be problematic, we need to define what we mean by 'idealism'. The terms 'ideal theory' and 'utopianism' and 'non-ideal theory' and 'realism' are often used interchangeably in the literature; however, a few, more nuanced, distinctions can be drawn with respect to these terms. A common approach in the literature is to distinguish between 'ideal' and 'non-ideal' theory. As with most trends in contemporary political theory and political philosophy, this distinction can be traced back to the influence of John Rawls' work. One of the distinctions Rawls drew in his *Theory of Justice* was that between ideal and non-ideal theories which reflected the two parts of this theory of justice.[27] The first part is aimed at working out 'the principles that characterize a well-ordered society under favourable conditions'.[28] This first 'ideal'[29] part 'presents a conception of a just society that we are to achieve if we can'[30] and, crucially for subsequent critiques, entails the assumption of '*strict compliance*'.[31]

The second part of the theory of justice, on the other hand, asks how this goal can be achieved, usually 'in gradual steps'.[32] This non-ideal theory looks

[26] 'impossibilism, n.' *OED Online*. Oxford University Press, https://www-oed-com.ezproxy.is.ed.ac.uk/view/Entry/92600?redirectedFrom=impossibilism#eid, accessed 22 June 2021.
[27] John Rawls, *A Theory of Justice* (Harvard University Press 1973); A John Simmons, 'Ideal and Nonideal Theory' (2010) 38 Philosophy and Public Affairs 5.
[28] Rawls (n 27), 216.
[29] ibid.
[30] ibid.
[31] ibid 245.
[32] John Rawls, *The Law of Peoples: With, the Idea of Public Reason Revisited* (Harvard University Press 1999) 89.

for courses of action that are 'morally permissible and politically possible as well as likely to be effective'.[33] Moreover, it relates to the principles 'that govern how we are to deal with injustice'.[34] The idealism in the first part of the *Theory of Justice*, which makes it *ideal* theory, stems from the fact that the assumption of strict compliance envisages, counterfactually, that everyone, in fact, accepts the principles of the theory of justice, helps to uphold just institutions, and acts precisely according to the dictates of justice.[35]

O'Neill develops the idea of idealism in normative theory by introducing a distinction between idealization in the premises of normative theory and 'abstraction'.[36] Abstraction relates to 'bracketing'[37] aspects of the real world in developing a normative theory but crucially does not deny that those aspects are true of the real world. All reasoning abstracts in one sense or another and, as such, it is important, unavoidable, and useful.[38] Idealization in the premises of normative theory, on the other hand, is more problematic in that it can lead to 'falsehood'.[39] For O'Neill, an assumption or a theory idealizes 'when it ascribes predicates that are *false* of the case in hand, and so denies predicates that are true of that case'.[40] Assumptions about human capacities and capabilities such as 'rational choice or self-sufficiency or independence from others'[41] are not evidently traits of many humans and are therefore, not mere abstractions but a form of idealization. Any theory involving such idealized assumptions is an ideal theory.

More generally, utopianism and political realism have a longer history, stretching back to Moore, Machiavelli, and beyond.[42] There has recently been a renewal of interest in realism in normative political theory,[43] defined as a position which does not 'seek to regiment politics through morality'.[44] Realists charge ideal theories, such as those of Rawls', with attempting to specify 'pre-political'[45] normative commitments which are taken to float free of politics

33 ibid.
34 Rawls (n 27), 8.
35 Simmons (n 27), 8.
36 Onora O'Neill, *Towards Justice and Virtue: A Constructive Account of Practical Reasoning* (Cambridge University Press 1996) 40.
37 ibid.
38 ibid.
39 ibid 41.
40 ibid.
41 ibid.
42 Thomas More, *Utopia* (Robert M Adams ed, 3rd edn, Cambridge University Press 2016); Niccolò Machiavelli, *The Prince* (Quentin Skinner and Russell Price eds, Cambridge University Press 2019).
43 William A Galston, 'Realism in Political Theory' (2010) 9 European Journal of Political Theory 385.
44 Enzo Rossi and Matt Sleat, 'Realism in Normative Political Theory' (2014) 9 Philosophy Compass 689.
45 ibid 689.

and enjoy 'antecedent authority'[46] over the political.[47] In contrast to utopian theory, realist normative theory is concerned in particular with questions of feasibility.[48] As such, realism can be summarized as insisting upon a clear distinction between the norms of ethics and the norms of politics as being concerned with more than merely questions of justice, as well as having an interest in political judgement.[49]

Generally speaking, then, ideal theory or idealization in normative theory, given that it includes false predicates,[50] leads to 'falsehood' and, therefore, produces theories which are 'fact-insensitive'[51] in respect of the real world in which we live. Two problems have been identified with this: first, such theories fail as a form of *practical reasoning* because they fail to provide action-guiding recommendations[52] and, second, they come at an *unacceptable moral cost*.[53]

With regard to the problem of practical reasoning (or lack thereof), O'Neill argues that normative theory *qua* practical reason aims at 'guidance rather than explanation'[54] and 'seeks to guide action whose aim is to fit the world (in some measure) to its recommendations, rather than its conclusions to the world'.[55] By idealizing, a theory becomes unfeasible in that its prescriptions are too far removed from the realities on the ground, making it 'impotent'[56] or 'deficient'[57] normative theory.

Ideal theory has also come in for criticism based on the fact that the implementation of idealized normative theory can be morally perverse, for example by creating more, rather than less, injustice. Mills' critique of ideal theories argues that idealization ignores or is oblivious to oppression and power disequilibria in actual real world societies.[58] The idealization in ideal theory thus comes at an unacceptable moral cost in that it fails to recognize and factor in the fact that, in real world societies, not all individuals enjoy the same levels of freedom and equality due to in-built structural and institutional biases

[46] ibid.

[47] See Williams, who critiqued Rawls' account of legitimacy in terms of a 'structural model' of 'political moralism'. Bernard Williams, *In the Beginning Was the Deed: Realism and Moralism in Political Argument* (Geoffrey Hawthorn ed, Princeton University Press 2005) 3.

[48] Rossi and Sleat (n 44), 690.

[49] ibid 691–94.

[50] O'Neill (n 36), 41.

[51] Colin Farrelly, 'Justice in Ideal Theory: A Refutation' (2007) 55 Political Studies 844, 846.

[52] Zofia Stemplowska, 'What's Ideal About Ideal Theory?' (2008) 34 Social Theory and Practice 319, 324.

[53] Charles W Mills, '"Ideal Theory" as Ideology' (2005) 20 Hypatia 165.

[54] O'Neill (n 36), 42.

[55] ibid.

[56] Farrelly (n 51), 848.

[57] ibid.

[58] Mills (n 53), 168.

which have led to the disadvantaging of certain classes of society, whether it be women, racial minorities, the working class, or others.[59] In not seeing oppression in societies and institutions, ideal theory does not (need not) address this oppression. Indeed, in some cases, it may *exacerbate* it in claiming a higher moral authority for dominant structures and perspectives than they otherwise deserve. Ideal theory, Mills argues, therefore becomes a form of *ideology*: a 'distortional complex of ideas, values, norms and beliefs that reflects the non-representative interests and experiences of a small minority of [society]'.[60] Another, related, moral cost associated with ideal theory relates to what has been called the 'problem of second best'.[61] The problem here is that if the prescriptions of a theory are too far removed from the realities on the ground, the theory becomes radical or revolutionary, requiring such structural change that even the attempt to implement the prescriptions of the theory would violate moral principles. The idea being expressed here is something along the lines of the road to hell being paved with ideal theory.[62]

In the case of transnational constitutional pluralism, the idealization involved revolves around assuming facts about transnational law and governance which are false, namely that there is a level of social integration, solidarity, or reflexive self-identification as a political community at this level when in reality there is no such thing, such that any theories based on these assumptions will fail to provide action-guiding recommendations or will perpetuate or produce injustice. Thus, in the particular context of legitimacy under the circumstances of constitutional pluralism, constitutionalism is 'impotent'[63] as normative theory, given its reliance on false assumptions like a transnational demos. Furthermore, transnational constitutionalism is potentially morally costly because it perpetuates structural injustices in the transnational realm borne of the 'new constitutionalism' we considered in Chapter 6,[64] or because it

[59] ibid.

[60] ibid.

[61] David Estlund, 'Utopophobia' (2014) 42 Philosophy and Public Affairs 113, 125. See also Richard G Lipsey and Kelvin Lancaster, 'The General Theory of Second Best' (1956) 24 Review of Economic Studies 11.

[62] The original—'the road to hell is paved with good intentions'—can be traced as far back as St Bernard of Clairvaux. See John Simpson and Jennifer Speake (eds), *The Oxford Dictionary of Proverbs* (6th edn, Oxford University Press 2008).

[63] Farrelly (n 51), 848.

[64] In this regard, for example, Krisch argues that applying constitutionalism to the transnational realm in the light of the idealization of its assumptions runs the risk of sanctifying that which ought not to be sanctified due to the normative costs involved. Such a move, he argues, 'represents a capitulation to contemporary circumstances when we should instead denounce the gap between our political ideals and what can currently be achieved. Only by naming that gap can we retain a sense for the challenge that constitutionalism . . . poses for the postnational space.' Krisch (n 4), 58.

makes prescriptions that would be so radical or revolutionary that moral principles would be invariably violated in the attempt to achieve such ideals.[65]

In the remainder of this chapter, we will argue that we have good reasons to be sceptical of the 'no demos' critique of transnational constitutionalism based on its idealized tendencies. The first reason to be sceptical about such scepticism relates to the chosen ground for the transnational constitutional sceptical charge: the concept of a demos. The second reason for scepticism relates to a broader scepticism about the charges levelled at ideal theory by political philosophy more generally.

4. What (Kind of Normative Theory) is a Demos?

Like its close relation, the concept of constituent power considered in Chapter 5, the concept of a demos has a considerable historical pedigree and, even in contemporary political discourse has been subject to a variety of meanings and uses.[66] However, given the fact that the context of the current debate relates to questions of *legitimacy* at the transnational level under the circumstances of constitutional pluralism, the conceptions of a demos at stake in these debates are necessarily, as Krisch emphasizes, 'normatively rich'[67] ones; that is, normative theories of a demos as opposed to purely descriptive, empirical, or historical accounts.[68] As such, as a theory of the legitimacy of governing authority, the concept of a demos cannot create an ought from an is; that is, normatively speaking, it cannot claim that a governing authority is legitimate merely because it exists.[69] What this means, then, is that the claims of

[65] ibid 54.

[66] Loughlin (n 5).

[67] Krisch (n 4), 39.

[68] Some accounts of a demos and its cognates, such as constituent power, remain firmly in a descriptive register and are not of concern to us here. Some, for example, argue that a constituent power is an account of historical constitutional founding or constitutional development. It is a common trope in constitutional theory to posit the French and American revolutions (and many since) and the constitutions to which they gave birth as the acts of historical constituent powers. Bruce Ackerman has famously attempted to explain constitutional change in the United States—'constitutional moments'—in these terms. Bruce A Ackerman, *We the People, Volume 1: Foundations* (Harvard University Press 1991). For discussion of the different uses of the concept see Matthias Kumm, 'Constituent Power, Cosmopolitan Constitutionalism, and Post-Positivist Law' (2016) 14 International Journal of Constitutional Law 697, 701. See also Loughlin (n 5).

[69] Two clarifications are in order with regard to this claim. First, it adopts, along with this part of the book more generally, a normative conception of legitimacy and is therefore not concerned with purely descriptive accounts of legitimacy of which Weber's is perhaps the most well-known account. See Max Weber, *Economy and Society* (Guenther Roth and Claus Wittich eds, University of California Press 1978). That transnational constitutional sceptics assume a similar conception of legitimacy is evidenced by the fact that they see legitimacy problems arising in transnational *de facto* authorities such as the European Union. If it were the case that belief in legitimacy evidenced through submission to authority

transnational constitutional scepticism involving the concept of a demos must be attached to specific normative claims about what we ought to do. Thus, such normative statements must, at a minimum, prescribe particular courses of action.[70] As much is clear from the charges of 'impotence' levelled at ideal theory by its critics.[71] As Macdonald notes, considering the concept of a demos in the context of the legitimacy of authority requires 'not only an empirical account of... social commonalities, but also a *normative* account of what kinds of political commonalities *should* count as politically significant in determining which social groups are entitled to democratic self-rule'.[72] This, therefore, necessitates closer scrutiny of the concept of a demos and its normative use in transnational constitutional scepticism.

The concept of a demos is used offensively by transnational constitutional sceptics to support the charge of idealism in transnational constitutional theory in two distinct but related ways: ontological and institutional. The ontological use of the concept of a demos to reject transnational constitutionalism based on its false or idealized assumptions involves the stipulation of necessary and sufficient conditions of the concept and the application of that concept to transnational governance to conclude that, in contrast to state-based societies, the conditions are far from suitable to support transnational constitutionalism at this level. A classic version of the ontological use of the concept can be found in the EU-related *Maastricht* and *Lisbon* decisions of the German Federal Constitutional Court (GFCC).[73] While the Court found that, ultimately, German ratification of the Maastricht and Lisbon Treaties did not violate the right to vote and the democratic nature of the German state as protected by the German basic law, its main line of argument was based on the fact that the European Union was not a competing source of democratic legitimacy for German political institutions and the German basic law.[74] This was

was sufficient for the legitimacy of an authority along Weberian lines, then there would be little problem with transnational authorities, as many can make plausible claims to be *de facto* authorities. See Cormac Mac Amhlaigh, 'Harmonising Global Constitutionalism' (2016) 5 Global Constitutionalism 173, 199. Relatedly, *de facto* authorities can, within certain moral parameters, be considered legitimate. However, even here, the legitimacy of a *de facto* authority is subject to normative constraints which are more demanding than the mere existence of a *de facto* authority. For an example along these lines, see Joseph Raz, 'On the Authority and Interpretation of Constitutions: Some Preliminaries' in Larry Alexander (ed), *Constitutionalism: Philosophical Foundations* (Cambridge University Press 1998).

[70] Although not necessarily exclusively. See section 5 below.

[71] Farrelly (n 51), 845.

[72] Terry Macdonald, 'Boundaries beyond Borders: Delineating Democratic "peoples" in a Globalizing World' (2003) 10 Democratization 173, 174, emphasis added.

[73] 2 BvR 2134/92 and 2159/92 JZ 1993, 1100; [1994] 1 CMLR 57 (hereafter *Maastricht*). BverfG, 2 BE 2/08, 30 June 2009 (hereafter *Lisbon*).

[74] *Lisbon* (n 73), para 256.

due to the fact that democratic constitutional legitimacy presupposed a demos, defined as 'pre-legal'[75] conditions including 'language, history and culture'.[76] According to the Court, these factors create a 'cultural area'[77] sustaining a political community 'bound by ... tradition ... and convention',[78] something that was notably absent at the transnational EU level. As such as a matter of empirical observation, then, the Court concluded, in Weiler's words, that 'there is no European demos, not a people not a nation'.[79]

The institutional use of the concept of a demos to dismiss transnational constitutionalism as utopian builds on the ontological use and involves the claim that current transnational institutions and infrastructures are far from being able to express, manage, and support a transnational demos. Krisch offers one such example. While he criticizes the GFCC's account of a demos as overwrought, he comes to similar conclusions regarding the societal barriers to a transnational demos based on similar reasoning. In his account of the ontological use of a demos, he argues that transnational constitutional theory must 'clarify what self-government through a constitution could mean'[80] in a space where there is 'no uncontested collective that could express its will in constitutional terms'.[81] This is all down to the 'power and wealth differentials, language and culture barriers, and the lack of identification of a common project'[82] at the transnational level, which undermine the existence of the necessary 'pre-legal' conditions for transnational constitutionalism. From this ontological premise regarding the transnational realm, he argues that institutional factors present another, further, barrier to transnational constitutionalism. If constitutions are tools to 'translate moral ideals into institutional practice',[83] Krisch argues certain institutional pre-requisites are necessary to allow it to discharge this particular function. For Krisch, we don't need to fetishize the state to understand that it is the only form of political organization which has successfully claimed

[75] *Maastricht* (n 73), para 41l.
[76] *Lisbon* (n 73), para 227.
[77] ibid para 236.
[78] ibid.
[79] Joseph HH Weiler, 'Does Europe Need a Constitution? Demos, Telos and the German Maastricht Decision' (1995) 1 European Law Journal 219, 229. This view was reprised in the context of the European Union in more recent times by former British Prime Minister David Cameron in his fateful 'Bloomberg Speech', where he first committed to holding a referendum on the UK's EU membership, which ultimately led to the United Kingdom voting to leave the bloc in 2016: 'There is not, in my view, a single European demos. It is national parliaments, which are, and will remain, the true source of real democratic legitimacy and accountability in the EU.' David Cameron, 'EU Speech at Bloomberg' (23 January 2013) <https://www.gov.uk/government/speeches/eu-speech-at-bloomberg> accessed 5 April 2018.
[80] Krisch (n 4), 55.
[81] ibid.
[82] ibid 56.
[83] ibid 50.

the monopoly of coercive legitimate force to which the comprehensive ambitions of constitutionalism could be attached.[84] The realities of the transnational context are far removed from these conditions; they are characterized by forms of 'organic growth which are not steered by a definable centre but determined by the rationalities of social subsystems and the interests and position of particular actors'.[85] As such, the institutional challenges that constitutionalism faces in a global context are high, making the idea of transnational constitutionalism 'utopian'.[86]

4.1 Whither the Normative Claim?

While it is clear that the use of a demos by sceptics speaks to a particular view of the empirical realities, both societal and institutional, which exist at the transnational level, the precise normative significance of this state of affairs, and its relationship to constitutional theory is less clear. That raises the question of what types of normative claims are associated with this use of the concept of a demos?

As we have seen in our survey of the concept of 'constitutive' constitutionalism in Chapter 5, a variety of normative claims can be based on the concept of a demos and its cognates, such as constituent power, depending on the specific context in question.[87] For example, the concept can play a normative role in respect of questions of institutional design, the separation of powers, constitutional amendment or reform, representation, and decision-making.[88] In the context with which we are concerned here, however—the circumstances of constitutional pluralism with an emphasis on the transnational context—the claims associated with a normative theory of demos relate to the demarcation of legitimate *boundaries*, and particularly the boundary between state and transnational governance. As much is clear from the use of the idea of a demos in the transnational constitutional sceptical accounts outlined earlier, where the boundaries of legitimate democratic communities are defined in terms of the particular 'pre-legal' features of that community which are assumed to be present in state-based communities but not transnational ones.

[84] ibid 47–49. See also Grimm (n 12), 459.
[85] Krisch (n 4), 54.
[86] ibid 55.
[87] See, for example, Lucia Rubinelli, *Constituent Power: A History* (Cambridge University Press 2020).
[88] For examples see Joel Colón-Ríos, 'Five Conceptions of Constituent Power' (2014) 130 Law Quarterly Review 306.

In this context, then, the normative claims entailed in the idea of a demos relate to the question of where the legitimate boundaries of sovereign democratic communities *should* lie; in other words, which types of communities *should* be self-governing.

Generally speaking, democratic theory contains two normative conceptions of a demos which justify normative claims surrounding the boundary question: a solidaristic conception and a jurisdictional conception.[89] The solidaristic account picks out the pre-political features of a particular group—empirical traits such as language, history, or culture—as normatively significant in two ways: as being *per se* normatively valuable or being valuable to achieve other normative ends, such as justice. They argue that it is only within groups which share, empirically, such features that political goods such as 'collective autonomy'[90] or republican ideals of self-governance can be achieved.[91] More instrumental defences of democratic boundaries rely on other values, such as justice, to delineate the boundaries of legitimate self-governing groups.[92] However, even if the concept of a demos is deemed to be a means to other ends, the claim is the same: only solidaristic groups sharing such empirical features constitute the legitimate objects of, for example, justice, as they are the only groups which enjoy the requisite level of mutual understanding and mutual trust necessary to support justice-based institutions and initiatives based on their common traits.[93]

The jurisdictional account of legitimate democratic boundaries, on the other hand, looks at the empirical realities of power in the world and bases solutions to boundary problems on these empirical facts.[94] This account endorses an 'all affected interests' view of democratic boundaries; that is, that the boundaries of democracy can only be legitimately drawn around all individuals who are affected by the exercise of that power in fact. As such, the jurisdictional account favours a more cosmopolitan approach to democratic boundaries, albeit that it is a bounded form of cosmopolitanism.[95]

[89] See Macdonald (n 72). It should be noted that the terminology used here differs slightly from Macdonald's.

[90] David Miller, *On Nationality* (Oxford University Press 1995) 88–89.

[91] ibid.

[92] See Michael Walzer, *Spheres of Justice* (Oxford University Press 1983); Miller (n 90).

[93] ibid.

[94] David Held is perhaps one of the best-known proponents of this conception of democracy. See, for example, David Held, *Democracy and the Global Order: From the Modern State to Cosmopolitan Governance* (Polity 1995).

[95] See, for example, Joshua Cohen and Charles Sabel, 'Directly Deliberative Polyarchy' (1997) 3 European Law Journal 313.

This, then, reveals the crux of the normative claim embedded in accounts of constituent power or demos with respect to the boundary problem: that democratic boundaries *should* coincide with whichever of the two accounts of democracy the particular theory endorses. In the solidaristic case—that which is employed by the no demos thesis—the claim becomes one that the boundaries of constitutional democracy *should* be based around state-based communities as they are the only types of communities which make plausible claims to enjoy the 'pre-legal' characteristics associated with a demos, and therefore the requisite level of solidarity for self-governance, justice, or constitutionalism. In the jurisdictional account, the boundaries of constitutional democracy *should* be redrawn to coincide with the way power is actually exercised in contemporary society, within and across state boundaries.

In considering the normative claims which underpin the use of a demos in the context of transnational constitutionalism, and legitimacy beyond the state more generally under the circumstances of constitutional pluralism, the jurisdictional account initially appears to be the more radical of the two. This view, as noted, takes the exercise of power, whatever its formal status and however formally designated, as the starting point for the consideration of the legitimate boundaries of democracy and the identification of a demos for constitutional purposes. In the transnational context, then, the demos or constituent power becomes merely those affected by the exercises of that power, making the idea of a European demos eminently plausible.[96] Even a global demos could be concocted on this account with regard to exercises of power with a global reach, such as certain decisions of the UN Security Council.[97] Viewed in this way, it can be seen how transnational constitutional scepticism presents itself as the more realistic account of transnational governance.[98] Taking the solidaristic account of democratic boundaries, and its expression in state-based communities as a given, it argues that any attempt to replicate practices, institutions, and structures predicated on the features of solidaristic communities at the transnational level, given its institutional weakness and the weak nature of cross-border or transnational solidarity, is wholly unrealistic or utopian.

However, on closer inspection, it is not clear that the solidaristic account employed by transnational constitutional sceptics is any less radical or utopian

[96] See, for example, Chris Thornhill, *A Sociology of Transnational Constitutions* (Cambridge University Press 2016).

[97] In some ways, the jurisdictional account has a strong affinity with transnational constitutional theory, a putative 'utopian' project which is divorced from the realities of transnational law and governance.

[98] Krisch (n 4), ch2, 'The Promise and Perils of Postnational Constitutionalism'.

than the jurisdictional account. It is a central pillar of these sceptical positions that states are the only legitimate governing arrangements for sovereign power or proper locus for democracy and constitutionalism, the justification being that state-based societies enjoy or, at least, best approximate the requisite degree of solidarity or homogeneity necessary for the existence of a demos based on the empirical features of that particular group. However, this is in itself a necessarily contingent matter. Some states could be said, empirically, to enjoy these features but others not.[99] Moreover, the actual experience of statehood in the contemporary world betrays a large degree of variance in terms of the existence of these prerequisites and associated levels of solidarity: internally divided states, plurinational states, multicultural societies (which characterize most Western societies), multi-linguistic and multi-ethnic federations are all features of many contemporary states, yet they fall short of the conditions considered necessary for the legitimate exercise of sovereign power or democracy by transnational constitutional sceptics.[100] As such, there is a misalignment between the empirical realities of many if not most contemporary states and the demands made by the idea of a demos.[101] Furthermore, the realities of transnational governance under the circumstances of constitutional pluralism, which even transnational constitutional sceptics adopt as a premise of theorizing transnational and global relations and structures, mean that there is a further misalignment between the contemporary status quo in terms of the boundaries of governance and groups sharing the pre-political features of the solidaristic account.

Thus, the solidaristic basis of transnational constitutional scepticism itself runs into two problems when viewed in the light of the charges made against transnational constitutionalism. First, the theory itself seems to rely on idealized assumptions about states in the real world. The fact that a good number, if not a majority, of state-based societies do not literally fulfil the criteria of a demos, and that other social groupings do, but are not formed around states, makes the assumptions that transnational constitutional sceptics make about the legitimacy of states necessarily counterfactual or idealized.[102] Moreover,

[99] For example, recent referendums or attempted secession in Scotland in 2014 and Catalonia in 2017 question whether the boundaries of even reasonably stable and well-established European states share the requisite level of solidarity entailed in the solidaristic (and therefore transnational constitutional sceptical) account.

[100] This is not to mention the arbitrary boundaries of post-colonial states, where little if any consideration was given to the extent of solidarity in terms of common empirical features of social groups when the boundaries were drawn.

[101] Stephen Tierney, *Constitutional Law and National Pluralism* (Oxford University Press 2006).

[102] As Macdonald notes, 'the theoretical demand [for alignment between solidarity and power] is not necessarily easily satisfied in practice'. Macdonald (n 72), 177.

as the concept of a demos relies on idealized assumptions, it runs the risk of succumbing to the charges of impotence and moral cost outlined earlier. This is clear in that the prescriptions of a demos as practical reasoning—that is, as making action-guiding recommendations—potentially entail a quite radical set of claims involving the redrawing of current boundaries to reflect solidaristic communities based on these empirical criteria. Thus, for example, the solidaristic account of legitimate democratic boundaries could potentially prescribe that the boundaries of post-colonial states should be redrawn to improve the reflection of the solidaristic groupings extant on these territories, that plurinational states should be split up to better reflect the different solidarities which exist on these territories, that multiculturalism should be halted or even reversed to align democratic boundaries with solidaristic groupings, or, most relevant to the current context, that the realities of the circumstances of constitutional pluralism with its varieties of transnational governance should be radically redesigned or even dismantled to align solidarity to democratic decision-making. One doesn't require a great deal of imagination to foresee the moral problems embedded in such designs.

Of course, transnational constitutional sceptics could counter that at least most states are more aligned with solidaristic communities on the whole than are not, particularly when viewed in the light of the nationalist rhetoric of populist politicians in recent times, and that redesigning boundaries according to the jurisdictional account would be more problematic. That is, one doesn't have to commit to a radical redesigning of sovereign boundaries or transnational governing arrangements in order to argue that there is more solidarity currently within state boundaries for just the types of reasons that theories of a demos provide (common language, culture, history) than there would be if the boundaries were redesigned on purely jurisdictional lines in terms of transnational governance. As is often noted, arguably the majority of even EU Member States currently enjoy a level of allegiance and authority much higher than EU institutions and enjoy more legitimacy than a hypothetical EU state ever would.[103] Again, however, all of this is a relative matter; it may be truer for some EU Member States than others.[104] Furthermore, it suppresses the normative claims associated with solidaristic accounts of a demos, failing to make

[103] Krisch (n 4), 96.

[104] A fact borne out in the Eurobarometer results relied on by Krisch. For example, the most recent Eurobarometer data available from May 2021 shows a wide variance between Member State citizens with respect to trusting EU institutions and having a positive image of the European Union vis-à-vis their national state institutions. Eurobarometer, 'Public Opinion in the European Union' (May 2021) <https://europa.eu/eurobarometer/surveys/detail/2355>

the case for states as they currently exist, and highlights that more needs to be done, including potentially dismantling state boundaries to achieve or at least approximate the alignment between sovereign power and societal solidarity based on the empirical features of a demos.

What all this serves to illustrate is that once the grounds of transnational constitutional scepticism in terms of the normative claims associated with the concept of a demos is interrogated, strong reasons for scepticism about this scepticism are revealed.

5. What's the Problem with Ideal Theory Anyway?

The second ground for scepticism relating to the 'no demos' critique of transnational constitutionalism has to do with the assumption that idealistic or utopian theory is, itself, problematic. As noted earlier, idealization in political theory is usually considered to be problematic because its fact-insensitivity can undermine its ability to guide action and it can be morally costly. However, normative theory must also not merely endorse the status quo; that is, it must do more than claim that what we should do about poverty, conflict, or helping refugees, or more closely related to the issue at hand, addressing the legitimacy problems in the circumstances of constitutional pluralism, is what we are already doing. As we have seen above, normative theory which merely endorses the status quo *also* comes at a moral cost in that it is likely to mask or affirm actual injustices in the world which normative theory should make prescriptions to remedy.[105] As such, normative theory must 'make demands on the world' in some sense, albeit possibly not demands that run the risk of the dangers highlighted above. Normative theory, then, faces a particular Procrustean dilemma: idealize too little and we affirm extant structural injustice, idealize too much and the theory can fail to be action-guiding or can be morally costly. The question is: how do we go about resolving this particular Procrustean dilemma?

One tack would be to follow O'Neill's distinction between idealization and abstraction, and particularly the function of normative theory as giving reasons for action. As noted above, for O'Neill, normative theory *qua* practical reasoning aims at guidance rather than explanation,[106] the aim of such

[105] Mills (n 53). Such 'complacent realism', says Estlund, involves recommending that people and institutions 'be exactly as they are already'. Estlund (n 61), 115.

[106] O'Neill (n 36), 42.

action-guidingness being to 'fit the world (in some measure) to its recommendations, rather than its conclusions to the world'.[107] Ideal theories fail to do this as they rely on false predicates whereas theories that merely abstract can achieve these aims.

However, in assessing how much is too much (or how little is too little) in normative theory, the usefulness of O'Neill's distinction seems to run into problems. This is because it is not exactly clear what the difference between idealization and abstraction actually is or, at least, what the precise relevance of the distinction is for normative theory. To recap, for O'Neill, an assumption or a theory idealizes 'when it ascribes predicates that are *false* of the case in hand, and so denies predicates that are true of that case',[108] whereas it abstracts when it brackets rather than denies predicates that are true of the issue at hand.[109] However it is not clear how abstraction, by bracketing aspects of the real world, is not really (or also) a form of falsehood. Take, for example, one target of O'Neill's critique of ideal theory: rational choice theories, which see individuals as being truly equal and rational in their interactions with each other, which is common in economic modelling of human behaviour.[110] On one reading, we could say that this involves idealization, given that we know in reality that individuals are not actually free and equal to the same extent due to a variety of social factors (birth, sex, race, social status, wealth, and so on) and that they do not always act rationally. As such, these assumptions will contaminate the theory in the ways outlined above. However, in making assumptions about autonomous and equal individuals acting rationally, we *are* drawing on certain aspects of reality: that humans are autonomous mammals, that they have the capacity to reason, and can interact in rational ways, albeit not all to the same extent and not all of the time. Thus, to take a model of autonomous rational humans interacting according to the dictates of reason is not necessarily a *misrepresentation*—that is, a false representation—of social reality but rather a *partial* one. As such, when presenting individuals in a theory as autonomous rational individuals interacting in, for example, commercial transactions according to the dictates of reason, rather than involving false predicates, we could be said to be *bracketing* the non-rational, non-autonomous aspects of human behaviour. That is, in making these assumptions about society, we are bracketing, rather than idealizing, certain aspects of an individual's situation in order to develop a particular theory. Thus, there seems to be little difference

[107] ibid.
[108] ibid 41.
[109] ibid 40.
[110] ibid 41.

between idealizing and bracketing because bracketing, like idealizing, seems to rely on a type of falsehood in the sense of not giving a completely accurate picture of the world.[111] Following on from this, there is a sense that all normative theories must rely on literally false assumptions in the form of *approximations* to reality[112] rather than literal descriptions of reality in order to be able to make advances on understanding what, for example, justice requires. This cannot mean that all theories are ideal theories and therefore useless, because then normative theory could only deal with very narrow and relatively simple problems.[113] If abstraction and idealization are forms of the same thing at least for the matters with which we are concerned here,[114] then we can see how some form of abstraction/idealization or, to adopt a more neutral term, *generalization*,[115] is a necessary step in *any* normative theorizing. The question then becomes: how much or little are we to *generalize* in normative theory?

We have already identified a 'floor' of the Procrustean dilemma in that normative theory cannot merely prescribe the status quo. With regard to a 'ceiling' of generalization, we can assume that the principle 'ought implies can'[116] sets a clear outer limit to generalization.[117] That is, we cannot be morally required to do things that are impossible for us to do. This rules out any theory which requires what Parfit calls the 'deeply impossible',[118] such as prescriptions that violate the laws of nature like the capacity of humans to fly unaided.[119] However, the space between the 'floor' of a status quo bias and the 'ceiling' of the 'deeply impossible' is a potentially large one, which leaves potentially considerable

[111] Hamlin and Stemplowska make a similar point. They offer the following example to highlight the problem: '[I]magine that we are concerned to include a treatment of the motivation of agents in our theory, and we recognise that in the "real world" there is considerable heterogeneity of motivation. Recognising the relevant degree of heterogeneity may make our model too unwieldy to be useful, so we consider adopting an assumption that limits the heterogeneity within the theory. This is clearly a false assumption, but is it an idealisation or an abstraction? One might answer that it is an abstraction if there is no reason to think that the assumption changes what we conclude from our theory. But how can we know?' They conclude that 'there is no straightforward, and perhaps no helpful, distinction between idealisation and abstraction'. They see it as a 'complex continuum'. Alan Hamlin and Zofia Stemplowska, 'Theory, Ideal Theory and the Theory of Ideals' (2012) 10 Political Studies Review 48, 50–51.

[112] Stemplowska (n 52), 327.

[113] ibid.

[114] There may be instances where this is a useful distinction, such as in cases of 'deep impossibility', see (n 119) below.

[115] Stemplowska (n 52), 327.

[116] See also Rawls (n 27), 236 et seq.

[117] Estlund (n 61).

[118] Derek Parfit, *Reasons and Persons* (Oxford University Press 1986) 219.

[119] In fact, it is possibly in the range of deep impossibility where the idealization/abstraction distinction drawn by O'Neill can arguably do some work. Assuming that humans can fly unaided is clearly a falsehood and cannot be rescued by claiming that flying humans is somehow 'bracketing' human ability in the manner outlined at pp. 174–75. As such, it seems relevant to these outer constraints. However, in the context at hand, we are already working within these constraints, so the distinction is, it is submitted, less relevant to the questions being addressed here.

latitude for generalization in normative theory. Within this space, then, there is much room for manoeuvre in terms of the generalizations made in the assumptions of normative theories and almost certainly more than critics of ideal theory assume.

Interrogating this space between the 'floor' and the 'ceiling' reveals that the relationship between purpose and generalization in the assumptions of normative theories is more complex than the simple 'action-guiding' criteria popular in critiques of ideal theory would suggest. First of all, while making action-guiding recommendations is clearly an important purpose of normative theory, it is a necessarily relative measure which will to some extent be informed by more specific motivations for the application of the theory. This, in turn, will have an impact on the level of generalization involved. If our stated purpose is to make specific recommendations in a particular policy area or apply the law to a given case, then the level of generalization required will be relatively low. However, if our purposes are the progressive realization of particular goals, such as the alleviation of poverty and malnutrition in a general sense, then the level of generalization of our theory will be necessarily higher. The variable nature of the action-guiding function of normative theory can be illustrated through an analogy with the implementation of human rights norms. Some human rights norms yield relatively specific prescriptions entailing limited levels of generalization, such as the right to life or prohibitions on torture or slavery.[120] Notwithstanding disagreement at the margins as to whether certain situations fit the relevant definitions, human rights norms such as these entail reasonably clear and direct action-guiding recommendations, such as: do not arbitrarily deprive other humans of their life, do not intentionally inflict pain and suffering on individuals with a view to achieving certain outcomes, and so on. However other rights, such as certain economic and social rights, are usually couched in more general terms, such as 'just and favourable conditions of work,'[121] the 'right to an adequate standard of living . . . including adequate food, clothing and housing,'[122] and the right to 'the enjoyment of the highest attainable standard of physical and mental health.'[123] The attainment of these quite general goals are correspondingly achieved through their '*progressive* realization,'[124] which does not yield recommendations as specific as the right to life or

120 Arts 6, 7, and 8 respectively of the International Covenant on Civil and Political Rights 1966 <http://www.ohchr.org/EN/ProfessionalInterest/Pages/CCPR.aspx>.

121 International Covenant on Economic, Social and Cultural Rights 1966 (ICESCR), Art 7. Full Covenant available at: <http://www.ohchr.org/EN/ProfessionalInterest/Pages/CESCR.aspx>.

122 Art 11 ICESCR (n 121).

123 Art 12 ICESCR (n 121).

124 Art 2 ICESCR (n 121).

prohibitions on torture. Thus, whereas all of these human rights norms involve action-guiding recommendations, the level of generalization involved in each is quite different, as is the precise form of action-guiding recommendation.

Furthermore, there are good reasons for supposing that action-guiding recommendations are not necessarily the only conceivable purpose of normative theory within the floor and ceiling set by the Procrustean dilemma.[125] David Estlund, for example, makes one such case for what he terms 'hopeless aspirational theory'.[126] These are normative theories which are morally sound in that they do not transgress moral principles and are technically achievable by humans as they are, but given other factors such as motivation, are unlikely ever to be achieved. He argues that such theories cannot be said to suffer from a defect in virtue of the fact that their prescriptions will never actually be met.[127] He identifies the terrain between the limits of status-quo bias and impossible theories as a 'noncomplacent nonutopian range of normative political theories',[128] and, while accepting that 'ought implies can', he argues that this does not entail the proposition that ought implies 'highly likely'.[129] As such, he argues it is important to separate probability from impossibility: the fact that it is improbable that something will happen does not make it impossible. This then brings theories which might be ruled out of the range of theories within the 'floor' and 'ceiling' of generalization on the grounds that they do not make action-guiding recommendations, within the range as not being impossible, strictly speaking. Estlund argues that such theories can be normative in the sense of being *evaluative*, whether or not the evaluation itself guides action.[130] That is, normative theory can provide insights by suggesting that 'society would be better like this', which might be true 'whether or not there is anything it makes sense to do in the light of this fact'.[131]

Stemplowska further fleshes out this idea by outlining a number of roles for theories involving highly generalized assumptions and offering alternative purposes for normative theory beyond guiding action.[132] For example, she argues that highly generalized theories can help us see more clearly the actual

[125] In this regard, Carens argues: 'There is no single correct starting point for reflection, no single correct set of presuppositions about what is possible ... The assumptions we adopt should depend ... on the *purposes* of our inquiry.' Joseph H Carens, 'Realistic and Idealistic Approaches to the Ethics of Migration' (1996) 30 International Migration Review 156, 169, emphasis added.

[126] See Estlund (n 61), 118.

[127] See ibid 114.

[128] See ibid 116.

[129] ibid.

[130] ibid 121.

[131] ibid.

[132] Stemplowska (n 52), 327–29.

real-world constraints on developing normative theories.[133] They can also help tease out the relationship between two principles or the values that underpin them, as this is easier to do in a radically simplified universe.[134] Furthermore, generalized theory can set out what is desirable when, for example, there is full compliance and inform our non-ideal theories by forcing us to inquire if we could innovate in order to come closer to an ideal and whether we must depart from the ideal when we are presented with the facts on the ground.[135] Similarly to Estlund, she argues that generalized theory can also provide evaluative benchmarks to help orient ourselves in the real world by providing a metric to show how far we are from our stated aims and how much would need to be done to approximate them.[136] In short, Stemplowska concludes that highly generalized normative theory can have purposes such as uncovering, clarifying, and safeguarding our 'normative commitments',[137] even if it cannot provide specific action-guiding recommendations.

What these examples show is that normative theory can have purposes beyond an action-guiding function and that this impacts upon the level of generalization appropriate to a particular normative theory. Therefore, the key point in distinguishing between unproblematic and problematic normative theory is not, as the 'no demos' critique suggests, an unspecified arbitrary level of 'idealism', or even a failure to guide action. Rather, the distinction should be based on a theory being within the range of the 'floor' and 'ceiling' set by the exclusion of status quo bias and 'ought implies can', the extent to which the purposes of the theory are clearly specified, and the extent to which the level of generalization made in the assumptions of the theory are appropriate to that particular purpose. If we want very specific prescriptions about how to act in particular contexts, then our theories should be much more factually informed of the context, that is, rely on limited generalization. If we want to serve broad evaluative aims, our theories should generalize much more.

6. Conclusion

In conclusion, our interrogation of the no demos critique in this chapter reveals that its core case relates to the question of what we can now call inappropriate

133 ibid 337.
134 ibid 328.
135 ibid 332.
136 ibid 336.
137 ibid 339.

generalization in normative theorizing. However, as we considered earlier, the question of how appropriate or inappropriate generalization is in a given theory will depend both on the purposes of our theorizing and our remaining within the broader moral parameters of 'making demands on the world' and 'ought implies can'. What this shows is that the no demos thesis does not, by itself, provide a 'knock-down' argument against even highly generalized, forms of transnational constitutional theorizing.[138] However, what our discussion in the current chapter reveals, is that if our theorizing is intended to guide action then our level of generalization should not be excessive. At least in this respect, the 'no demos thesis' contains a useful warning that in the context of transnational constitutional pluralism, the disagreement in fact about how to address the legitimacy problems at this level should act as a constraint upon our particular normative theories where they are intended to make recommendations which guide action. Thus, the no demos thesis can be understood in terms of advising caution in developing normative theories of constitutional pluralism to avoid assuming, counterfactually, that there is sufficient theoretical *agreement* on questions of legitimacy at this level when such agreement does not exist. Such a counterfactual assumption about theoretical agreement *in fact*, as opposed to attributing particular characteristics to individuals based on empirical traits, could result in problematic forms of generalization in normative theorizing. This caution will be borne in mind in our next, final, chapter which outlines a general approach to transnational constitutional pluralism.

[138] See, for example, Jürgen Habermas, *The Divided West* (John Wiley & Sons 2014).

8
What's Right with (Transnational) Constitutionalism?
Towards an Interpretive Transnational Constitutional Pluralism

1. Introduction: The 'First Constitutional Question'

In this final chapter we bring together the various threads considered in the previous chapters of this part of the book in an attempt to defend a normative account of transnational constitutional pluralism. In order to do this, it is worth taking stock of our argument. In Chapter 5 we considered the complexity of the concept of constitutionalism through a variety of 'dualisms'. This complexity then provided the basis for the 'cacophony critique' in Chapter 6 which questioned the utility of the concept in the light of the variety of meanings which have been attributed to it: constitutive, regulative, and the various sub-definitions and divisions within this overarching dualism within the concept. We then considered the argument that the tendency in constitutionalism towards entrenchment and judicial supremacy could result in delegitimizing rather than legitimizing authority both at state and transnational levels. Finally, we considered a critique of transnational constitutionalism which objected to the exportation of the concept of constitutionalism from its statist domicile to the 'foreign climate' of transnational law and governance based on the absence of a 'demos' in respect of the latter, which we argued was better understood as a critique of overgeneralization in normative theorizing.

This chapter will address these critiques to develop a normative account of transnational constitutional pluralism. In doing so, we have a strict order of priority. First we must address the cacophony critique before looking at the illegitimacy and category error critiques and defending a normative account of transnational constitutional pluralism. The cacophony critique involves a second-order critique of the concept of constitutionalism in that its resolution is necessary for the illegitimacy and no demos critiques to be taken seriously,

New Constitutional Horizons. Cormac S. Mac Amhlaigh, Oxford University Press. © Cormac Mac Amhlaigh 2022.
DOI: 10.1093/oso/9780198852339.003.0008

as well as for a normative account of transnational constitutional pluralism to get off the ground. As we have seen, the illegitimacy and 'category error' critiques rely on particular conceptions of constitutionalism which make up part of the cacophony. The illegitimacy critique relies on '*guarantiste*' conceptions of constitutionalism as the target of its critique whereas the 'category error' critique relies on particular 'constitutive' understandings of constitutionalism. However, if we fail to address the 'definitional conundrums'[1] surrounding the concept in a non-arbitrary way, these latter critiques merely contribute to, rather than move beyond, the cacophony and therefore succumb to the cacophony critique. Moreover, advancing and defending a normative account of transnational constitutional pluralism without addressing the cacophony critique would similarly result in more semantic or pseudo disagreement. The illegitimacy critique, the category error critique, as well as our normative account of transnational constitutional pluralism more generally, therefore all have an interest in prioritizing the resolution of the cacophony critique in order to advance their various positions.[2]

Thus, the resolution of the cacophony critique, as a second-order critique as opposed to the substantive first-order illegitimacy and category error critiques, enjoys a 'lexical priority' over them and is also a necessary step in developing and defending a normative account of transnational constitutional pluralism. In this regard resolving the cacophony critique in a non-arbitrary way becomes the 'first constitutional question'[3] in terms of addressing the disagreement around the concept before moving on to think about the other critiques of constitutionalism and transnational constitutionalism, as well as, perhaps more importantly for our current purposes, defending a normative account

[1] Jeffrey L Dunoff and Joel P Trachtman, 'A Functional Approach to International Constitutionalization' in Jeffrey L Dunoff and Joel P Trachtman (eds), *Ruling the World?: Constitutionalism, International Law, and Global Governance* (Cambridge University Press 2009) 9.

[2] Proponents of both the illegitimacy and category error critiques implicitly acknowledge the priority of the resolution of the 'cacophony critique' in that they note that the concept of constitutionalism they advance can be defined in different ways. For example, Waldron notes that constitutionalism 'means many things' and that there is a risk of constitutionalism degenerating into an 'empty slogan' which is 'sometimes used in a way which conveys no theoretical content at all'. Jeremy Waldron, *Political Political Theory: Essays on Institutions* (Harvard University Press 2016) 22. Similarly, as noted in Chapter 7, no demos critiques of the idea of transnational constitutionalism have accepted that some forms of constitutionalism might be 'export apt' in the form of 'constitutionalism lite'. Nico Krisch, *Beyond Constitutionalism: The Pluralist Structure of Postnational Law* (Oxford University Press 2010) ch2, 'The Promise and Perils of Postnational Constitutionalism'.

[3] In a similar manner to the way that Williams identified the 'first political question' in political theory in terms of the securing of 'order, protection, safety, trust, and the conditions of cooperation'. Bernard Williams, *In the Beginning Was the Deed: Realism and Moralism in Political Argument* (Geoffrey Hawthorn ed, Princeton University Press 2005) 3.

of transnational constitutionalism under the circumstances of constitutional pluralism.

In this chapter, we will answer the 'first constitutional question' by taking an *interpretive* approach to the concept of constitutionalism following Dworkin's interpretive account of political value.[4] In Dworkin's well-known approach, the focus is placed on identifying the substantive value of a particular object or social practice and understanding disagreement in terms of this substantive value. This approach, moreover, leads to a broader ethical obligation in theoretical inquiry which argues for the integration of political values into a complete whole.[5]

Characterizing constitutionalism as an interpretive concept in this way answers the 'first constitutional question' by seeking to establish second-order *agreement* about the point or value of constitutionalism upon which first-order disagreements can emerge. This approach helps to guide disagreement about the concept of constitutionalism around a common conception of its value. In doing this, the cacophony critique of the concept of constitutionalism loses its potency. While disagreement remains by taking an interpretive approach to the concept of constitutionalism, it becomes a bounded form of theoretical disagreement where interlocutors disagree in the shadow of agreement rather than disagreeing about semantics or talking past each other. Furthermore, addressing the cacophony critique by taking an interpretive approach to the concept of constitutionalism lays the foundation for tackling the illegitimacy critique. This is due to the idea of the unity of value which flows from an interpretive approach to political concepts and encourages a move away from 'lop-sided' accounts of political value such as constitutionalism which privilege certain substantive values (such as the rule of law) over others (such as democracy). As we will see later in the chapter, many forms of 'new constitutionalism' are the product of a deliberate move to *disaggregate* the concept of constitutionalism for its exportation to transnational contexts. If we understand our inquiry into constitutionalism as an inquiry into political value in general, however, following Dworkin, we can understand ourselves to be under an ethical obligation to attempt to *integrate* values in our account of constitutionalism.[6] As such, the interpretive approach points towards a holistic understanding of the political value of constitutionalism and therefore rejects the partial or *disaggregated* accounts of constitutionalism common in accounts

4 Ronald Dworkin, *Law's Empire* (Belknap Press 1986), ch2, 'Interpretive Concepts'.
5 Ronald Dworkin, *Justice for Hedgehogs* (Belknap Press 2011).
6 ibid.

of transnational constitutionalism which respond to the illegitimacy and particularly the 'new constitutionalist' critique.

Finally, with regard to the charges of overgeneralization implicit in the category-error challenges to transnational constitutionalism, assuming that the function or purpose of constitutional theory is practical reasoning, an interpretive approach retains a sufficient level of realism in that it is based on the actual circumstances of constitutional pluralism, rather than hypothetical alternatives. As such, it functions to provide a normative account of transnational constitutional pluralism without undermining the practical reasoning function of constitutional theory nor paying the moral cost involved in overgeneralization.

2. Harmonizing the Cacophony: Answering the First Constitutional Question

Our first step in defending an account of transnational constitutionalism, then, is answering the 'first constitutional question' by clarifying 'what it is we talk about'[7] when we talk about transnational constitutional pluralism in a non-arbitrary way. One tack to address the 'cacophony' would be to simply join the fray; conjuring up a stipulative definition of constitutionalism, articulating its core features into necessary and sufficient conditions, and armed with this conceptual paraphernalia, develop a normative theory of constitutionalism to attack or support the idea of (transnational) constitutional pluralism. This, as we have seen, is more or less the approach taken by many contributors to transnational constitutional debates, not least the sceptics who base their scepticism on the association between constitutionalism and the idea of a *demos*. They stipulate a definition of constitutionalism centred around the idea of a demos—for example Krisch's 'foundational constitutionalism'[8]—and use this definition to conclude that the concept of transnational constitutionalism is riddled with problems. This approach, of course, cuts both ways. It is as available to supporters of transnational constitutionalism as to its detractors. For example, using this methodology, '*guarantiste*' accounts of constitutionalism can be marshalled to argue for the 'constitutional' restraint of transnational governing authorities, thereby making the very idea of transnational constitutionalism

[7] Christine Bell, 'What We Talk About When We Talk About International Constitutional Law' (2015) 5 Transnational Legal Theory 241, 241.

[8] Defined in terms of a 'comprehensive ambition' to 'ground the entire system of government'. Krisch, *Beyond Constitutionalism: The Pluralist Structure of Postnational Law* (n 2), 41.

both imminently plausible as well as desirable on these terms. In this way, we can claim to have solved some of the core critiques of both the concept of constitutionalism as well as transnational constitutionalism *arbitrarily*, by definitional fiat. This is because we can fold the question of the desirability of (transnational) constitutionalism as normative theory into our premises as contained within our stipulative definition of constitutionalism, from which the conclusion as to its desirability inexorably follow.

The problems with this approach are twofold. Perhaps most obviously, such an approach merely exacerbates rather than contributes to 'harmonizing' the cacophony.[9] More substantively, assuming that our interventions are in good faith and are not ironic or strategic, in taking this approach it is not entirely clear what contribution our intervention would make to the questions of legitimate authority that constitutionalism is aimed at addressing. If we suggest, for example, that constitutionalism is 'really' about 'foundational constitutionalism' such as on Krisch's account, or alternatively is 'really' about legally limited government, as Sartori has insisted,[10] what must we say about alternative conceptions? That they are wrong? If so, what might the success conditions of our claims be? How would we articulate our case for 'our' conception of constitutionalism? That this is the most conventional account of constitutionalism in constitutional discourse?[11] That we have discovered an uncontested historical artefact which proves our claims?[12] If so, then what are we really arguing about? About the correct account of the semantic usage of constitutionalism in its history as Dworkin suggests?[13] If *this* is the case, then, we are left with two unattractive conclusions about our disagreement: either we are not really disagreeing about the concept of constitutionalism at all—we are simply talking past each other as our stipulative definitions immediately shut down any possibility of meaningfully engaging with divergent conceptions of constitutionalism—'I don't know what you're talking about but it's not constitutionalism (as I have defined it)', and therefore adding to the cacophony, or we are disagreeing, not on substantive issues of normative theory but on the rules surrounding the correct semantic usage of the term 'constitutionalism'

[9] Cormac Mac Amhlaigh, 'Harmonising Global Constitutionalism' (2016) 5 Global Constitutionalism 173.

[10] Giovanni Sartori, 'Constitutionalism: A Preliminary Discussion' (1962) 56 The American Political Science Review 853.

[11] This seems to be Krisch's view: 'Over two centuries thus, foundational constitutionalism has come to dominate the domestic tradition of constitutionalism.' Krisch, *Beyond Constitutionalism: The Pluralist Structure of Postnational Law* (n 2), 47.

[12] For a critique of this approach to the idea of constituent power, see Lucia Rubinelli, *Constituent Power: A History* (Cambridge University Press 2020) 'Introduction'.

[13] Dworkin, *Law's Empire* (n 4), ch1, 'What Is Law?'.

as evidenced by reference to some historical discourse in which the term appeared in the past.[14] If we are talking past each other, we fail to see the concerns raised by the other side. A stipulative definition of constitutionalism along '*guarantiste*' lines cannot engage with concerns about 'constitutive' constitutionalism based on, say, the idea of a constituent power.[15] Our disagreement is not substantive, then, but pseudo-disagreement. If, on the other hand, we are making a semantic point, then we are engaged in an enterprise entirely distinct from, or at least very obliquely related to, building a substantive normative theory of transnational constitutional pluralism; our disagreement, in Dworkin's terminology, becomes infected with a semantic 'sting'.[16]

It is for these reasons that we do better, it is argued, to think about our disagreements around the normative concept of constitutionalism by taking an 'interpretive' approach particularly as defended by Dworkin. His well-known interpretive approach to political concepts draws a distinction between 'criterial concepts'—such as the classic cases of 'bachelorhood' or 'equilaterality'—which are conducive to clear defining conditions, and 'interpretive' concepts—including the core concepts of political theory in which we can include constitutionalism, which are not.[17] Criterial concepts generally yield precise criteria, such as the criteria of an equilateral triangle involving a figure with three equal sides.[18] However, interpretive concepts are

[14] ibid ch2.

[15] This problem also affects those critics who do not cast their critique in explicitly constitutional terms. Unlike, say, Krisch, whose discontent with transnational constitutionalism is based on his own stipulative definition of foundational constitutionalism, Waldron argues against constitutionalism, not using the term 'constitutionalism', but using alternative interpretive concepts such as equality or democracy. However, this tack simply serves to delay, slightly, the question. If we were to say that by constitutionalism we 'really mean' equality and democracy then what objection could he have? Recasting our objections to, say, '*guarantiste*' constitutionalism in terms of a stipulative definition of another concept does not get us out of the woods as it simply intensifies the cacophony. Waldron (n 2).

[16] Dworkin, *Law's Empire* (n 4), 45–46.

[17] Ronald Dworkin, *Justice in Robes* (Belknap Press 2006) ch6, 'Hart's Postscript and the Point of Political Philosophy'; Dworkin, *Justice for Hedgehogs* (n 5), ch8, 'Conceptual Interpretation'.

[18] Dworkin, *Justice for Hedgehogs* (n 5), 158. However, even if defining conditions of criterial concepts are relatively precise, it does not mean that there will not be disagreement on individual cases of application; for example whether an unmarried 18-year-old male qualifies as a 'bachelor' or not. However, the types of disagreement we have about whether an 18-year-old male qualifies as a bachelor are disagreements about the application of the concept nested within agreement on a criteria about what the criteria for each concept is. That is, such disagreement involves the range of application—that is to say the *extension*—of the concept rather than what the core criteria of the concept is. Some criterial concepts yield more vague criteria such has 'baldness' or 'book' (ibid 158). With regard to these types of concepts, we may not only disagree about the extension of the concept, but we will also disagree about some of the defining conditions of the concept as well. However, what makes such disagreement meaningful is the fact that we can agree on some core features of the concept—such as the fact that baldness has to do with lack of hair on one's head—while disagreeing about some marginal cases such as whether it must be on the top of one's head or also at the sides. Thus, we can disagree about whether someone who is thinning at the temples is 'bald' within a broader agreement of the core features of the concept of baldness. However, if there is no agreement about the core features of the concept and hurling stipulative defining conditions at each other, we are not really disagreeing at all, but simply talking past each other in the

concepts which *we use, share, debate and disagree about despite the fact that we do not have precise agreement about what their criteria are.*[19] Interpretive concepts presuppose an interpretive attitude which recognizes that a particular object or practice such as constitutionalism has some point, that it 'serves some interest or purpose or enforces some principle', or in short, that it 'has value'.[20] This attitude imbues the object of our inquiry with a sense of the meaning beyond the mere enumeration of its core features.[21] Adopting this attitude to a particular object or social practice reveals the value of the practice by articulating 'some scheme of interests or goals or principles the practice can be taken to serve or express or exemplify'.[22] Moreover, this attitude involves attributing value to an object or practice in order to make of it 'the best possible example of the form or genre to which it is taken to belong'.[23] As Dworkin summarizes:[24]

> A conceptual claim about a political value aims to show ... the value in it: it aims to provide some account of its value that is comparably fundamental, by way of explanation, to the molecular structure of a metal ... it will try to show [the value] in its best light.

For our current purposes, the primary advantage of thinking about constitutionalism as an interpretive concept is that it provides a better explanation of the types of substantive disagreements that emerge in relation to the concept of constitutionalism than adopting the purely 'criterial' approach employed, for example, by the 'category error' critique. Thinking of constitutionalism as an interpretive concept rather than a criterial concept means taking disagreement about different accounts and interventions in debates about, say, the possibility or desirability of transnational constitutionalism seriously, as good faith disagreement about substantive value rather than semantic or pseudo-disagreement.

manner of the different definitions of constitutionalism outlined above. Or, alternatively, we are (implicitly) disagreeing about semantics; about the conventions of linguistic usage of particular concepts in the past.

19 Dworkin, *Justice for Hedgehogs* (n 5), 160.
20 Dworkin, *Law's Empire* (n 4), 47.
21 ibid 47.
22 ibid 52.
23 ibid 52. This, as Dworkin acknowledges, is consistent with Quine's 'principle of charity'.
24 Dworkin, *Justice in Robes* (n 17), 155.

3. Types of Disagreement and Interpretive Concepts

In thinking about constitutionalism as an interpretive concept, it is useful to first delimit the broad parameters of disagreement about political value in general. Dworkin distinguishes between the different types of disagreements that we can have when we disagree about interpretive concepts. The first type of disagreement at stake is a distinction between external and internal scepticism with regard to the very possibility of truth in relation to political value. External scepticism with regard to political concepts such as justice and democracy (or constitutionalism) involves a view that there can be no objective truth about what democracy or justice (or constitutionalism) means, there can only be disagreement based on rival subjective formulations. As Dworkin notes:

> External skepticism is a metaphysical theory, not an interpretive or moral position. The external skeptic does not challenge any particular moral or interpretive claim ... His theory is ... a second-level theory about the philosophical standing or classification of these claims. He insists they are not descriptions that can be proved or tested like physics: he denies the aesthetic or moral values can be part of what he calls ... the 'fabric' of the universe. His skepticism is external because disengaged: it claims to leave the actual conduct of interpretation untouched by its conclusions. The external skeptic himself has opinions about Hamlet and slavery and can give reasons for preferring these opinions to those he rejects. He only insists that all these opinions are projected upon, not discovered in, 'reality'.[25]

One type of external sceptic identified by Dworkin argues that all moral judgment is false because there are no moral facts in the world.[26] On this view, trying to explain disagreement about political values is of utterly no consequence as everyone engaged in disagreement is propagating false positions. We can take or leave different views about political value because there is simply no truth of the matter (other than the fact that there are no moral facts in the world). Alternatively, external sceptics argue that when we advance propositions of political value—such as that North Korea is not a democracy, or that the European Union is not constitutional—we are simply emoting, projecting particular psychological or emotional states, but nothing more than this.[27]

[25] Dworkin, *Law's Empire* (n 4), 80.
[26] What Dworkin calls 'error scepticism'. Dworkin, *Justice for Hedgehogs* (n 5), 32.
[27] What Dworkin calls 'status' external scepticism. ibid, 32–33. As noted in Chapter 6, following the cacophony critique to its logical conclusion could result in a form of external skepticism.

Internal scepticism, on the other hand, captures a form of disagreement about political values where interlocutors believe that political values do exist and that we can, in principle, speak meaningfully about the truth of particular values such as democracy or justice. Internal scepticism is therefore a form of scepticism 'within the enterprise of interpretation';[28] that is, it involves advancing propositions about what the best interpretation of a concept or a practice is against rival propositions with which it disagrees. Thus, the primary difference between internal and external scepticism is that the former type of scepticism believes that there is, in principle, a best interpretation of a practice or a concept and it therefore 'plays the interpretive game' in a non-ironic sense, whereas the external sceptic denies the idea of a best interpretation of a concept or a practice. For internal sceptics, then, their disagreements about moral or political value are based on moral or political positions 'because they must assume the truth of some very general moral claim in order to establish their skepticism about other moral claims'.[29] They rely on morality 'to denigrate morality'.[30] External sceptics, on the other hand, are sceptical about morality 'all the way down'.[31]

4. Explaining Constitutional Disagreement

Thus, within disagreement about political value we encounter this threshold question about whether, when we disagree about political values such as constitutionalism, we are disagreeing from the viewpoint of internal or external scepticism; that is, whether we believe that in principle there is a truth about the matter of advancing propositions of value in their best light or whether this is impossible as there can never be any truth of the matter. With respect to our focus on disagreement surrounding the concept of constitutionalism in particular, one example of external scepticism is Carl Schmitt's constitutional theory, and in particular his account of the relationship between constitutional law and the concept of the political. On Schmitt's view, constitutional theory is 'derivative of the political'[32] which Schmitt famously defined in terms of a distinction between friend and enemy.[33] For Schmitt,

[28] Dworkin, *Law's Empire* (n 4), 78.
[29] Dworkin, *Justice for Hedgehogs* (n 5), 32.
[30] ibid 32.
[31] ibid 32.
[32] Martin Loughlin, *Political Jurisprudence* (Oxford University Press 2017) 126.
[33] Described in terms of the 'utmost degree of intensity ... of an association or dissociation'. Carl Schmitt, *The Concept of the Political* (George Schwab tr, University of Chicago Press 2007) 26. A political

the political is autonomous, not only from the 'aesthetic and economic' but also, significantly, from 'the moral'.[34] Furthermore, given that the friend/enemy distinction is the consequence of an 'intensity of an association or dissociation of human beings',[35] and can arise in any social situation, it is difficult, Loughlin remarks, 'to see how any form of predictability, let alone *normative rationality*, can apply to this dimension of human experience'.[36] For Schmitt, moreover, 'all political concepts, images and terms ... have a polemical meaning'; that is that they are 'focused on a specific conflict ... whose ultimate consequence ... is a friend-enemy grouping'.[37]

It is, therefore, relatively easy to interpret this form of constitutional theory in terms of an external scepticism about the existence of political values in the world.[38] If the political is autonomous, both from positive law but also, significantly, from morality, and constitutionalism properly so called is derived from the autonomy of the political and particularly its friend/enemy distinction, then Schmitt's constitutional theory can be interpreted, with relative ease, as a form of external constitutional scepticism.

Our forms of constitutional scepticism considered in Chapters 6 and 7 do not fit this Schmittian style of constitutional theorizing. Each of these critiques of constitutionalism themselves rely on robust normative foundations in order to critique (transnational) constitutionalism, whether it be democracy, political equality in respect of the illegitimacy critique, or the *moral* costs in ideal theorizing in the no demos critique. They therefore emphatically rely on political value to denigrate particular political concepts (such as constitutionalism)

unity, then, which constitutes the constituent power, comprises a degree of association in *fact* which is commensurate with a 'willingness to fight and die for and together with other members of one's group'. (ibid 38) Thus, for Schmitt, the bonds of unity of a people which make up a constituent power as expressed by the friend/enemy distinction at the root of the concept of the political are *existential* in the form of ultimate survival.

[34] Schmitt (n 33), 25–6.

[35] ibid 38.

[36] Loughlin, *Political Jurisprudence* (n 32), 130.

[37] Schmitt (n 33), 30.

[38] See Karl Löwith, 'The Occasional Decisions of Carl Schmitt' in Richard Wolin (ed), *Karl Löwith, Martin Heidegger and European Nihilism* (Columbia University Press 1995); Hjalmar Falk, 'The "Theological Nihilism" of Friedrich Gogarten. On a Context in Karl Löwith's Critique of Carl Schmitt' (2014) 22 European Review 217; Roberto Farneti, 'Paradoxes of Normativity: On Carl Schmitt's Normative Skepticism' (2013) 34 History of Political Thought 114. For a contrasting view, see Loughlin, *Political Jurisprudence* (n 32), where he argues for a more 'nuanced' reading of Schmitt beyond the basic 'law of the political' equating with 'might is right'. However, he acknowledges that Schmitt's writings are not 'consistent on this point' (ibid 131–32).

and are therefore better considered as forms of internal scepticism rather than external scepticism.[39]

Discounting, then, an external scepticism about constitutionalism as inappropriate to the types of disagreement about transnational constitutionalism that we have been considering over Chapters 5, 6, and 7, our interest, then, in characterizing and understanding the type of disagreement surrounding the concept of constitutionalism in Chapter 5 is that of *internal* scepticism. That is, that disagreement entails a scepticism about particular values such as, say, the legitimacy of legal constraints on governing authority, rather than scepticism about the truth of value in general.[40]

4.1 Constitutional Disagreement as Internal Scepticism

Within internal scepticism, then, adopting an interpretive attitude, we can encounter three different stages of interpretation of a concept or practice. The first stage is the 'pre-interpretive' stage, where there is general agreement on the object of study; that is, the various characteristics of a social practice of law or government or, in artistic interpretation, the individuation of the particular artistic work as the object of our interpretation.[41] As Dworkin notes, this stage already involves some measure of interpretation; however, some general consensus is required if our interpretation is to move beyond semantic or pseudo-disagreement. The second stage of interpretation is the identification of some general justification for an objective, a political concept, or a particular practice, which will identify the value of that object, or why it is worth pursuing.[42] Then there is the post-interpretive stage, where the interpreter revises their

[39] Schmitt's own conception of international law and international relations tended towards the 'realist'. Carl Schmitt, *Der Nomos Der Erde Im Jus Publicum Europaeum* (Dunker & Humbolt 1950); Martti Koskenniemi, 'Carl Schmitt and International Law' in Jens Meierhenrich and Oliver Simons (eds), *The Oxford Handbook of Carl Schmitt* (Oxford University Press 2017).

[40] Dworkin speaks of a variety of forms of internal scepticism which need not unduly detain us here—internal error skepticism and global internal scepticism. The former attempts to deny the application of moral ideals to particular contexts—such as moral questions relating to sexual acts between consenting adults or the application of moral standards to foreign policy—whereas the latter attempts to reject all moral claims based on a counter-factual (such as the existence of a deity). However, both of these forms of internal skepticism rely on the (potential) truth of moral claims—morality requires deference to the choices of consenting adults or the existence of a deity—and can therefore be distinguished from external scepticism. Dworkin, *Justice for Hedgehogs* (n 5), 34–35. We could interpret Loughlin's defence of Schmitt in this way; recasting Schmitt as an internal error sceptic such that for Schmitt true moral claims do exist but that the morality of the political (such as it is) defeats conventional constitutional morality such as the rule of law or fundamental rights protections. Loughlin, *Political Jurisprudence* (n 32), 126.

[41] Dworkin, *Law's Empire* (n 4), 66.

[42] ibid 66.

sense of what the practice 'really' requires so as to achieve the aims established at the interpretive stage.[43] Thus, the interpretation of political concepts involves *agreement* about what the general contours of the object are and what its general point or purpose is, but *disagreement* about what the best representation of that point or purpose is; what best represents that purpose in its best light.[44]

Our first step in understanding disagreement about the concept of constitutionalism understood as an interpretive concept, then, is to identify the broad pre-interpretive agreement about the practices to which the concept relates, around which the substantive disagreement can take place. As Dworkin suggests, when considering interpretive concepts, our identification of the pre-interpretive agreed object of our inquiry is mainly conventional, constrained by the 'history or shape of a practice or object'.[45] This will generally be uncontroversial. For example, in artistic interpretation it takes the form of delimiting the text that is to count to individuate, for example, *Pangur Bán* as a poem, *Normal People* as a novel, or *Philadelphia, Here I Come!* as a play. In terms of a social practice, it will involve picking out the relevant sociological or historical facts that are relevant to the identification of a practice such as law.[46] For the concept of law, specifically, Dworkin argues that our pre-interpretive consensus involves '[l]egislatures and courts and administrative agencies and bodies, and the decisions their institutions make [which are] represented in a canonical way'.[47]

With respect to our disagreement surrounding the concept of constitutionalism more broadly, we can identify a common thread, a pre-interpretive agreement, in the various accounts of constitutionalism considered in Chapter 5 as drawing on the 'history and shape' of the concept *relating to the practices of government*. Here Loughlin's formulation of the type of thing we would associate with the pre-interpretive agreement surrounding the concept of constitutionalism is as good as any:[48]

[43] ibid 66. Of course Dworkin notes that these stages are stylized in the sense that actual disagreement most likely involves all three at once. However they are useful to parse for analytical purposes to understand the nature of substantive theoretical disagreement.

[44] ibid 67. Dworkin summarizes these stages in the following way: '[F]irst a background identification of a practice or tradition to which the interpretation belongs . . .; second, a set of assumptions about the purpose of that practice; and third, a claim that the proffered interpretation realizes those purposive assumptions better than any alternative understanding.' Dworkin, *Justice for Hedgehogs* (n 5), 134.

[45] Dworkin, *Law's Empire* (n 4), 52.

[46] ibid 52.

[47] ibid 91.

[48] Martin Loughlin, *The Idea of Public Law* (Oxford University Press 2004) 5.

> As a general phenomenon, the activity of governing exists whenever people are drawn into association with one another ... to be able to develop and flourish, such groups must establish some set of governing arrangements, however rudimentary [...] Whatever the type of governing arrangement established, an iron law of necessity holds sway. Since it simply is not possible for associations of any significant scale and degree of permanence to be capable of governing themselves, the business of governing invariably requires the drawing of a distinction that has become fundamental to the activity: the division between rulers and ruled, between a governing authority and its subjects'.

That is, the 'pre-interpretive' intuitions that we have about the concept of constitutionalism—the consensus as to the primary features or characteristics of constitutionalism in the 'history and use' of the concept in the understandings identified in Chapter 5—relate to the idea that the object to which constitutionalism refers is the practice of governing with all the institutions and rules which go along with it. Moreover, the type of governing in question is *political* governing involving, potentially, the application of coercion.[49]

Having identified the activity of governing as the pre-interpretive agreement about what 'counts' as constitutional practice, our next stage is the identification of the purpose of the practice of constitutionalism and in particular, the identification of the political value of the tradition which is then subject to rival interpretations as to how that purpose or value can be best achieved or what presents that value in its 'best light'. Dworkin argues that a 'central concept'[50] of the point or purpose of an object or practice, while desirable, is not necessary. A general explanation of the value or purpose of an object can suffice to 'organize further argument' based on a particular political value.[51] In this spirit, then, our gambit here is to claim that what links the various accounts of constitutionalism considered in Chapter 5 is the fact that they all understand the purpose of constitutionalism as *legitimating governing authority* in some sense. Thus, even if the development of constitutionalism in the state context was 'varied'[52] between different states, as evidenced by the different meanings attributed to the concept considered in Chapter 5, there is, as Loughlin argues,

[49] See generally Dworkin, *Law's Empire* (n 4), ch3, 'Jurisprudence Revisited'; Dworkin, *Justice in Robes* (n 17), ch6; Dworkin, *Justice for Hedgehogs* (n 5), ch14, 'Obligations'.

[50] Dworkin, *Law's Empire* (n 4), 92–93.

[51] ibid 92–93.

[52] Martin Loughlin, *Foundations of Public Law* (Oxford University Press 2010), 158.

a 'coherent trajectory'[53] of Western constitutional development which can be understood as generally aimed at reflecting upon what legitimate governing authority requires.[54] This is the common thread which brings the at times varied practices of government together, making up what can be described as a 'Western Constitutional Tradition'.[55] Thus, to summarize the first two steps of our interpretive inquiry into the concept of constitutionalism we can say that they correspond to the two elements of Bernard Williams's political theory of legitimacy: a response to the 'first political question' in the form of securing 'order, protection, safety, trust and the conditions of cooperation',[56] that is, the activity of governing, and its accompanying 'basic legitimation demand'[57] in the form of advancing arguments about what legitimate governing authority requires.

From here we can move on to the next stage of our interpretive inquiry regarding the concept of constitutionalism: to present its point or purpose in its best light. Here we can make two distinctions in the ways in which constitutional discourse attempts to present the value of legitimate governing authority in its best light: from the viewpoint of substantive value and from the viewpoint, downstream of this value, of particular institutional prescriptions as to how those particular values can be best achieved. With regard to showing the purpose of constitutionalism in its best light, one key general cleavage within this tradition relates to those who deem the best interpretation of legitimate governing authority to be inspired by the values of liberalism, and those who deem the best interpretation of legitimate governing authority to be inspired by the values of republicanism, as well as a variety of positions in between.[58] Downstream of this particular disagreement, disagreement emerges with respect to what specific institutional prescriptions our combination of substantive values of liberalism or republicanism requires. This is, for example, the locus of disagreement about whether judicial review is supportive or

[53] ibid, emphasis added.

[54] 'In these articulations, humans are assumed to be free and equal beings who collectively determine the nature of their political existence and who, as the ultimate source of political authority, are conceived to be authors of the governing regime under which they live. Since this principle of self-actualization is made operational through the institution of law, the works of these jurists simultaneously provide us with an explanation of the law establishing and maintaining the public sphere. This body of work provides the intellectual foundations of public law.' ibid 157.

[55] ibid 158.

[56] Williams (n 3), 3–4.

[57] ibid 4–5.

[58] Mac Amhlaigh, 'Harmonising Global Constitutionalism' (n 9); J Tully, 'The Unfreedom of the Moderns in Comparison to Their Ideals of Constitutional Democracy' (2002) 65 Modern Law Review 204; J Habermas, 'Constitutional Democracy: A Paradoxical Union of Contradictory Principles?' (2001) 29 Political Theory 766.

detrimental to liberal ideals of liberty[59] or supportive or detrimental to ideals of republican freedom.[60]

In this way, we can organize our disagreement around the concept of constitutionalism by identifying the common purpose of constitutionalism based on a particular (and particularly Western) post-Enlightenment history of thinking about what legitimate governing authority requires. Such an account, it is submitted, is 'sufficiently abstract and uncontroversial' to allow for 'a great many competing claims'.[61]

In this way, we can say that legitimate governing authority can be said to be 'tied' to constitutionalism such that it would be 'natural for people to regard that tie as special and in the way of conceptual' to say that legitimate governing authority is 'part of the "very meaning" of constitutionalism'.[62] It provides the 'general justification for the main elements'[63] of the object or practice of constitutionalism. As such, each of the accounts of constitutionalism presented in Chapter 5, and the disagreement which emerges between them, are best viewed as 'subinterpretations'[64] of this more abstract idea.

We can round out our account of an interpretive concept of constitutionalism with some arboreal metaphors again furnished by Dworkin. The debates about constitutionalism identified in Chapter 5 can be said to follow a 'tree-like structure'.[65] People by and large agree about the most general and abstract propositions about constitutionalism which 'form the trunk of the tree': that constitutionalism relates to the practices of governing and the general aspects of these practices both normative and institutional, and whose primary purpose is to approximate values of legitimate political authority, but they disagree about 'more concrete refinements or sub-interpretations of these abstract propositions'.[66] These disagreements constitute the 'branches of the tree'.[67] The 'trunk' of legitimate governing authority therefore, provides a 'kind of plateau on which further thought and argument are built'.[68]

[59] John Rawls, *Political Liberalism* (Columbia University Press 1993), Lecture VI; Waldron (n 2), ch9.
[60] Contrast Philip Pettit, *On the People's Terms: A Republican Theory and Model of Democracy* (Cambridge University Press 2012), with Richard Bellamy, *Political Constitutionalism: A Republican Defence of the Constitutionality of Democracy* (Cambridge University Press 2007).
[61] Dworkin, *Law's Empire* (n 4), 93.
[62] ibid 70.
[63] ibid 66.
[64] ibid 71–72.
[65] ibid 70.
[66] ibid 70.
[67] ibid 70.
[68] ibid 70.

4.2 Constitutional Disagreement as Constitutionalism's Dualisms

In order to substantiate our claim regarding the benefits of viewing the concept of constitutionalism, or perhaps more accurately, *disagreement* about the concept of constitutionalism, in terms of an interpretive concept, it is worth revisiting the variety of 'dualisms' identified in Chapter 5, recasting them as 'branches' of the constitutional 'tree'. Building on the first cleavage of our constitutional discourse between substantive values of liberalism and republicanism, we can argue that regulative constitutionalism in the form of limited government and constitutive constitutionalism in the form of the justification of the foundations of government provide rival interpretations or conceptions of the concept of constitutionalism as an account of legitimate authority based on ideals of liberty and equality. Within our first limb of our 'tree' of constitutionalism, moreover, we encounter the further spilt between 'legal' and 'structural' conceptions of regulative constitutionalism based on the idea of legal limitations and structural limitations respectively. These can further branch out into different sub-conceptions; for example, the idea of legal limitations involving a minimal rule of law requirement—'rule by law', meaning that the authority uses the means of law to act—or more substantive conceptions of the rule of law involving some form of minimal entrenchment of constitutional norms, along with further splits into the desirability or otherwise of judicial supremacy. Similarly, the structural limitations on the regulative branch of constitutionalism further bifurcate into weaker or stronger, more minimal or maximal prescriptions surrounding the separation of powers into executive, judicial, and legislative branches.

The constitutive limb of the initial fork in the trunk, moreover, is concerned with the idea of constitutionalism providing the foundations of legitimate governing authority. This in turn can be split into a conception of constitutionalism which sees legitimate governing authority emerging from the instrumental function of constitutionalism as facilitating the achievement of political equality in the form of democracy as Waldron argues, and a concept of constitutionalism which prioritizes foundational or constitutive agency as the key feature in legitimate government, for example, in the form of a constituent power.

The most important feature of the tree metaphor, however, is that all of those engaged in 'internal disagreement' agree that the 'tree' exists, that it has value which can have truth value (they are not external sceptics), and that they all understand themselves to be interpreting the same 'tree' involving the idea of legitimate governing authority informed by a 'Western Constitutional Tradition'. The different branches of the 'tree' then represent different interpretations of the 'trunk' in terms of how its core values can be best achieved.

Thinking of constitutionalism in this way helps us understand disagreement surrounding the concept in a way which makes the disagreement genuine; that is, disagreement about substantive value, rather than pseudo- or semantic disagreement.[69] Of course, it is to be expected that our characterization of constitutionalism in terms of legitimate political authority and the disagreement which emerges with regard to the different functions of different parts of constitutionalism could, itself, be the subject of disagreement. The decision to understand particular concepts such as constitutionalism as an interpretive concept is, itself, as Dworkin notes, an interpretive exercise;[70] after all, interpretation is 'interpretive all the way down'.[71] As such, the 'tree of constitutionalism' presented here itself involves an interpretation of the disagreement surrounding the concept presented in its best light. That is, it involves a claim that the best way to understand disagreement about the concept of constitutionalism in the series of dualisms outlined in Chapter 5 is to take it seriously as substantive disagreement about political values and not semantic or pseudo-disagreement which is, in turn, best understood according to this tree-like structure building on the 'trunk' of legitimate political authority informed by ideals of liberty and equality. This does not make it immune to disagreement or critique. However, any putative disagreement or critique of this particular interpretation surrounding disagreement about the concept of constitutionalism will, if it is not to constitute a form of external scepticism, have to advance a case that disagreement about the concept of constitutionalism can be understood in another way which presents that disagreement in its best light.

5. Interpretive Constitutionalism and the Constitutional Cacophony

Understanding our disagreements about the concept of constitutionalism in terms of interpretive concepts therefore helps us tackle the 'first constitutional question' entailed in the cacophony critique.

[69] ibid 71.
[70] Dworkin, *Justice for Hedgehogs* (n 5), ch8.
[71] ibid 162.

In terms of our tree model of disagreement about constitutionalism as an interpretive concept, we can see that the disagreement between, say, those who endorse legal limitations and judicial supremacy and those who endorse legislative supremacy can be mapped out as different 'branches' on the 'trunk' of legitimate political authority which provides the core shared political value of constitutionalism. In this way, then, we can see that the prescriptions of different 'constitutional dualisms' is one way of thinking about legitimate governing authority in terms of the blend of liberalism and republicanism in the Western Constitutional Tradition, while its sceptics can be seen to be pursuing another branch of that tree. Thus, we can see that the disagreement here is a substantive disagreement about what legitimate governing authority requires as opposed to pseudo- or semantic disagreement. This serves the purpose of 'harmonizing' the cacophony and addressing the 'definitional conundrums' by providing an important 'fulcrum of disagreement'[72] for the various positions in constitutional discourse. Harmonizing the cacophony in this way is, in itself, an important advance in how we understand the concept of constitutionalism and might help us hone our conceptions and our ideas with greater accuracy and sophistication which cannot but be a good thing.[73] Moreover, it also secures our good faith attempts to establish truth in questions of value and wards against scepticism or cynicism about political values.

However, as we noted earlier, answering the 'first constitutional question' in terms of an interpretive concept also allows us to gain deeper understanding of the particular types of disagreements involving the illegitimacy and no demos critiques of transnational constitutionalism, as well as help us establish a solid foundation for a normative account of transnational constitutional pluralism.

[72] Timothy AO Endicott, 'Herbert Hart and the Semantic Sting' (1998) 4 Legal Theory 283.

[73] As Dworkin notes, exposing this structure of disagreement 'may help to sharpen argument and will in any case improve the community's understanding of its intellectual environment'. Dworkin, *Law's Empire* (n 4), 71. This sentiment has an affinity with Gallie's aims in presenting certain political concepts as essentially contested which we encountered in Chapter 6. See Walter B Gallie, 'Essentially Contested Concepts' (1955) 56 Proceedings of the Aristotelian Society 167. As noted there, Gallie argued that even if contestation doesn't lead to consensus on the meaning or value of a concept, it can provide beneficial consequences in the form of allowing us to gain deeper insights and a better understanding of our interpretation of concepts and what is valuable about them and what is not. Dworkin has endorsed Gallie's idea of an essentially contested concept in various parts of his work Ronald Dworkin, *Taking Rights Seriously* (Duckworth 1977) 103; Dworkin, *Justice in Robes* (n 17), ch7, 'Thirty Years On'. For discussion and critique of Dworkin's use of the idea of an essentially contested concept, see Kenneth M Ehrenberg, 'Law Is Not (Best Considered) an Essentially Contested Concept' (2011) 7 International Journal of Law in Context 209.

5.1 Constitutional Illegitimacy and the Unity of Constitutional Value

Thinking about constitutionalism in an interpretive way not only allows us to make sense of disagreement about the concept; that is, to 'harmonize' the 'cacophony' into substantive disagreements of value and not merely semantic or pseudo-disagreements. It also helps us to understand how our values relate to each other. As Dworkin notes, the interpretive enterprise 'weaves together hosts of values and assumptions of very different kinds' which are 'drawn from very different kinds of judgment or experience'.[74] It is therefore 'pervasively holistic'.[75]

That interpretation is holistic in this way means that our identification of political values as interpretive concepts and understanding disagreement surrounding political value in terms of 'best interpretations' is a more ambitious proposal that it might seem at first. It forces us to think beyond our own 'best interpretations' of the value of a particular object such as legitimate governing authority and reflect upon the (potentially vast) normative hinterland which support and justify our values. It forces us to take seriously a *unity of value*.

Dworkin's most ambitious thesis about the unity of value is the 'one big thing' that the hedgehog knows in the eponymous title of his last book. The unity of value in its most expansive and basic form involves the basic proposition that 'the truth about living well and being good and what's wonderful is not only coherent but mutually supporting: what we think about any one of these must stand up, eventually to any argument we find compelling about the rest'.[76] With respect to ethical and moral value in particular, Dworkin argues that we must try to understand our ethical and moral values as integrated. We must, he argues, 'try to understand them holistically and interpretively, each in the light of the others, organized not in hierarchy but in the fashion of a geodesic dome'.[77] We understand values and their importance better 'by seeing which conception of each and what assignment of importance to them best fits our sense of the other dimensions of living well, of making a success of the challenge of living a life'.[78] This is because, for Dworkin:

[74] Dworkin, *Justice for Hedgehogs* (n 5), 154.
[75] ibid 154.
[76] ibid 1.
[77] Dworkin, *Justice in Robes* (n 17), 160–61.
[78] ibid 160–61.

> [e]thics is a complex structure of different goals, achievements, and virtues, and the part each of these plays in that complex structure can only be understood by elaborating its role in an overall design fixed by the others. Until we can see how our ethical values hang together in that way, so that each can be tested against our provision account of the others, we do not understand any of them.[79]

For this reason, Dworkin argues that political concepts '*must* be integrated with one another'.[80] We cannot defend a conception of any of them without showing how 'our conception fits with and into appealing conceptions of the others'.[81]

Once we start down the path of taking an interpretive approach to concepts of political value such as constitutionalism, there is an inexorability about thinking of value in holistic terms.[82] However, Dworkin's case for the unity of value does not only rest upon the consequences of an interpretive approach to value. To this interpretive case, Dworkin adds a second, higher-order justification based on a *correct approach to inquiring into and acting on values in general*.[83] Dworkin's approach to thinking about value involves, an 'integrated epistemology' whereby 'we must make assumptions about what is true in order to test theories about how to decide what is true'.[84] This means that the epistemological part of our value theory, the part that 'tells us how to inquire *responsibly* into values' is *itself* 'governed by certain ethical values that define what it means to be a responsible agent'.[85]

This approach therefore involves an *ethical* requirement to think about and act on values as an integrated whole. Inter-operation operates also at this meta-level for Dworkin such that thinking and acting coherently according to a coherent set of values appropriately interpreted is central to human dignity in the sense of acting with self-respect and authenticity.[86] In this way, then, the unity

[79] ibid 160–61.
[80] Dworkin, *Justice for Hedgehogs* (n 5), 7.
[81] ibid 7.
[82] ibid 1. As MacInnis notes, 'the unity thesis underlies Dworkin's influential interpretive theory of law', Luke MacInnis, 'Dworkin's Unity of Value: An Interpretation and Defense' (2020) 26 Res Publica 403, 404. More generally MacInnis argues that Dworkin's case for the unity of value is made up of three related theses: the independence thesis, that the domain of value is an autonomous domain and propositions can only be defined using other value judgments; the interoperation thesis, 'the positive side of the independence thesis'; and the interpretation thesis, which explains 'how value judgements can be defended within the domain of value by relating value judgments to each other through a process of interpretation'. ibid 407.
[83] MacInnis (n 82), 410.
[84] Dworkin, *Justice for Hedgehogs* (n 5), 82.
[85] MacInnis (n 82), 411–12.
[86] ibid 410; Dworkin, *Justice for Hedgehogs* (n 5), 204.

of value is 'neither an epistemic axiom nor a metaphysical generalization'[87] but an 'essential dimension of ethical responsibility'.[88]

Engaging in an inquiry into political value, then, involves finding the 'place of each value in a larger and mutually supporting web ... that displays supporting connections among moral and political values generally and then places these in the still larger context of ethics'.[89]

Dworkin recognizes the weight of this obligation of moral responsibility that his more general approach to ethical inquiry involves. He urges that this approach 'would be impossible to achieve fully, even if we set out self-consciously to achieve it'.[90] 'We cannot', he argues, 'hope to construct a dense, detailed, interwoven, wholly coherent filter of conviction wrapped around our will that is effective without exception and that brings us a constant glow of fittingness.'[91] We must treat this responsibility in ethical inquiry as a 'work *always in progress*'.[92] We are morally responsible, Dworkin argues, provided we accept 'moral integrity and authenticity as appropriate ideals' and deploy a '*reasonable effort* towards achieving them'.[93]

5.2 The Unity of Value and the Illegitimacy Critique

Dworkin's insights into the relationship between inter-operability and the unity of value provide the basis for addressing the illegitimacy critiques of constitutionalism we met in Chapter 6. For these purposes, we can narrow our lens from Dworkin's immense canvas of value *as a whole* to focus on the more parochial disagreements outlined in Chapter 5 regarding the meaning of constitutionalism. In order to begin to address the illegitimacy critique of constitutionalism, it is worth summarizing its core features. As will be recalled, this form of constitutional scepticism consisted of a dual attack: not only was constitutionalism in practice illegitimate but it fraudulently made claims to legitimize the exercise of governing power. The twin features of constitutional

[87] MacInnis (n 82), 404.
[88] ibid.
[89] Dworkin, *Justice in Robes* (n 17), 168. MacInnis presents the idea in the following terms: 'deliberation about and conduct upon an integrated conception of values is an essential dimension of ethical responsibility. Since we each have a sovereign responsibility, constitutive of our agency and essential to our dignity, to live our lives according to our own convictions about what is good and right, and since it is not possible to execute this assignment unless we strive to act upon a coherent scheme of values, then we are obligated to strive for unity among our values.' MacInnis (n 82), 409.
[90] Dworkin, *Justice for Hedgehogs* (n 5), 109.
[91] ibid 109.
[92] ibid 109.
[93] ibid 109, emphasis added.

entrenchment and judicial supremacy served to violate particular interpretations of liberal equality or republican freedom.[94] Moreover, the illegitimacy critique of *transnational* constitutionalism, in particular, built on these normative premises to argue that such developments at the transnational level exacerbated the effects of entrenchment and judicial supremacy given that they served externally to constrain the democratic life of a political community.

As noted earlier, taking an interpretive approach to constitutionalism allows us to see these particular understandings of political value in terms of liberal equality or republican freedom as particular 'forks' or 'branches' on the more general 'tree' of constitutionalism. As such, the illegitimacy critique of constitutionalism can be understood, on an interpretive account, as a 'best interpretation' of legitimate governing authority based on democratic procedure as against constitutional entrenchment or judicial supremacy. It is, moreover, a form of internal scepticism in that it relies on moral propositions (of liberal equality or republican freedom) to 'denigrate' these particular interpretations of the representation of legitimate governing authority in its best light. This reflects a common approach to thinking about constitutionalism and democracy in oppositional terms: that we must have either one or the other, or more of one and less of the other, and that this is simply a tragic feature of our politics. However, an interpretive approach trained upon the unity of value encourages us to think of these face value conflicts in unitary terms. In advancing the thesis about the unity of value, Dworkin argues that he doesn't want merely to offer a method of resolving conflicts of value based on some 'reflective equilibrium' which might offer solutions to conflicts in individual cases.[95] Rather, accepting the thesis of the unity of value involves denying that the conflict even exists.[96] For the unity of value, 'there are no genuine conflicts in value' that require adjudication.[97] Our conflicts between, say, a value of 'democracy' and a value of 'constitutionalism' as set up by our critics, are merely 'apparent'[98] conflicts. As noted earlier, our moral responsibility in inquiring into value is 'never complete'.[99] We are, Dworkin argues, 'constantly reinterpreting our concepts as we use them'.[100] Thus, when facing our apparent conflicts such as the putative conflicts between democratic process and entrenchment, or judicial supremacy as set up by our discontents in Chapter 5, we must further refine our conceptions

[94] Waldron (n 2); Bellamy (n 60).
[95] Dworkin, *Justice for Hedgehogs* (n 5), 119.
[96] ibid 119.
[97] ibid 119.
[98] ibid 119.
[99] ibid 119.
[100] ibid 119.

of these values. In attempting to determine what we should do in the face of an apparent conflict along the lines of our example, we must simply 'reinterpret our concepts to resolve our dilemma'.[101] 'The direction of thought', Dworkin argues, is towards '*unity, not fragmentation*'.[102] Whatever resolution of the apparent conflict we adopt, we have, Dworkin concludes, 'taken a step towards a more integrated understanding of our moral responsibilities'.[103] This is the natural consequence of an interpretive approach. Political values do not merely exist, our political values are supported not by appeals to 'reality' but through justifications which, in turn, draw upon other, further values. Political value is normative 'all the way down'. The correct use of political concepts is therefore a matter of interpretation.

What we can take from this idea in respect of our disagreements about constitutionalism is that we must strive to integrate our different conceptions of constitutionalism in terms of the best representation of legitimate political authority. In terms of our stylized dichotomy between regulative and constitutive constitutionalism, we must continually attempt to integrate these interpretations into a coherent conception of constitutional value. Our task as interpreters of the concept of constitutionalism is to show how our conception fits into 'appealing conceptions of the others'.[104]

What this implies for our approach to the concept of constitutionalism is that an interpretive approach to constitutionalism involves normatively important reasons, moral reasons, to deploy a reasonable effort to integrate our 'best interpretations' of our core political value of constitutionalism. On this approach, then, we fail in our moral responsibilities as interpreters of the concept of constitutionalism if we only take the first step in an interpretive approach to political value; that is, presenting our own 'best interpretation' of the constitutional value of legitimate political authority in the Western Constitutional Tradition. To discharge our moral responsibilities on an interpretive scheme fully, we must also take the next, further, step of illustrating and justifying how our particular conception is integrated with other conceptions of that value. Thus, as theorists of the interpretive concept of constitutionalism whose 'point' or 'purpose' is the value of legitimate political authority, our question becomes how we can integrate our 'best interpretations' of the concept in terms of, for example, limitations on governing power (whether legal or structural) with

[101] ibid 119.
[102] ibid 119.
[103] ibid 119.
[104] ibid 7.

constitutive conceptions of constitutionalism based on the values of consent or values associated with constituent power.

Emphasizing the holism promoted in interpretive approaches to political concepts allows us to address the critiques of the concept of constitutionalism considered earlier, in a better way. When viewed as 'best interpretations' of the political value of legitimate political authority, the target of the illegitimacy critique, '*guarantiste*' conceptions of constitutionalism prescribing, for example, a measure of constitutional entrenchment or judicial supremacy, take on a new light which takes much of the sting out of these illegitimacy critiques. For example, the case for entrenchment and judicial supremacy as the 'best interpretations' of the political value of legitimate political authority, are based, at least in part, as noted in Chapter 5, on political values such as the rule of law or fundamental rights which are, themselves, set in a particular relationship with liberty and equality. For many, it is these prescriptions stemming from the values of the rule of law, fundamental rights and equality which show the constitutional value of legitimate political authority in its best light. And it is precisely these mechanisms and the elevation of these values which have attracted the attention of some of constitutionalism's critics. However, if we are taking seriously our moral responsibilities in taking an interpretive approach to the concept of constitutionalism, we cannot simply leave matters there. We must also take the second step, which involves taking seriously rival conceptions of the political value of constitutionalism based on, for example, democratic consent based in the same way on ideals of liberty and equality as conceptions of the political value of constitutionalism, and force ourselves to think about how our conceptions (or the intermediate level values which inspire them) can be integrated with each other. Thus, if we are discharging our ethical obligations properly as constitutional theorists,[105] we have to undertake this second step of trying to integrate our conception with other conceptions to provide a holistic account of the political value of constitutionalism as legitimate political authority. When viewed in this light, we can critique conceptions of constitutionalism—for example Sartori's rather narrow '*guarantiste*' conception—not for failing to provide an account of legitimate political authority *per se* but rather for failing to take this second step in interpreting and integrating their conceptions with rival, particularly constitutive, conceptions and therefore failing to take the moral responsibilities of inquiry under an interpretive approach seriously. Thus, it is not a matter of determining that the conception is incorrect or illegitimate on its own terms. It only becomes problematic, on an interpretive

[105] ibid 101.

view, if we only go halfway along our interpretive exercise and fail to make a good faith attempt to integrate our conceptions with others in order to present a holistic conception of the integrated values of the concept of constitutionalism.[106] For this reason, then, we can meet the illegitimacy critiques of constitutionalism by critiquing them, as well as their target '*guarantiste*' conceptions, for stopping at endorsing their own 'best interpretation' of the value of the concept and therefore failing to take the extra necessary step of striving for an integrated conception of the value of constitutionalism, and failing to illustrate how particular conceptions relate to other conceptions. On this view, the critiques of constitutionalism are not insurmountable and do not inhere in the interpretive concept of constitutionalism itself. They relate, rather, to a failure to discharge our ethical responsibilities surrounding an inquiry into value on an interpretive approach in full.[107] This deficiency can be remedied by endorsing a fully interpretive approach to the concept of constitutionalism based on the unity of (constitutional) value. In order to avoid the pitfalls of partial accounts of the political value of constitutionalism, and attract the types of critique that we considered in Chapter 6, we simply need to attempt in good faith to pursue our ethical obligations as identified by Dworkin, ensuring that we complete the second step in our theorizing in illustrating how our best interpretation of the political value of constitutionalism relates to other conceptions in order to present a holistic and complete account of the political value of constitutionalism. As noted earlier, this is itself an interpretive exercise and adopting this approach will not solve disagreement. Moreover, as Dworkin acknowledges, the bar for integrating our values is extremely high and it is unlikely that any individual theorists will ever achieve the ideal.[108] However, we come closer to discharging our ethical and moral responsibilities, in adopting this unitary and holistic approach, through our reasonable efforts.

6. Interpretive Transnational Constitutional Pluralism

The legitimacy critique of constitutionalism is, as we have seen, exacerbated in relation to the idea of transnational constitutionalism in terms of 'new

[106] ibid 109.

[107] It hardly needs mentioning that this admonition towards a holistic approach also applies to other accounts such as Waldron's and Bellamy's based on liberal equality and republican freedom endorsing democratic procedures as the 'best interpretation' of the political value of constitutionalism *qua* legitimate governing authority. See Chapter 7.

[108] Dworkin, *Justice for Hedgehogs* (n 5), 109.

constitutionalism'. As noted earlier, as an expression of the concept of constitutionalism, transnational constitutionalism shares the problems associated with its state-based counterpart, in particular, its 'definitional conundrums' and its potential lack of democratic credentials. However, it also has to reckon with the other axis of disagreement considered at length in Chapter 7; that is, whether constitutionalism is a concept which is suited to or aptly 'exported' to the 'foreign climate' of transnational governance in the light of the fact that this climate entails significant disanalogies with the state context in terms of particularly acute disagreement at this level with regard to questions of political value such as constitutionalism. As intimated in Chapter 7, the 'category error' objection and the illegitimacy critiques of 'new constitutionalism' are linked. To a significant degree, the problems associated with 'new constitutionalism' are the product of a deliberate strategy by transnational constitutional theories to manage the 'gap' between state and suprastate levels of government to cater for the different order of magnitude of political disagreement at this level. This involves the stripping down of the concept of constitutionalism—from big 'C' to small 'c'—to manage the particular 'problems of translation'[109] between these levels. The concept of *transnational* constitutionalism in particular, then, potentially faces particularly acute illegitimacy problems: entailing both the conventional illegitimacy critiques of constitutionalism as well as the critiques of the exportation of the concept to the 'foreign climate' of transnational governance.

A concern with the latter issue, the 'exportation' problem, can be seen in the tendencies in theories of transnational constitutionalism to *disaggregate* the concept of constitutionalism in order to accommodate the novel foreign climate of the transnational level. This approach to transnational constitutionalism involves, in Walker's terms, the idea that:

> one can pick some features out of the state constitutional mix, such as a Charter of Rights or a system of inter-institutional checks and balances, and these features will remain of significant value despite being deprived of either the fuller legal framework or the deeper socio-cultural context of the state.[110]

[109] Neil Walker, 'Postnational Constitutionalism and the Problem of Translation' in Joseph HH Weiler and Marlene Wind (eds), *European Constitutionalism beyond the State* (Cambridge University Press 2003).

[110] Neil Walker, 'Beyond the Holistic Constitution?' in Petra Dobner and Martin Loughlin (eds), *The Twilight of Constitutionalism?* (Oxford University Press 2010) 295.

Thus, disaggregation becomes the solution to manage the issue of exporting the concept of constitutionalism from the state to the transnational level by taking a fragment of the concept and transporting it to address legitimacy problems at this level of government. Elements of disaggregated constitutionalism can be found in a variety of accounts of transnational constitutionalism; however, here we will consider two forms of disaggregated transnational constitutional theory which are exemplars of the type of move which has attracted 'new constitutionalist' critiques: Walker's disaggregated constitutionalism and Krisch's defence of Global Administrative Law (GAL).

6.1 Disaggregated Transnational Constitutionalism

Walker has developed a nuanced and theoretically informed defence of a disaggregated transnational constitutionalism based on the specific problems affecting the exportation of the concept of constitutionalism to the transnational level. Adopting an approach to the concept of constitutionalism similar to the interpretive approach adopted here, he argues that the 'holistic' form of constitutionalism as developed in the state is, in fact, a series of 'distinct layers' of 'situated "constitutional" practice that have operated separately or in different combinations in the past'.[111] Constitutionalism, for Walker is a 'cluster concept'[112] made of layers which offer a 'frame for the "constitutive" representation and regulation of... social reality'.[113]

From this, then, we can conceptualize, Walker argues, forms of constitutionalism which entail combinations of these 'layers' or made up of one of these layers exclusively. Thus, we can think about transnational constitutionalism in more or less unitary terms as embracing more or less of the different layers which are aggregated into a holistic concept of constitutionalism. Using this method, then, he argues that we can analyse transnational governance in more or less constitutional terms, identifying governance regimes that are more like, and less like, the holistic constitutionalism of the state. The European Union, for example, is perhaps the most state-like being made up, as it is, of a 'layered set of holistic frames'.[114] Others, such as the World Trade Organization (WTO) or the United Nations (UN) are less so; constitutional debate here being limited to the 'thin legal and politico-institutional registers'.[115] Beyond these settings,

111 These are 'juridical, politico-institutional, popular and societal'. ibid 298.
112 ibid 298.
113 ibid 298.
114 ibid 301.
115 ibid 301.

constitutionalism becomes even more etiolated, relying less and less on the holistic frame of the state-based model such as the types of societal constitutionalism of ICANN (the Internet Corporation for Assigned Names and Numbers) or the *lex mercatoria*.[116] Considering the variety of 'registers' of transnational constitutionalism extant in the context of transnational governance, Walker concludes that 'none of the connecting elements—the "holism of holisms"—of state constitutionalism can be guaranteed' at this level.[117]

Thus, Walker concludes that, what he calls 'transnational societal constitutionalism' is a constitutionalism 'that is reconfigured in each of its framing aspects'.[118] It represents a 'complex mix of discrete self-constitution and diffuse external constitution across all four registers—legal, politico-institutional, popular and societal'.[119]

6.2 'Global Administrative Law'

Notwithstanding its rebranding as 'administrative law', a similar disaggregated form of constitutionalism has been promoted by an influential group of scholars under the banner of 'Global Administrative Law' (GAL). It tracks developments in transnational governance and in particular the development of norms and principles which it identifies as a 'global administrative law' which operates at national, transnational, and international levels[120] and is defined in terms of the 'mechanisms, principles, practices and supporting social understandings that promote or otherwise effect the accountability of global administrative bodies, in particular by ensuring they meet adequate standards of transparency, participation, reasoned decision, and legality, and by providing effective review of the rules and decisions they make'.[121] These take place within a 'global administrative space' which is distinct from the 'space of inter-state relations governed by international law and the domestic regulatory space governed by domestic administrative law, although encompassing elements of each'[122] and views them as 'closely intertwined in many areas of regulation and administration'.[123]

[116] ibid 293.
[117] ibid 302.
[118] ibid 303.
[119] ibid 304.
[120] Benedict Kingsbury, Nico Krisch, and Richard B Stewart, 'The Emergence of Global Administrative Law' (2005) 68 Law & Contemporary Problems 16, 15–61.
[121] ibid 17.
[122] ibid 26.
[123] ibid 26.

However, proponents of GAL do not merely track and map these developments but also make a normative case for the emergence of GAL as a key support of the *legitimacy* of transnational governance.[124] Global administrative lawyers envisage three sets of 'normative goals'[125] which GAL can achieve in transnational governance: inter-administrative accountability, protection of private rights or the rights of states, and promotion of democracy.[126] More generally, Krisch has promoted GAL as an attenuated form of normative theorization of transnational governance for the same reasons that Walker has argued for a disaggregated transnational constitutionalism. However, for the reasons which we considered in Chapter 7, and which we need not rehearse here, Krisch argues that his version of holistic constitutionalism—'foundational' constitutionalism—is too 'holistic'[127] and too thick to be legitimately applied to transnational governance. For this reason, he endorses the much more attenuated form of GAL as a way of approaching the legitimacy questions and concerns which emerge in the context of transnational governance.[128] However, unlike certain disaggregated models of transnational constitutionalism which argue for the replication of constitutional modes of governance at transnational level, even in limited form such as judicial review or procedural justice, GAL serves, Krisch argues, as 'an inspiration and contrast'.[129] It serves as a 'framework for identifying converging and diverging developments in institutional practice, and it helps us sharpen our sensitivity to the problems and possibilities of establishing accountability mechanisms on the global level'.[130] Like Walker's disaggregated constitutionalism, Krisch's account of GAL also has a more limited normative ambition.[131] It doesn't aim at a 'full account of the conditions under which global governance, or global administration, would be legitimate' but rather at 'elucidating the respective normative values and presuppositions of particular institutional alternatives'.[132] GAL therefore trades on a certain 'working consensus' and normative premises which it deems to be

[124] ibid 26

[125] ibid 45.

[126] ibid 43.

[127] Nico Krisch, 'Global Administrative Law and the Constitutional Ambition' in Petra Dobner and Martin Loughlin (eds), *The Twilight of Constitutionalism* (Oxford University Press 2010) 254.

[128] 'The holistic ambition of foundational constitutionalism ... sits uneasily with the societal and political circumstances of contemporary global politics: less comprehensive approaches might fare better in this context.' ibid 255

[129] ibid 256.

[130] ibid 256.

[131] ibid 257.

[132] ibid 257.

'less contested' than broader, more expansive accounts of the legitimacy of governance more generally.[133]

6.3 Disaggregation and Constitutional Illegitimacy

With regard to the disaggregationist tendency in transnational constitutionalism to manage the problems associated with exporting the concept to the transnational level, we can immediately anticipate, given our previous discussion on the concept of constitutionalism more generally, the potential problems with this approach. First, going back to our question of definitional conundrums, a disaggregated transnational constitutionalism must be careful not to succumb to the problem of pseudo-disagreement or the 'semantic sting'. If we 'slice and dice' the concept of constitutionalism in the way that these approaches endorse, are we not exacerbating the disagreement surrounding the concept considered in Chapter 5?

Walker anticipates this problem, noting that a disaggregated constitutionalism of the type he promotes could have 'divisive and mutually alienating consequences'[134] along the lines of semantic or pseudo-disagreement. He parries this risk by arguing, in a seemingly Dworkinian vein, that we must identify a 'common point' from which to investigate the differences between different conceptions of constitutionalism such as those outlined in Chapter 5.[135] This can be achieved, Walker argues, by recasting debates about the concept of constitutionalism in 'functional terms'.[136] This involves approaching the concept of constitutionalism not as a debate over 'diverse and rival conceptions of the ends of constitutionalism understood as ends that either are or are not exclusively associated with the state' but as a debate over 'diverse and rival conceptions of the constitutional means necessary to ends that would themselves be capable of commanding general agreement across state-centered and post-state positions'.[137]

Identifying these means and ends, Walker concedes, involves proceeding at a 'very high level of abstraction'[138] and he identifies the function

133 ibid 258.
134 Walker, 'Beyond the Holistic Constitution?' (n 110) 307.
135 ibid 296.
136 ibid 296.
137 Walker, 'Beyond the Holistic Constitution?' (n 110), 296, emphasis added.
138 ibid 296.

of constitutionalism as a 'meta-political' one involving 'shaping the domain of politics broadly conceived—of literally "constituting" the body politic'.[139]

Thus, this core function of constitutionalism is what holds everything together, what connects the different 'frames' or 'layers' into a holistic conception of constitutionalism. From this we can assume that provided we retain sight of this core function, then we can avoid the types of problematic disagreement we are keen to avoid.

However, if this strategy fails and we end up with pseudo- or semantic disagreement through this disaggregated approach, Walker argues that we simply have to make do and that it may be a price worth paying for the normative payoff in thinking about transnational governance in (albeit disaggregated) constitutional terms. He argues that the contemporary circumstances of constitutional pluralism no longer permit a simple holistic model of constitutionalism; that in a transnational context 'a more holistic solution is not always the better or more "constitutionally" appropriate' and that a *non*-holistic constitutionalism can 'lay claim to many political virtues'[140] including a dispersal of power in a transnational context. In this respect, disaggregated constitutionalism can retain, Walker argues, 'a crucial long stop function as a kind of "placeholder" for certain abiding concerns we have'.[141] It provides an important way of retaining the idea of a 'common' in the context of the circumstances of transnational constitutional pluralism.[142] To give up on the idea of constitutionalism completely in this foreign climate due to the risks of pseudo- or semantic disagreement is to risk losing something 'of great and irreplaceable value'.[143]

If Walker is more keenly aware of the problems of semantic or pseudo-disagreement with respect to disaggregated constitutionalism, Krisch, in his defence of GAL vis-a-vis 'foundational' constitutional alternatives, is more aware of the types of critiques of transnational constitutional regulation highlighted by the 'new constitutional' critique. He notes that approaches such as GAL may favour the rule of law in any trade-offs between democracy and the rule of law and that it could reflect certain liberal, 'even libertarian' biases to the extent to which GAL attempts to bracket the bigger problems of the legitimacy of transnational governance.[144] Such approaches, Krisch concedes, may lead

139 ibid 296.
140 ibid 305, emphasis added.
141 ibid 307.
142 ibid 307.
143 ibid 307.
144 Krisch, 'Global Administrative Law and the Constitutional Ambition' (n 127), 260.

to 'distorted normative assessments'.[145] However, acknowledging these problems, he argues that GAL should simply 'retain awareness' of the institutional contexts in which such mechanisms operate 'and the broader normative questions they raise'.[146] Thus, any normative assessments GAL makes about particular instances of transnational governance will be 'relative and provisional' and will depend on 'assumptions about elements of a broader theory, and these assumptions need to remain explicit'.[147] Moreover, cognizant of the charge that a limited approach to governance may serve to sanctify that which ought not to be sanctified, he argues that we have no alternative on the grounds that the problems associated with more ambitious proposals—such as transnational foundational constitutionalism—are more intractable. Thus, he concludes a more 'circumscribed project' is more 'attractive as long as its goals and limitations are kept explicit'.[148] As such, when faced with the difficulties and complexities of contemporary transnational governance 'proceeding in small steps, with limited ambition, may be the only sensible option'.[149]

Initially Walker's approach to transnational constitutionalism seems promising in terms of avoiding pseudo- or semantic disagreement. His approach to the concept of constitutionalism in terms of identifying the common 'ends' of constitutionalism and viewing disagreement about the concept as relating to means has an obvious affinity with the interpretive approach endorsed here. On Walker's account, our core political value of constitutionalism equates with his 'function' and our rival 'best interpretations' of that value equate with his disagreement about constitutional means. However, problems emerge with respect to the application of this approach to the different levels of governance, particularly at the transnational level. After endorsing rival conceptions of constitutionalism—his 'layers'—as particular means to common ends, he proceeds to exclude certain layers as inappropriate to different levels of governance which heightens the risks of eliding substantive theoretical disagreements about legitimacy. If we accept a conception of transnational constitutionalism exclusively in terms of, say, a juridical frame of ordering under the disaggregated approach to constitutionalism because it is the only conception 'permitted' at a given level of transnational governance, then how are we to understand disagreement at this level that suggests that constitutionalism is, say, 'really' about constituent agency as some proponents of the no demos

145 ibid 261.
146 ibid 261.
147 ibid 262.
148 ibid 262.
149 ibid 266.

thesis argue? If it is the case that each of these layers or frames can operate independently, what makes them conceptions of a common conceptual core of constitutionalism? As noted earlier, he identifies the core function of constitutionalism as shaping and ordering a domain of politics around some notion of common interest.[150] However, if the different 'layers' of constitutionalism which speak to this function can and have operated distinctively, to the extent that the cluster can be 'parsed' and we can unproblematically apply and utilize different frames in different contexts, then the core function identified needs to do a lot of work to ensure that our disagreement about the concept of constitutionalism doesn't descend into pseudo- or semantic disagreement. That is, on our interpretive approach, our core political value, or on Walker's approach our key 'meta-political function',[151] must provide the anchor for our concept such that disagreement is understood in terms of rival interpretations of that core political function. The case for constitutionalism along the lines defended here—as reflecting the core political value of legitimate governing authority—it is submitted, provides a satisfactory anchor in this regard. It is not clear that Walker's functional account, on the other hand, does. In disaggregating the concept of constitutionalism once we move to the transnational level, Walker seems to collapse a potentially broad and capacious understanding of constitutional ends into one of its discrete 'means' at the cost of excluding other, rival, interpretations of those means and ends. His account of the function of the concept of constitutionalism in terms of the ordering of common interests and as 'literally 'constituting' the body politic',[152] seems at once too thick and too thin to garner the necessary substantive agreement necessary in order for rival 'best interpretations' to emerge. It seems too thick in that, notwithstanding the abstraction in his formulation, the key 'function' or 'ends' of constitutionalism seem to be loaded in favour of the values of the 'constitutive' branch of the constitutional 'tree', thereby potentially demoting or even excluding regulative understandings of constitutionalism. By the same token it is potentially too 'thin' to anchor the disagreement around constitutionalism in the sense that an attenuated functional account of constitutionalism based around underspecified ends of common interest seems too underdetermined to anchor our disagreements about the concept.

It is submitted that in disaggregating the concept of constitutionalism into its various conceptions, Walker's approach runs a serious risk of becoming

150 Walker, 'Beyond the Holistic Constitution?' (n 110), 296.
151 ibid 304
152 ibid 296.

distinctly 'criterial', involving claims that transnational constitutionalism is 'really' about a juridical frame of ordering, for example, such that our disagreement about whether a disaggregated transnational juridical constitutionalism really is a conception of constitutionalism—because I prefer or understand constitutionalism to mean 'foundational constitutionalism'—therefore becomes pseudo- or semantic disagreement.

Moreover, if, as is argued here, part of our moral and ethical responsibility in theorizing political value is to integrate our own conceptions of constitutionalism with others in order, *inter alia*, to overcome the illegitimacy charge, then it is easy to see how Walker's collapsing of ends into means fails to discharge this responsibility. If we can do without an ethical responsibility to strive to integrate our political values at the transnational level then we risk endorsing a morally problematic account of constitutionalism as identified by the 'new constitutionalism' critique in particular. It is not clear, and Walker does little to convince us, that the value of the normative language of constitutionalism, even if used in an explicitly and self-consciously disaggregated way at transnational level, as providing a 'placeholder' for 'certain abiding concerns we have' about the idea of 'common interest', is worth the cost of the morally problematic outcomes of an unbalanced understanding of the political value of constitutionalism identified by constitutionalism's critics.

With regard to Krisch's admonition to 'retain awareness' of the limitations of the approach and the broader questions in which they are nested, Krisch's approach seems to suffer even more directly from the pathologies of 'new constitutionalism' identified earlier, in the sense that it fails to even contemplate an approach which involves the integration of values at this level. As noted, on Krisch's account, GAL picks out some discrete and limited normative goals for practices within the 'Global Administrative Space' as providing a form of legitimacy for transnational governance more suited to this 'space' than (particularly 'constitutional') alternatives. In this way, GAL presents a value of legitimate political authority at the transnational level but deliberately refuses to take the second step to integrate values in an ethically responsible way. Indeed, in identifying discrete 'normative goals' which GAL can pursue, and in even recognizing that they are necessarily related, embedded even in 'broader normative questions'[153] and broader 'assumptions about elements of a broader theory',[154] his failure to take the second step seems less excusable than it might be for committed 'new constitutionalists'. If 'new constitutionalists' can plead

[153] Krisch, 'Global Administrative Law and the Constitutional Ambition' (n 127), 261.
[154] ibid 262.

ignorance as to the awareness and understanding of an interpretive approach and the fact that their conceptions of constitutionalism should be seen as best interpretations of a core political value which must ultimately be somehow set in relation to other rival best interpretations, Krisch seems to acknowledge or at least hint towards this broader normative hinterland but simply refuses to contemplate it. Like Walker, he pleads the complexity of the transnational realm in excusing such lack of ambition. However, the problem here is if he fails to investigate the normative hinterland behind his immediate normative goals, it is not clear that he can claim as unambiguously as he does, that a more limited ambition is 'more attractive'[155] and that proceeding in 'small steps' is the only 'sensible option'.[156] This is because, in refusing to contemplate the broader normative hinterland (as the interpretive approach for example does), it may be *less* attractive and *less* sensible to pursue such limited goals. We cannot know unless we understand how our normative goals connect to a clear and elucidated core political value, how others interpret that value and how our goals connect with and may require revision in the light of these other rival conceptions of a core political value.

There is a danger, then, that in addressing questions of legitimacy at the transnational level in this disaggregated way, both of these accounts succumb to the cacophony and illegitimacy critiques of constitutionalism considered earlier. That is, in advancing conceptions of legitimacy in disaggregated constitutional or GAL terms, we contribute to, rather than resolve, the cacophony and inadvertently sanctify that which ought not to be sanctified; that is, bestow the imprimatur of legitimacy on governing regimes which do not deserve such designation. In heeding the nature of the 'foreign climate' of constitutionalism at the transnational level, there is a clear and present danger that these approaches to the idea of transnational constitutionalism capitulate to their circumstances and end up with a form of 'complacent realism'.[157]

7. Transnational Constitutional Pluralism and Generalization

This discussion brings us back to a question raised in Chapter 7 but yet to be given a satisfactory answer. Assuming that an interpretive approach to the

155 ibid 262.
156 ibid 266.
157 David Estlund, 'Utopophobia' (2014) 42 Philosophy and Public Affairs 113, 115.

concept of constitutionalism based on the constitutional 'tree' and its 'trunk' of legitimate political authority is a better approach to thinking about constitutionalism and legitimacy at the transnational level, how do we reckon with the facts 'on the ground' about transnational governance with its 'mysteries'?[158] What characterizes Walker's, Krisch's, and the no demos thesis approaches to transnational constitutionalism, it is argued, is arguably an oversensitivity to the 'foreign climate' of the transnational level of governance and the extent to which the concept of constitutionalism which developed in the state can survive and take root in such a climate; that is, an oversensitivity to our 'circumstance of constitutional pluralism' in terms of disagreement at this level. It may be the case that in taking the interpretive approach to political value endorsed here, we should simply acknowledge that the problems with transnational constitutionalism are a natural consequence of trying (and possibly failing) to serve two distinct masters: the need to take our context seriously in thinking in normative terms to avoid problems of generalization in normative theory considered in Chapter 7 on the one hand, and our ethical obligations to integrate values according to the unity of value on the other. At the very least we can acknowledge that this is potentially a key tension in transnational constitutional theorizing. Disaggregated constitutionalism and GAL and, more clearly, the no demos thesis take the former very seriously at the cost of the latter. However, we can do better than characterizing the issue as a series of Procrustean trade-offs. This involves taking an interpretive approach also to the question of generalization in normative theorizing in a manner which retains our aims of the unity of value.

7.1 Holism and Exportation

As noted in Chapter 7, the key issue commonly identified with the exportation of the concept of constitutionalism between the state and transnational levels in the form of the 'no demos' thesis is the risk that an attempt to theorize in constitutional terms at the transnational level would generalize too much, assuming a level of political agreement and institutional development which simply does not exist at this level. In this regard, there were two factors relevant to the appropriate level of generalization: a general and a particular one.

[158] David Kennedy, 'The Mystery of Global Governance' in Jeffrey L Dunoff and Joel P Trachtman (eds), *Ruling the World?: Constitutionalism, International Law, and Global Governance* (Cambridge University Press 2009).

At a general level we identified the outer parameters of acceptable normative theorizing: a 'floor' and a 'ceiling'. The 'floor' of generalization in normative theorizing involves a requirement that a normative theory should generalize to some extent so as not merely to endorse the status quo; that is that what we should be doing about poverty, homelessness, arms sales, assisting refugees, or climate change is what we are already doing. A theory which fails to generalize from particular facts fails to provide any normative standards and either sanctifies that which ought not to be sanctified or collapses into purely descriptive theory. Such an approach is likely to mask or affirm actual injustices in a world which normative theory should make prescriptions to remedy.[159] The outer bounds of generalization in normative theorizing, the 'ceiling', is set by the idea that 'ought implies can': we cannot be required to do things that are impossible for us to do.

More specifically, as noted in Chapter 7, our metric of whether a normative theory is appropriate will depend on the purposes of our theorizing. Broadly speaking, if the purposes of our theorizing relate to practical reasoning, the level of generalization will be lower; if the purpose of our theorizing is broadly evaluative, or to illustrate alternative hypothetical possibilities, then the level of our generalization can be higher.[160] Thus, acknowledging the purposes of our theorizing helps us navigate the potentially large space between the outer parameters of theorizing set by the 'floor' and the 'ceiling'.

In this way, the two levels are related. The purpose of our theorizing will, to a certain extent, determine whether the floor or ceiling has been transgressed. For example, a normative theory whose purpose is evaluation will have a much higher threshold of permissible generalization than one which makes detailed prescriptions about, for example, how a particular norm should be applied by a judicial body or whether and which institutional reforms are required in a particular governing regime. Thus, a normative theory could make wildly idealized assumptions which could be appropriate for comparative purposes to gauge how far our current circumstances are from such a society.[161] That it is unlikely that it could be achieved is not a problem as we are merely comparing and evaluating, even if the utility of our theorizing in this way may be called into question. On the other hand, if we wanted to find out what we must do to improve, say, our policy on arms sales, immigration and asylum, corruption and financial influence in politics, or whether our 'winner takes all' voting

159 Estlund (n 157); Charles W Mills, '"Ideal Theory" as Ideology' (2005) 20 Hypatia 165.

160 Zofia Stemplowska, 'What's Ideal About Ideal Theory?' (2008) 34 Social Theory and Practice 319, 336

161 ibid 336

system satisfies the value of democracy, then our theory must be based on more context-specific assumptions about the world. Therefore, in taking seriously the message about the perils about overgeneralization in normative theorizing which is implicit in the no demos critiques considered in Chapter 7, and disaggregated constitutionalism and GAL in this one, we need to pay more attention to what the *purposes* of a *transnational* constitutional theory might be.[162]

7.2 Generalization and Disagreement

In terms of constitutionalism as normative theory, we are, as we have seen earlier, bound by the 'history and usage' of the concept which provides the necessary consensus to allow disagreement to emerge. That is that the conventional purposes of constitutionalism as normative theorizing will, to an extent, be 'baked' into the consensus surrounding the concept of constitutionalism in our pre-interpretive stage of inquiry. To this extent, then, the level of generalization in our theory must be appropriate to these purposes. Here our gambit surrounding the purposes of constitutionalism as normative theory is that it relates to *practical reasoning*.[163] That constitutionalism is a form of practical reasoning has, it is argued, sufficiently widespread support in constitutional discourse to allow us to assume a level of agreement around this particular point.[164]

[162] In emphasizing the purposes of theory in this way we should avoid any confusion between the 'purposes' of theorizing in terms of the use to which a theory is being put at stake here, and the way in which the political value of an interpretive concept has been sometimes described as the 'purpose' of the concept. The latter is essentially a synonym of value and relates to the value which a particular interpretive concept pursues. The former, on the other hand, relates to the different tasks of theory and the different way we use theory for particular ends. A useful way to clarify the distinction is to think about the distinction along the lines of Rawls' dichotomy between 'ideal' and 'non-ideal' theory. As Simmons notes, Rawls' distinction between 'ideal' and 'non-ideal' represented his attempt to grapple with the problem of the relationship between philosophical theory and political practice. A John Simmons, 'Ideal and Nonideal Theory' (2010) 38 Philosophy and Public Affairs 5. In Rawls' account, the ideal part of his theory of justice sets out to establish and clarify the principles of justice whereas the non-ideal part of his theory of justice relates to the ways in which the goals of his theory can be achieved in the long term 'using gradual steps'. John Rawls, *The Law of Peoples: With, the Idea of Public Reason Revisited* (Harvard University Press 1999) 89. In this way, in Simmons's words, '[w]here ideal theory dictates the objective, nonideal theory dictates the route to that objective' (Simmons, 'Ideal and Nonideal Theory', 12). Thus, we can understand our two senses of 'purpose' in the manner suggested by Rawls. The 'purpose' of our interpretive concept in the first sense relates to the valuable aims or goals of that object—achieving a just society, legitimating governing authority—whereas the 'purposes' in the second sense of the purposes of our particular theory relate to the means to achieve those purposes in a given context; what is practically possible "here and now" within the "historical conditions of our age' (ibid 11–12).

[163] See generally Joseph Raz, *Practical Reason and Norms* (Oxford University Press 1999); Neil MacCormick, *Practical Reason in Law and Morality* (Oxford University Press 2008).

[164] Richard H Pildes, 'Why Rights Are Not Trumps: Social Meanings, Expressive Harms, and Constitutionalism' (1998) 27 The Journal of Legal Studies 725; Robert Alexy, *A Theory of Constitutional Rights* (Julian Rivers tr, Oxford University Press 2002); L Alexander, 'Constitutionalism' in Mortimer

To recall O'Neill's popular definition considered in Chapter 7, then, we can say that practical reasoning aims at 'guidance rather than explanation'[165] and 'seeks to guide action whose aim is to fit the world (in some measure) to its recommendations, rather than its conclusions to the world'.[166] As a form of practical reasoning, then, constitutionalism as a normative theory involves making particular 'recommendations' involving 'specific proposals for actions, policies and/or institutional reforms that are able to achieve improvements now or in the not too distant future'[167] when measured against the specific values implicated in the normative theory. Moreover, to remain within our parameters of acceptable generalization, these recommendations must be 'viable' in the sense of being 'achievable and desirable, as far as we can judge, in the circumstances we are facing, or likely to face in the not-too-distant future'.[168]

If our purpose of constitutionalism as normative theory is practical reasoning, then, this impacts upon the level of generalization that will be appropriate to this enterprise as well as the extent to which the moral parameters of normative theorizing will be transgressed. As practical reasoning involves action to 'fit the world', then we must take seriously the 'world' as it is, in constitutional terms; institutions, societies, laws, and individuals as they are and not as they might be.[169] This speaks to a relatively low-level of generalization as compared with comparative or evaluative purposes; what might in other terminology involve the more 'realistic' or 'non-ideal' end of the real–ideal spectrum but what we will here call non-utopian requirements associated with the purposes of practical reasoning.[170] From the perspective of transnational constitutional theory in particular, then, constitutionalism must take the transnational world as it is, replete with deep-seated theoretical disagreement about

Sellers and Stephan Kirste (eds), *Encyclopedia of the Philosophy of Law and Social Philosophy* (Springer 2020); Neil Walker in particular has repeatedly endorsed the role of constitutionalism as a form of practical reasoning in the context of transnational constitutional discourse. See, for example, Neil Walker, 'Taking Constitutionalism beyond the State' (2008) 56 Political Studies 519; Walker, 'Postnational Constitutionalism and the Problem of Translation' (n 109); Neil Walker, 'Multilevel Constitutionalism: Looking Beyond the German Debate' in Suvi Sankari and Kaarlo Tuori (eds), *The Many Constitutions of Europe* (Routledge 2016).

165 Onora O'Neill, *Towards Justice and Virtue: A Constructive Account of Practical Reasoning* (Cambridge University Press 1996) 42.

166 ibid.

167 Stemplowska (n 160), 323.

168 ibid 324.

169 Jean-Jacques Rousseau, *Rousseau: The Social Contract and Other Later Political Writings* (Victor Gourevitch ed, Victor Gourevitch tr, 2nd edn, Cambridge University Press 2019). See also Rawls (n 162), 13.

170 See Chapter 7.

legitimacy as emphasized by disaggregationist transnational constitutional theories and particular versions of the no demos thesis.[171]

Moreover, this disagreement is more complex than political disagreement at the state level, revolving as it does, around less path-dependent institutional and political possibilities when compared with political disagreement in states. Even if disagreement is a core 'realist' tenet in many (state-based) constitutional theories,[172] in taking this disagreement seriously for the purposes of a transnational constitutional theory, we must acknowledge that there is a qualitative difference between the intensity and scope of theoretical disagreement within state societies and the trenchant disagreement that exists at the transnational level.[173] With the best will in the world, we cannot wish into existence a level of consensus or agreement about policy or institutions with global reach, or even regional reach,[174] that can compare with the (admittedly variegated) forms of consensus around institutions, societies, and laws that exist at the state level. In this respect, we can easily see the attraction of taking a more modest approach to thinking about legitimate transnational government, involving more disaggregated accounts of constitutionalism, GAL alternatives, or generally thinner modes of accountability. As we have seen, it is precisely because they take this disagreement seriously while acknowledging the institutional and legal structures that exist that the no demos thesis, disaggregated constitutionalism, as well as GAL all, in different ways, endorse variations of constitutionalism which depart, sometimes radically, from a 'holistic' concept of constitutionalism, up to and including a rejection of the idea of transnational constitutionalism itself. Our question then becomes whether the complexity and intensity of theoretical disagreement at the transnational level inexorably leads to either an attenuated 'disaggregated' concept of constitutionalism or an alternative way of thinking about questions of legitimate transnational authority altogether. We argue that it is possible to answer this question in the

[171] For example, in this regard Krisch observes that '[t]he divided character of the global polity appears indeed as the single greatest challenge to the globalisation of constitutionalism … international society is characterised by a high degree of diversity and contestation, and even the small signs of increasing convergence that we can observe are by no means unambiguous'. Krisch, *Beyond Constitutionalism: The Pluralist Structure of Postnational Law* (n 2), 59.

[172] Cormac Mac Amhlaigh, 'Friend or Foe?: Bernard Williams and Political Constitutionalism' (2021) 27 Res Publica 219–34. Putting it somewhat crudely, we can differentiate between disagreement in reasonably stable states about particular policies with reasonable *agreement* about second-order questions of whether we even *should* be acting together, and disagreement both about policies as well as the second-order question of whether and to what extent we should be acting together which is arguably a more prominent feature of transnational law and governance.

[173] Generally speaking, that is. There will, of course, be exceptions where the disagreement in states is perhaps more intense than at the transnational level, leading to the dissolution of the state.

[174] As the EU's contemporary multiple crises—rule of law, refugee, economic, pandemic—can attest.

negative. To see why, we need to return to our account of constitutionalism as an interpretive rather than a criterial concept and how it approaches disagreement on questions of political value.

8. Interpreting Transnational Disagreement

Taking an interpretive approach to political disagreement at the transnational level involves identifying the point or purpose of transnational legal and political practices. The interpretive approach demands that we identify the point or value of an object and view our disagreement as rival best interpretations of that value. This avoids the conclusion that our political disagreements, generally more intense than at the state level, constitute pseudo- or semantic disagreement. Thus, if we must take disagreement seriously as a feature of transnational law and governance, and this presents a non-utopian constraint in our normative theory of transnational constitutionalism, we need to take this disagreement itself seriously, as genuine substantive theoretical disagreement.

We therefore must also follow the steps of the interpretive approach in respect of disagreement about transnational law and governance in the same manner employed with respect to the concept of constitutionalism outlined earlier; namely, identifying a pre-interpretive agreement about our object of inquiry as well as identifying a reasonable consensus about what the purpose or value of that object is. With regard to our pre-interpretive agreement about the *object* of our inquiry, the practices of transnational law, and governance, we can garner a reasonable consensus around the fact that transnational law and governance exists and that it includes the norms, institutions, and forums of transnational governing regimes in all their kaleidoscopic diversity. Whatever their contested legitimacy, and notwithstanding the strains put upon them in the past decade or so,[175] a reasonably developed structure of law and institutions exists at transnational level: a global rules-based order, with all its foibles, is (still) a reality of our current world rather than a utopia or a chimera.

Our next step, then, in theorizing this fact in normative terms in a way that makes sense of the theoretical disagreement which emerges at this level is to identify in broad terms the value of the practices of transnational governance. As with the concept of constitutionalism at the state level, our claim with regard to this form of agreement is that it involves the *value of transnational governing*

[175] G John Ikenberry, *A World Safe for Democracy: Liberal Internationalism and the Crises of Global Order* (Yale University Press 2020).

authority. Thus, notwithstanding our disagreement, sometimes intense and radical, about the legitimacy of practices of transnational governance, our disagreement, if it is to make sense as substantive and not pseudo- or semantic disagreement, is based on agreement about the political value of transnational political authority. There are several aspects of this feature of disagreement at the transnational level which we can develop further.

First, the disagreement about transnational constitutional theory presupposes, it is argued, an agreement about the political value of transnational authority. The political value of transnational authority is part of the political value of authority in general as encapsulated in Williams's idea of the 'first political question' considered earlier.[176] Political authorities can provide important political and normative goods borne of their cooperative and coordination functions. Perhaps the most well-known articulation of the political value of authority in general—at least in the Anglophone world—is that provided by Hobbes.[177]

Thus, the first step in understanding our disagreement at transnational level is acknowledging the existence of transnational law and governance as well as appreciating the political value of transnational authority as a response to the 'first political question' of transnational authority, and the particular goods which come from cooperation and coordination at this level. However, in line with our purposes of practical reasoning and being sensitive to the generalization in our concept of constitutionalism, we need to ensure that we are sensitive to the nature and justification of authority at the transnational level which may diverge from the justification of political authority at the state level, given its differing levels of agreement and institutional development. Our transnational constitutional theory, being sufficiently non-utopian to suit our aims of practical reasoning, must take this into account. However, the political value of transnational authority, can, at the abstract level of political value, be seen to *share* the core justification of political authority at the *state level*. No less an authority than Kant has articulated the political value of transnational authority by drawing analogies between state-based and transnational political

[176] Williams (n 3).

[177] 'The finale Cause, End, or Designe of men (who naturally love Liberty, and Dominion over others) in the introduction of that restrain upon themselves (in which we see them live in Commonwealths), is the foresight of their own preservation, and of a more contented life thereby; that is to say, of getting themselves out form the miserable condition of Warre, which is necessarily consequent (as hath been shown) to the natural Passions of men, and thereby to secure them in such sort, as that by their own industry, and by the fruits of the earth, they may nourish themselves and live contentedly.' Thomas Hobbes, *Leviathan* (Richard Tuck ed, Cambridge University Press 1996), 120.

authority. In a well-known tract from his essay on perpetual peace, he argued that:[178]

> People who have grouped themselves into nation states may be judged in the same way as individual men living in a state of nature, independent of external laws; for they are a standing offence to one another by the very fact that they are neighbors. Each nation, for the sake of its own security, can and ought to demand of the others that they should enter along with it into a constitution, similar to the civil one, within which the rights of each could be secured. This would mean establishing a federation of peoples ... peace can neither be inaugurated nor secured without a general agreement between the nations; thus a particular kind of league, which we might call a pacific federation (pactum pacis) [would] seek to end all wars for good.

Of course, the nature of, and justification for, transnational governance has evolved considerably since Kant's times beyond basic considerations of security, and much of the cooperation and coordination problems between, rather than within, contemporary societies arise from the 'time space compression'[179] of our contemporary globalized world which make up our circumstances of constitutional pluralism. Thus, more contemporary accounts of the political value of transnational authority emphasize the necessity of transnational authorities in the light of the particular challenges raised by contemporary globalization and in particular the scale and capacity problems associated with unilateral state action. These include a variety of governance questions whether relating to environmental protection,[180] climate change,[181] tax evasion,[182] or, more generally, in Dworkin's words, the prevention of 'economic, commercial, medical or environmental disaster'.[183] The recent rapid transboundary spread of SARS-CoV-2 merely serves to underscore these global-level challenges.[184]

178 Immanuel Kant, 'Perpetual Peace: A Philosophical Sketch' in Hans Reiss (ed), *Kant's Political Writings* (Cambridge University Press 1971) 102.

179 Jan Aart Scholte, 'Defining Globalisation' (2008) 31 World Economy 1471.

180 Elisa Morgera, 'Bilateralism at the Service of Community Interests? Non-Judicial Enforcement of Global Public Goods in the Context of Global Environmental Law' (2012) 23 European Journal of International Law 743.

181 Remi Moncel and Harro van Asselt, 'All Hands on Deck! Mobilizing Climate Change Action beyond the UNFCCC' (2012) 21 Review of European Community & International Environmental Law 163.

182 Thomas Piketty, *Capital and Ideology* (Harvard University Press 2020).

183 Ronald Dworkin, 'A New Philosophy for International Law' (2013) 41 Philosophy and Public Affairs 2, 17–18.

184 Curtis A Bradley and Laurence R Helfer, 'Introduction to "The International Legal Order and the Global Pandemic"' (2020) 114 American Journal of International Law 571; Eyal Benvenisti, 'The

Thus, banal as it might seem, the political value of transnational authority, and the capacity it creates to solve collective action problems through cooperation and coordination, particularly in our contemporary circumstances of constitutional pluralism, provides the core political value around which intense and substantive disagreement rotates in our transnational constitutional theory. Much like in our discussion of the political value of constitutionalism more generally, the political value of transnational constitutionalism in terms of the capacity produced by transnational political authority provides the 'fulcrum'[185] for the widespread and intense disagreement which emerges at this level. Furthermore, ever mindful of the non-utopianism necessary for our purpose of practical reasoning, it is necessary to emphasize that our transnational constitutional theory relates to *actually existing transnational political authorities*; that is, to extant practices of transnational law and governance. This, in turn, permits our transnational constitutional theory to make action-guiding recommendations.[186]

Therefore, our transnational constitutional theory relates to disagreements about the best interpretation of the political value of transnational governing authority based on the actual practices of transnational governing authorities, whether they address security, trade, climate change, human rights, economic development, or otherwise. In our transnational constitutional theory we are not concerned with hypothetical transnational authorities, or world-state utopias (or dystopias).[187] There are many possible permutations and combinations of how we can go about achieving a legitimate global order, reflected in our theoretical disagreements. However, in the light of the non-utopianism necessary for our practical reasoning, we are concerned with the practices of actually existing organizations such as the African Union, or the Organization of American States, or the European Union. Our normative approach to transnational constitutionalism, therefore, can make specific recommendations about individual policies or institutional reforms that are achievable now or in the not-too-distant future, all understood as relating to the political value of transnational political authority.

Furthermore, our transnational constitutional theory, presented through this interpretive lens, recasts our disagreements at transnational level about the

WHO—Destined to Fail?: Political Cooperation and the COVID-19 Pandemic' (2020) 114 American Journal of International Law 588.

185 Endicott (n 72), 39.
186 Stemplowska (n 160), 323.
187 See, for example, Jürgen Habermas, *The Postnational Constellation: Political Essays* (Polity 2001).

legitimacy of this or that organization, or their specific policies, or their institutional arrangements, or proposals for improvements, as rival—often antagonistically rival—'best interpretations' of presenting the *political value of the existence of the relevant transnational authority in its best light*. In this way we can understand calls for, for example, reform of the UN Security Council in terms of the status of the P5,[188] or their terrorist listing procedures,[189] or of the role of human rights considerations in the Southern African Development Community,[190] or for the accession of the European Union to the European Convention of Human Rights,[191] or the question of environmental or human rights issue 'linkage' in international trade law,[192] or the role of the rule of law or human rights considerations in deliberations of transnational courts in the Caribbean and Latin America,[193] as interventions involving the presentation of the political value of a particular transnational authority expressed in institutional terms in their best light. Even those who trenchantly critique, along 'new constitutionalist' lines, particular transnational governing authorities such as the Bretton Woods institutions, can be understood in this way, using 'best interpretations' of transnational political authority to critique existing transnational political authorities.[194]

These debates can all be understood, according to the general approach to transnational constitutionalism defended here, as interpretations of the political value of transnational authority in what they perceive to be their best light, including in order to critique the status quo and offer proposals for improvement.[195]

188 Jean L Cohen, *Globalization and Sovereignty: Rethinking Legality, Legitimacy, and Constitutionalism* (Cambridge University Press 2012).

189 Matej Avbelj, Filippo Fontanelli, and Giuseppe Martinico (eds), *Kadi on Trial: A Multifaceted Analysis of the Kadi Trial* (Routledge 2014); Gráinne de Búrca, 'The European Court of Justice and the International Legal Order after Kadi' [2009] Harvard International Law Journal 1.

190 Frederick Cowell, 'The Death of the Southern African Development Community Tribunal's Human Rights Jurisdiction' (2013) 13 Human Rights Law Review 153; Erika de Wet, 'The Rise and Fall of the Tribunal of the Southern African Development Community: Implications for Dispute Settlement in Southern Africa' (2013) 28 ICSID Review—Foreign Investment Law Journal 45.

191 Paul Gragl, *The Accession of the European Union to the European Convention on Human Rights* (Bloomsbury Publishing 2013). Tobias Lock, 'The EU before the European Court of Human Rights after Accession' in Sionaidh Douglas-Scott and Nicholas Hatzis (eds), *Research Handbook on EU law and Human Rights* (Elgar 2017).

192 Andrew TF Lang, 'Reflecting on "Linkage": Cognitive and Institutional Change in The International Trading System' (2007) 70 The Modern Law Review 523.

193 See Salvatore Caserta, *International Courts in Latin America and the Caribbean: Foundations and Authority* (Oxford University Press 2020).

194 Olena Sihvo, 'Global Constitutionalism and the Idea of Progress' (2018) 12 Helsinki Law Review 10; Ntina Tzouvala, *Capitalism As Civilisation: A History of International Law* (Cambridge University Press 2020).

195 Unsurprisingly, given its interpretive emphasis, the general approach to transnational constitutional theory defended here, particularly against charges of idealism or utopianism, has an affinity with Dworkin's posthumously published account of the legitimacy of international law entailing

9. An Example: Constitutional Conflicts in the European Union

It is beyond the scope of this chapter to provide an extensive illustration of how this approach to transnational constitutionalism can work in the practices of discrete sites of transnational law and governance. The interpretive approach to transnational constitutionalism is presented as a general approach or methodology to the very idea of a transnational constitutional theory by addressing the three common objections to the idea we have considered in previous chapters. As such, rather than presenting a detailed blueprint for *a* theory of transnational constitutional pluralism, it clears the way for a variety of different constitutional theories to proceed, focused on specific institutional arrangements and transnational governing practices whose legitimacy is understood in terms of disagreement of rival 'best interpretations' of the political value of that particular governing authority while also paying heed to our ethical obligations to strive to integrate our rival 'best interpretations'. Any specific constitutional theory of, for example, the UN or the WTO, will necessarily have to engage in much more contextual detail in the same way that particular constitutional theories of individual states must be sensitive to the particular historical, political, and institutional contexts of the governing arrangements of

principles of mitigation and salience considered in Chapter 4. Significantly, Dworkin's account, without engaging explicitly in the issues associated with generalization in normative theories considered in detail here, adopts an approach to theorizing international law which tracks the non-utopianism endorsed here. First, he argues that theories of international must be realistic in the sense that they must have a prospect of 'general endorsement' (Dworkin, 'A New Philosophy for International Law' (n 183), 15) by the international community and that a moral obligation of states to try to improve the international systems demands only 'what in the circumstances if feasible' (ibid 17) Moreover, his approach to the principle of mitigation, particularly through its progeny, the principle of salience, shows a sensitivity to questions of generalization in a similar manner to the account defended here. As is clear in the principle of salience, Dworkin's approach to the legitimacy of international law takes its transnational governing arrangements as it finds them and leads to a duty to support *existing institutional arrangements* which support the principle of mitigation notwithstanding the fact that there are a myriad of possible ways in which the principle of mitigation could be satisfied: 'In many circumstances, a number of very different regimes of international law would each serve to improve the legitimacy of the international system, were it enacted and enforced, and states may reasonably disagree about which would be best ... [however] if a significant number of states, encompassing a significant population, has developed an agreed code of practice, either by treaty or by other form of coordination, then other states have at least a prima facie duty to subscribe to that practice as well, with the important proviso that this duty holds only if a more general practice to that effect, expanded in that way, would improve the legitimacy of the subscribing state and the international order as a whole' (ibid 19). The salience principle, moreover, has an 'obvious snowballing effect' in that 'as more nations recognize a duty to accept and follow widely accepted principles, those principles, thus even more widely accepted, have greater moral gravitational force' (ibid 20).

the particular states in question.[196] However, we would be remiss if we didn't provide some indication of how all this cashes out in practice and how this general interpretive approach to the concept of transnational constitutionalism can illuminate constitutional discourses in respect of particular transnational governing regimes. We will therefore briefly consider how this approach applies, for the sake of convenience, to a puzzle in transnational constitutional pluralism which we have already met earlier in the book: the puzzle of constitutional conflicts within the European Union.

In our discussion in Chapter 4, we looked briefly at the question of what happens when a norm designated 'external' to the legal system is deemed by a state court to conflict with a designated 'internal' norm of the system. In Chapter 4 we noted how this is an increasing risk under the circumstances of constitutional pluralism and how such conflicts are, in reality, conflicts between the political purposes of the supremacy and openness of the legal system seized of the conflict. However, we neglected to explore further how such questions *should be resolved* in terms of a normative theory of conflicts resolution for interacting legal systems and competing authority claims. This is the role for our general approach to transnational constitutional pluralism as a normative theory involving practical reasoning about what we should do when faced with disagreement regarding legitimacy.

This is a subject which has received considerable attention in the voluminous literature on constitutional conflicts involving EU law.[197] As noted in Chapter 4, the basis of *disagreement* in such conflicts—and in particular in the EU context—is frequently presented in terms of a dispute about the appropriate nature and locus of authority and in particular which level of governance, or perhaps more accurately which court, *should* have the final say on the norms applicable in the conglomerate system that is the EU's legal order. A variety of solutions have been advanced which attempt to provide an answer to this question. More 'radical' accounts have argued that it should be left open and resolved on an *ad hoc* and mutually accommodative basis, implying that normative theory has a limited, or no, role here.[198] Others have argued

196 See, for example, Richard H Fallon, 'How to Choose a Constitutional Theory' (1999) 87 California Law Review 535.

197 See generally Gareth Davies and Matej Avbelj (eds), *Research Handbook on Legal Pluralism and EU Law* (Edward Elgar 2018); Matej Avbelj and Jan Komárek, *Constitutional Pluralism in the European Union and Beyond* (Hart 2012).

198 Neil MacCormick, *Questioning Sovereignty: Law, State and Nation in the European Commonwealth* (Oxford University Press 1999). Nico Krisch, 'Who Is Afraid of Radical Pluralism? Legal Order and Political Stability in the Postnational Space' (2011) 24 Ratio Juris 386, 412. These prescriptions could be interpreted as a form of internal error skepticism: whereas normative resolution of norm conflicts do have a role in certain contexts (such as, possibly, internally within legal systems pursuant to the ideals of the rule of law), they do not have any role in conflicts *between* legal systems. For discussion see

for a strict supremacy of EU law.[199] The idea here is that EU law should provide second-order content-independent reasons for resolving the conflict in favour of EU law each time.[200] And yet others have advanced solutions based on a supremacy of international law or based on an overlapping consensus and deliberative solutions.[201] What is key to the areas of interacting legal systems and constitutional pluralism in the EU context, however, is disagreement: both about how putative conflicts should be characterized as well as disagreements about how they should be resolved; that is, what is the most legitimate way to proceed given the fact of potential conflict.

As will by now be familiar, a key tenet of the interpretive approach is that societal or political disagreement should be understood as *substantive* disagreement and not pseudo- or semantic disagreement. In this regard, our interpretive approach wards us away from characterizations of the interactions and relationships involved in disagreements where, for example, the two sets of courts—EU and national—are essentially talking past each other. As will be recalled, the puzzle in potential conflicts between EU law and state law is the following: Member States argue that EU law derives its validity and authority from the Treaties established by Member States and for this reason, that Member States remain the 'master of the treaties' and ultimately the final arbiters of any clashes between EU law and the law of Member States; the EU institutions, on the other hand, believe that EU law is autonomous from the law of its Member States, that its validity and authority is self-generating and that *it* remains the ultimate arbiter of any clashes between EU law and Member State law. Characterizing the interaction in this way

Ralf Michaels and Joost Pauwelyn, 'Conflict of Norms or Conflict of Laws? Different Techniques in the Fragmentation of Public International Law' (2012) 22 Duke Journal of Comparative & International Law 349; Dworkin, *Justice for Hedgehogs* (n 5), 33.

199 For a discussion of the EU's primacy doctrine as providing second-order content-independent reasons for the resolution of conflicts, see Cormac Mac Amhlaigh, 'Concepts of Law in Integration Through Law' in Daniel Augentstein (ed), *'Integration through Law' Revisited: The Making of the European Polity* (Routledge 2012). For a more wide-ranging discussion endorsing this idea in relation to more recent conflicts, see R Daniel Kelemen, 'On the Unsustainability of Constitutional Pluralism: European Supremacy and the Survival of the Eurozone' (2016) 23 Maastricht Journal of European and Comparative Law 136; Federico Fabbrini, 'After the OMT Case: The Supremacy of EU Law as the Guarantee of the Equality of the Member States' (2015) 16 German Law Journal 1003; R Daniel Kelemen and Laurent Pech, 'The Uses and Abuses of Constitutional Pluralism: Undermining the Rule of Law in the Name of Constitutional Identity in Hungary and Poland' (2019) 21 Cambridge Yearbook of European Legal Studies 59.

200 Mac Amhlaigh, 'Concepts of Law in Integration Through Law' (n 199).

201 See, for example, MacCormick's 'pluralism under international law', MacCormick (n 198), 117; Charles Sabel and Oliver Gerstenberg, 'Constitutionalising an Overlapping Consensus: The ECJ and the Emergence of a Coordinate Constitutional Order' (2010) 16 European Law Review 511.

raises the spectre of pseudo-disagreement, however.[202] This is due to the fact that, as with the other types of disagreements we have considered in previous chapters, the different approaches reflect disagreement about the necessary and sufficient conditions for authoritative decision-making. As with our discussion of the no demos thesis, the different positions in the dispute advance their own conceptions of what ultimate authority requires under these circumstances of constitutional pluralism—a 'demos', say, or the coordinating function of supranational authority to reap the rewards of transnational cooperation—to the extent that they are talking past each other. This is due, as should be now familiar, to their taking a *criterial* approach to the question of legitimate authority—and particularly legitimate judicial decision-making—under the circumstances of constitutional pluralism.

If our understandings—or conceptions—of legitimate authority are answered in a such a *criterial* way then there is no conflict and no disagreement: both positions assume they have settled the disagreement in favour of their own understanding of ultimate authority in interactions between EU law and national constitutional law. Any risk of conflict is pre-emptively settled by the criteria of authority endorsed by either side. In such a scenario there is no 'interaction' between the legal systems which would leave space for a normative theory of constitutional pluralism to guide and provide practical reasoning in the interactions between state and EU constitutionalism. There is no common ground—no consensus around a conception of political value—which would allow for such a normative theory to resolve conflicts. Moreover, a prescriptive normative theory applied to such pseudo-disagreement—such as that the EU courts' interpretation of the conflict is the correct one,[203] or that national courts are always correct given that they are the 'Masters of the Treaties'[204]—could result in problematic counterfactual theory in the manner of the 'semantic sting' affecting accounts of legal positivism on Dworkin's reading, assuming an agreement or consensus about the idea of legitimate authority when there is

202 For example, if our interpretation of the practices of state courts applying EU law and EU courts applying state law are predicated on the adoption of the point of view of one legal system; that is adopting a national or EU point of view on interactions. To argue for the locus of ultimate authority from this perspective results in a form of pseudo disagreement.

203 Kelemen (n 199); Fabbrini (n 199).

204 Such as espoused by the German Federal Constitutional Court. See generally Christian Calliess, 'Constitutional Identity in Germany: One for Three or Three in One?' in Christian Calliess and Gerhard van der Schyff (eds), *Constitutional Identity in a Europe of Multilevel Constitutionalism* (Cambridge University Press 2019).

none.[205] This, as we saw in Chapter 7, moreover, comes with particular problems of failing to provide action-guiding recommendations or being morally costly.[206]

This characterization of the disagreement between national courts and EU courts when their norms potentially conflict has been encouraged by certain comments made by theorists of these conflicts in the EU context. One characterization of this issue presented by Neil MacCormick, who launched the constitutional pluralist 'movement'[207] in respect of the interactions between EU law and national constitutional law, puts it in the following terms:[208]

> the interpretive power of the highest decision-making authorities of the different systems must be, as to each system, ultimate. It is for the ECJ to interpret in the last resort and in a finally authoritative way the norms of [EU] law. But equally, it must be for the highest constitutional tribunal of each member-state to interpret its constitutional and other norms, and hence to interpret the interaction of the validity of [EU] law with higher level norms of validity in the given state system.

Culver and Giudice aptly capture the problem with this characterization in terms of pseudo-disagreement:[209]

> if the highest decision-making authorities are each claiming supremacy to interpret the relation between Member State law and EU law, what MacCormick claims are interacting systems look more like *two hierarchal systems talking past each other*. Both systems include both the norms of Member States and the EU, but they differ in their view of which norms are supreme and who has supreme authority to interpret the norms. *So where is the interaction*?

205 Dworkin, *Law's Empire* (n 4), ch1, 'What Is Law?'; Scott J Shapiro, 'The "Hart–Dworkin" Debate: A Short Guide for the Perplexed' in Arthur Ripstein (ed), *Ronald Dworkin* (Cambridge University Press 2007).

206 As well as failing to explain a particular practice such as law in Dworkin's case. Cormac Mac Amhlaigh, 'The Anatomy of Constitutional Pluralism in the European Union' in Gareth Davies and Matej Avbelj (eds), *Research Handbook on Legal Pluralism and EU Law* (Elgar 2018).

207 Julio Baquero-Cruz, 'The Legacy of the Maastricht-Urteil and the Pluralist Movement' (2008) 14 European Law Journal 389.

208 MacCormick (n 198), 118.

209 Keith Culver and Michael Giudice, 'Not a System but an Order: An Inter-Institutional View of European Union Law' in Julie Dickson and Pavlos Eleftheriadis (eds), *Philosophical Foundations of European Union Law* (Oxford University Press 2012); see also Pavlos Eleftheriadis, 'Pluralism and Integrity' (2010) 23 Ratio Juris 365.

Unlike our previous inquiry in Chapter 4, where we attempted to make sense of such putative interactions from the point of view of the concept of legal systems, here, to avoid pseudo- or semantic disagreement in terms of a *normative* account of constitutional pluralism, then, to avoid the semantic sting or problematic idealization of the interactions based on an erroneous account of agreement, we need to understand the situation in terms of rival 'best interpretations' of a common political value.

Our interpretive approach to transnational constitutional pluralism can help us refocus the discussion and reappraise the disagreement around a core political value in which the various stakeholders—including national apex courts and the EU courts—are invested. Taking our general interpretive approach to transnational constitutional pluralism to this particular type of disagreement, then, encourages us to recast these putative 'interactions' not as 'laundry lists'[210] of criteria of legitimate authority resulting in the pseudo- or semantic disagreement outlined earlier, but as an *interpretive disagreement about legitimate transnational political authority*. Our interpretive approach recasts the issues raised in respect of EU constitutional conflicts in terms of *substantive agreement* about the political value of transnational political authority which EU constitutionalism represents. The disagreement, then, relates to how to understand that core political value in its best light. Applying the normative account of constitutional pluralism developed here, then, we can view political disagreement about authority in the EU system as, first, based on an *agreement* of the political value of transnational political authority: in this case, the political value of EU constitutionalism with its broad aims of continental 'peace and prosperity'.[211] Approaching the interactions between the legal systems in this way allows for a common agreement on the part of all of the stakeholders in the debate regarding the political value of EU constitutionalism. From this basis, our interpretive approach to transnational constitutionalism—here EU constitutionalism—involves *recasting disagreements about the locus of ultimate authority between EU and state constitutions into disagreements about the best interpretations of the political value of EU constitutionalism*. For some, especially the Court of Justice of the European Union and its supporters, it is the political autonomy of the EU institutions and its legal system, the interpretive autonomy of the EU courts as well as the primacy of its legal system which ensures equality and the values of the rule of law in the integration process,

210 Mattias Kumm, 'The Jurisprudence of Constitutional Conflict: Constitutional Supremacy in Europe before and after the Constitutional Treaty' (2005) 11 European Law Journal 262, 276.

211 Joseph Weiler, *The Constitution of Europe: 'Do the New Clothes Have an Emperor?' And Other Essays on European Integration* (Cambridge University Press 1999), 246.

which presents the political value of EU constitutionalism in its best light.[212] For others, it is state consent, state-based democracy, the presentation of EU Member States as 'Masters of the Treaties' and the values associated with transnational legality—and in particular, the requirement that EU institutions exercise their powers within the confines of the legal restrictions put in place by the EU's Member States as understood by their apex courts—which provides the best interpretation of the political value of EU constitutionalism.[213] What this approach provides, then, is a concrete 'fulcrum' of disagreement about the political value of EU constitutionalism in a way which captures the nuances and complexities of the disagreement as opposed to a simple binary 'criterial' choice between the supremacy of domestic constitutionalism or the supremacy of EU constitutionalism. Moreover, it avoids the risks associated with characterizing the issue of EU constitutional conflicts as competing claims to ultimate authority in terms of pseudo-disagreement.[214]

Moreover, our general approach to transnational constitutional pluralism defended here requires that the various 'best interpretations' of EU constitutionalism, whether in terms of the autonomy or supremacy of the EU legal system, Member State consent, or transnational legality, attempt to integrate their best interpretations with the other values at stake, guided by our ethical obligations corresponding to the 'unity of value'. In terms of our constitutional theory offering recommendations, then, in the types of disagreement which have characterized the field of EU constitutional conflicts, each position must strive to integrate their 'best interpretations' of transnational EU political authority in a way which engages and integrates with other rival conceptions. Thus, at a general level, the recommendations of our transnational constitutional pluralism will involve the idea that we should reason practically—that is make decisions in concrete cases—which realizes, as far as possible, the unity of value of transnational political authority. Thinking of transnational constitutionalism in this interpretive way highlights the fact that disagreement in the circumstances which give rise to EU constitutional conflicts are substantive political disagreements, and not pseudo-disagreement. Perhaps more

212 Fabbrini (n 199); Kelemen (n 199).

213 See, for example, the recent Weiss case of the German Constitutional Court. See generally, D. Grimm *et al.*, 'Special Section: "The German Federal Constitutional Court's PSPP Judgment"' (2020) 21 German Law Journal.

214 For an alternative Dworkinian-inspired view, see Samantha Besson, 'From European Integration to European Integrity: Should European Law Speak with Just One Voice?' (2004) 10 European Law Journal 257. Besson views Member State law and EU law to be part of one 'complex single legal order' and endorses an integrity-based approach to this complex system as supporting the authority of EU law.

importantly, it exposes and emphasizes the 'normative core'[215] of EU constitutional conflicts, understood as *agreement* as to the political value of EU constitutionalism in the context of disagreement of its 'best interpretation', and a shared commitment to the project of European integration in general.[216]

215 Jessica C Lawrence, 'Constitutional Pluralism's Unspoken Normative Core' (2019) 21 Cambridge Yearbook of European Legal Studies 24.

216 Referring back to our discussion in Chapter 4 regarding the individuation of legal systems, we are now in a position to develop the conclusions of that chapter to argue that the interpretive approach to the values of supremacy and openness of legal systems involves a duty to view them as rival 'best interpretations' of the role law can play in legitimating coercion and that we are under an ethical obligation to try to integrate them according to the unity of value. The general approach to EU conflicts endorsed by the normative theory of transnational constitutional pluralism defended, here, moreover, has some similarities to approaches to conflict avoidance such as those of Letsas, Kumm, and Maduro. George Letsas, 'Harmonic Law: The Case Against Pluralism' in Julie Dickson and Pavlos Eleftheriadis (eds), *Philosophical Foundations of European Union Law* (Oxford University Press 2012); Mattias Kumm, 'The Cosmopolitan Turn in Constitutionalism: On the Relationship between Constitutionalism in and beyond the State' in Jeffrey L Dunoff and Joel P Trachtman (eds), *Ruling the World?: Constitutionalism, International Law, and Global Governance* (Cambridge University Press 2009); Miguel Poiares Maduro, 'Contrapunctual Law: Europe's Constitutional Pluralism in Action' in Neil Walker (ed), *Sovereignty in Transition* (Hart 2003). Letsas' non-positivist, Dworkin-inspired approach to constitutional conflicts largely avoids conflicts given his 'harmonic' characterization of constitutional pluralism. However, a core feature of Letsas' approach diverges from the current approach. Unlike the approach taken here where national constitutional values can play an important role in theorizing these constitutional conflicts in the form of 'best interpretations' of what legitimate transnational authority requires, he seems to downplay these sorts of claims as not being relevant to a moral resolution of the issue. Kumm and Maduro come closer to the approach endorsed here. Kumm's account of cosmopolitan constitutionalism, seeks to establish an 'integrative basic conceptual framework for a general theory of public law that integrates national and international law' (Kumm, 'The Cosmopolitan Turn in Constitutionalism', 264) that allows for the '*holistic construction of legitimate public authority*' (ibid 322, emphasis added). The potential problems emerge in Kumm's approach where he endorses particular principles of cosmopolitan constitutionalism which are aimed at resolving any disagreements. These principles underlie 'both national and international law' and will sometimes favour the application of international rules over national and vice versa. (ibid 274). Kumm posits a principle of international legality and 'countervailing' principles (ibid 277) of subsidiarity, due process and reasonableness and acknowledges that under his model 'the potential for legally irresolvable conflict between national and international law remains' (ibid 279) In the light of this it is not clear that the framework of cosmopolitan constitutionalism will necessarily result in 'a constructive debate about the delimitation of the sphere of the national and the international in specific legal and political debates' (ibid 291). If an international court decides in favour of a principle of international legality, and a state court fails to follow that decision based on a countervailing principle of, say, subsidiarity, then are they really disagreeing on substance? There is at least a question to be answered as to whether there is in fact any disagreement on the issue given that both courts argue that there is a solution to the resolution of particular based on different principles. This remains the case even if, as Kumm claims, that a 'direct conflict' between the cosmopolitan paradigm and national constitutional rules 'remains a theoretical possibility only' (ibid 278). Emphasizing the role and importance of national courts in recognizing the authority of EU constitutionalism for EU constitutionalism itself, and the ensuing 'multilogue' (Contrapunctual Law ibid 514) between courts in the building of EU constitutionalism, Maduro's characterization of interactions in terms of 'contrapunctual law' draws on the musical practice of counterpoint whereby different melodies are harmonized without being in a hierarchical relationship between themselves (ibid 523). Maduro's account sets out deliberately to avoid the problem of pseudo disagreement noting that for pluralism to be viable in a context of coherent legal order '*there must be a common basis for discourse*' (ibid 524, emphasis added). This involves, on Maduro's account, a commitment to a series of 'principles of contrapunctual law' which will set up the common basis for pluralism, the agreement necessary for meaningful disagreement to get off the ground (ibid 524). These principles include a principle of coherence where courts should make sure that legal decisions are coherent with previous legal decisions which involves 'a commitment to a coherent [EU] legal order' (ibid 528), both in terms of the decisions of the EU courts but also the decision of the national courts of other EU Member States (ibid 529) and universalizability

Of course, this is simply one, short (and somewhat parochial and admittedly Eurocentric) example of the application of the account of transnational constitutional theory being advanced here. The possibilities of application are only as finite as the number of existing transnational governing practices.

10. Persistent Objectors

Framing disagreement at the transnational level in these constitutional terms is, itself, interpretive: it attempts to provide a 'best interpretation' of disagreements about what the possibilities or values of transnational constitutional pluralism might be. The account defended here excludes disagreements which do not share the consensus about the practices of transnational law and governance and the political value of legitimate transnational governing authority about which disagreement about 'best interpretations' can emerge. We can envisage two views of legitimate authority which diverge from the way in which we have approached the question of disagreement at transnational level here: one which rejects the political value of transnational authority, and another which rejects the value of political authority more generally.

The first divergent view of legitimate authority rejects the political value of transnational authority. This view champions a particular understanding of state sovereignty as the only legitimate form of transnational ordering and elements of this view could be seen in recent populist denigrations of transnational organizations and transnational cooperation, as exemplified by the successful campaign to take the United Kingdom out of the European Union and endorsed by its subsequent 'Brexit' government.[217] This understanding of legitimate authority views international politics in classically imperialistic terms, where the only political value at stake is that of state sovereignty and the ability of states to pursue their strategic interest, expressed at the transnational level as actual (as opposed to tacit or assumed) state consent.[218] On this view,

requiring that national decisions on EU law be universalizable to other courts including the EU courts. The account defended here renders explicit what is left implicit in Maduro's account in clarifying the fact that the coherence and universalizability of decision-making in Maduro's account is not coherence for its own sake, or for aesthetic purposes analogous to counterpoint in music, but rather stems from an ethical duty to integrate our 'best interpretations' of the political value of transnational governing authority based on the unity of value.

[217] Paul Craig, 'Brexit a Drama: The Endgame—Part I' (2020) 45 European Law Review 163; Cormac Mac Amhlaigh, 'Back to a Sovereign Future?: Constitutional Pluralism after Brexit' (2019) 21 Cambridge Yearbook of European Legal Studies 41.

[218] For a refutation of a critique of the consent-based view see Dworkin, 'A New Philosophy for International Law' (n 183).

the only value of transnational political authority is its function in giving expression to the will of states. Our normative theories of transnational law and politics, such as they are, therefore, require a return to the supremacy of sovereign states and *ad hoc* inter-state bargaining based on national interests and balances of power.

An alternative view rejects the political value of transnational governing authority by endorsing a view of political authority in terms of a radically decentred, pluralistic, even cosmopolitan understanding of global legal and political ordering. On this view, states are, themselves, illegitimate, the product of coercion, oppression, cultural homogenization, and violence. Any transnational system built upon such foundations is necessarily contaminated by these illegitimate origins. Such a view might prescribe a vision of global politics and society built upon a radically cosmopolitan kaleidoscope of social and cultural political groupings and entities without any overarching coordinating authority.[219]

These interpretations of our disagreements at transnational level cannot be accommodated by the account of transnational constitutionalism defended here.[220] However, their exclusion need not worry us unduly in the light of the fact that their views of legitimate political authority depart, potentially radically, from the practices of transnational law and governance as they currently are. To this extent, then, it is not clear that their views are interpretations of the practices of transnational law and governance.[221] Given that the contemporary

219 See generally Krisch, *Beyond Constitutionalism: The Pluralist Structure of Postnational Law* (n 2); Joshua Cohen and Charles Sabel, 'Directly-Deliberative Polyarchy' (1997) 3 European Law Journal 313. For a particularly Marxist inspired view of the end of the state system in the light of globalization, see Michael Hardt and Antonio Negri, *Empire* (Harvard University Press 2001).

220 Although elements of both could be present in our account as 'best interpretations' of some transnational practices such as subsidiarity, state consent, pluralism or transnational democracy. For one example of how this might look see Cormac Mac Amhlaigh, '"Even Children Lisp the Rights of Man": International Human Rights Law and National Minority Jurisdictions' in Stephen Tierney (ed), *Nationalism and Globalisation* (Hart 2015).

221 As noted in Chapter 1, even the supposedly state sovereigntist Brexit 'event' has resulted in *more* rather than *less* legal and political pluralism. In this respect, such positions could be compared to an example provided by Dworkin of someone who departs radically from the agreements about pre-interpretive practices and the political value of a practice. Such radical departures from the consensus, Dworkin argues, do not contradict themselves nor speak thoughts 'no one can understand ... [w]e understand him only too well [and] it is not inconceivable (though it is unlikely) that he will be able to defend his view through a radical interpretation of [a] practice that is otherwise so appealing that it persuades us to abandon what was formally a cardinal paradigm'. 'We cannot be sure', he continues, 'his views are really the nonsense we suppose except by hearing him out and discovering whether we share his conviction. If we remain convinced that his views are not only wrong but fundamentally wrong, that his radical interpretation has missed some main point any successful interpretation must recognize, it will be enough for us to say that his views are absurd. We do not need to add the more dramatic but mistaken charge encouraged by the semantic sting: that his error is verbal or conceptual. We will think him very wrong, but not wrong in some different way from other claims we reject but think less preposterous.' (Dworkin, *Law's Empire* (n 4), 92.

world is made up of a web of transnational authorities, such views of transnational governance are, in some ways quite radically, counterfactual. As more abstract theories of transnational governance presented for the purposes of comparison or evaluation, they may have some function. However, in this respect they do not constitute transnational *constitutional* theories given that they fail as a form of practical reasoning. Where they *are* presented as forms of practical reasoning, then they come with a potentially very high moral price tag.[222]

A second objection to our account here is a version of the no demos thesis; however, this time it is refracted though our account of constitutionalism as an interpretive concept. In short, this objection argues that characterizing constitutionalism as an interpretive concept does not liberate us from the classic problems of bringing constitutionalism beyond the state, of which the no demos thesis is the most salient example.[223] This reformulation of the no demos thesis argues that the agreement necessary—even on an interpretive account—of the object of a theory of constitutionalism and its purpose or point necessarily implicates or presumes the society, politics, and institutions of *states*. On this view, the interpretive enterprise in respect of transnational constitutional theory defended here fails for lack of the necessary elements—pre-interpretive agreement and agreements about political value—which could make such an interpretive approach successful on its own terms.[224] As evidenced by the extensive consideration of the no demos thesis in Chapter 7, we simply do not agree that the political value of constitutionalism relates to the types of governing organizations considered here (transnational structures of law and governance). This objection will, therefore, argue that there is a sleight of hand in pre-emptively talking about transnational authority in constitutional terms in the face of such disagreement.

However, in order to take this objection seriously, it needs to provide us with reasons as to why the practices of law and governmence and the political value of authority is restricted to the practices of law and governance and the authority of *states*. What is it specifically about *states* that make the political value of constitutionalism limited to this historical governing arrangement? Therefore, our objector must pick out a feature of features of state-based constitutional practice—a demos, for example—and argue against our enterprise in the same way as the no demos thesis outlined in Chapter 7. However, once

[222] See Chapter 7.
[223] Walker, 'Taking Constitutionalism beyond the State' (n 164).
[224] See, for example, Martin Loughlin, 'Constitutional Pluralism: An Oxymoron?' (2014) 3 Global Constitutionalism 9.

she adopts *this* approach, our objector will encounter two familiar problems. In picking out a particular feature of state-based constitutional practice, our objector begins down the path of presenting a criterial concept of constitutionalism—constitutionalism 'just is really' about state-based forms of political ordering—therefore leading to semantic or pseudo-disagreement. Furthermore, it is for this reason that our objector cannot make sense of our disagreement about transnational constitutionalism. Given that our objector's intervention in transnational constitutional debates is based on a criterial concept of constitutionalism involving necessary and sufficient conditions of, for example, a demos, her intervention in these disagreements is pseudo-disagreement as she is not disagreeing with someone taking an interpretive approach.

Our objector, undeterred, may take another shot and dismiss our approach here based not on a criterial conception of constitutionalism, but on our co-option of a 'Western Constitutional Tradition' which organizes the values of our constitutional 'tree'. Here, the objection would be that our approach is problematic given that our reliance on the Western Constitutional Tradition, a tradition which unambiguously emerged in states, necessarily excludes novel governing sites such as those which exist at the transnational level. Therefore, our fundamental category error in talking about transnational constitutionalism does not stem from a criterial approach to the concept but is based, rather, on the building-blocks of our interpretive approach which do not permit the extension of the concept to the 'foreign climate' of transnational law and governance. However, we can meet this hypothetical objection in the same way we met the previous one. In determining the relevant agreement around the object of our inquiry as well as the elements of our political value, we take an interpretive attitude, even at this stage. As Dworkin notes, social practices such as law 'do not carry identifying labels'.[225] We therefore take an interpretive approach to determining what is included and what is excluded from our object, even at the stage of our pre-interpretive agreement. Thus, again, we need normative reasons to limit the elements of our object to the governing practices of *states*; that is why our 'tree' of the Western Constitutional Tradition implicating legitimate governing authority should be limited to the governing authorities of states. Again, our objector will have to rely on a normative interpretation of the tradition which does not succumb to the problems outlined above (ie not semantic or pseudo-disagreement and not making counterfactual assumptions).

We can clarify why the statist objection does not defeat the account of transnational constitutionalism provided here by examining the relationship

[225] Dworkin, *Law's Empire* (n 4), 66.

between the empirical or historical features of a practice and its normative purpose. As Dworkin suggests, the ascription of value to a concept or practice in terms of its point or purpose can be stated independently of the empirical features of the practice itself; these core features of the object are sensitive to the point of the practice, and can therefore change in order to achieve this point.[226] As such, for interpretive concepts, the empirical features of the object are contingent rather than essential (as is the case with criterial concepts) given that they express particular ways of pursuing the particular point or purpose of the concept, rather than exhausting the purpose or point of the concept in and of itself.[227] Thus, if this is the case, then the (contingent) fact that the key features of constitutional practice historically emerged in states is less important than the fact that they constitute interpretations of a political value of legitimate governing authority. As Dworkin notes:[228]

> It is only a historical fact that the present institution is the descendant of similar earlier examples. The changes from one period to another, or the differences from one society to another, may be sufficiently great so that the continuity should be denied. Which changes are great enough to cut the thread of continuity? That itself is an interpretive question, and the answer would depend on why the question of continuity arises.

Thus, in thinking about the analogies or *dis*analogies between the state and transnational contexts, we should ask whether the practice in the 'foreign climate' of transnational law and governance shares the point or purpose or value of the practice at the state level. That is, whether the point or purpose of the practice of transnational governance is the same as at the state level. We have already seen that this is the case through our identification of the political value of transnational political authority. In normative terms, then, the state-based history of the Western Constitutional Tradition which is the object of our conceptual inquiry is a contingent rather than an essential feature of our interpretive concept of constitutionalism.

If it is the case, as I have argued here, that the basis of our disagreement at transnational level is based on an agreement about the political value of transnational authority, then the question of 'taking constitutionalism beyond the state'—even a holistic constitutionalism as endorsed here—becomes much

[226] ibid 47.
[227] ibid 47.
[228] ibid 69–70.

less problematic. The core 'non-utopian' features of the transnational level of law and governance, a core reason for *denying* the appropriateness of constitutionalism (or holistic constitutionalism) at this level, becomes a feature, not a bug, of our transnational constitutional theory where our disagreement is recast as a disagreement about how to present the political value of transnational governing authority in its best light. The permutations and combinations of 'best interpretations' may be more varied and complex here than at the state level, not least given that transnational authority must always reckon with some form of federal arrangement—between individuals and groups (including states)—which is a contingent feature of state level governance. This means that part of our disagreement about how to present the political value of transnational legitimate authority in its best light may include interpretations which see a more limited role for transnational authority and a potentially greater role for, say, state autonomy (or state sovereignty if we want to call it that), alongside the more familiar disagreements on institutions, procedures and substantive policy questions which are more familiar to state-based constitutional disagreement, with the caveat that they are compatible with, or based upon, the actual practices of transnational law and governance. Nonetheless, the form of disagreement, based as it is on a core political value of legitimate transnational authority, make it an apt, as well as sufficiently realistic normative theory for transnational governance. Moreover, in thinking about our disagreements about specific transnational authorities in an interpretive vein, we must also, as Dworkin advises, recognize and engage with alternative 'best' interpretations—including critical interpretations as we have already seen in 'new constitutionalism'—with a view to striving for a unity of transnational constitutional value.

11. Conclusion

The interpretive method adopted for our account of constitutional pluralism as normative theory, it is argued, provides a better approach to thinking about transnational constitutionalism, and questions of transnational legitimacy more generally than alternative approaches. First, it answers the 'first constitutional question' borne of the definitional conundrums which surround the concept of constitutionalism, helping us on to the terrain of more substantive value-based disagreement. Furthermore, given that, as Dworkin has developed extensively over the course of his work, the interpretive approach leads to thinking about political value in unitary terms, it helps provide a broader perspective on questions of legitimacy which temper the 'illegitimacy' critiques of both constitutionalism as well as 'new constitutionalism'. The integration of value encouraged and promoted by the interpretive approach helps us address the critiques of constitutionalism based on the idea that constitutionalism picks out a small number of values—such as the rule of law—and privileges these over all other values. The interpretive approach leading to the unity of value does not follow this logic. If, in taking an interpretive approach to the concept of constitutionalism based on the political value of legitimate political authority, we understand rival conceptions to be alternative 'best interpretations' of that value, we can see how our individual conceptions of constitutionalism are related by the common value of legitimate political authority. This, in turn, encourages us to reflect upon and take alternative conceptions seriously, leading us to revise our own conceptions where appropriate in the light of our understanding of alternative conceptions. From here, it is but a short step to the development of an ethical obligation (on Dworkin's account) to provide a holistic account of the political value of legitimate political authority, involving the integration of our 'best conceptions' with rival conceptions into a unitary whole. As Dworkin noted, this is not an easy task; however, we discharge our ethical obligations in taking the task seriously and in good faith.[229] Rather than encouraging the distillation of core conceptions and privileging them at the expense of others, it forces an engagement and integration with rival conceptions with a view to achieving the core substantive value of our disagreement. Moreover, this holistic obligation also applies in our practical reasoning. In thinking about our disagreement and political value in holistic terms, we should strive to make decisions in a way which discharges this moral responsibility.

With regard to the transnational context, in particular, an interpretive approach to constitutionalism casts transnational constitutional discourse in an improved light. It allows us to take seriously the legitimacy concerns relating to transnational governance while at the same time acknowledging and respecting the differences between the state and transnational levels of governance. However, in respecting the differences between these levels of governance, it forces us to think about what the most salient features of difference are from a normative perspective. In this regard, institutional and political-cultural factors, while relevant, are not determinative. Even if there is an order of magnitude in disagreement at the transnational level when compared with the

[229] Dworkin, *Justice for Hedgehogs* (n 5), 109.

state level (generally speaking, there are of course state exceptions to this) the basic requirements of the interpretive approach apply. Part of our pre-interpretive agreement involves both the institutions and practices of transnational governance as well as the political disagreements which gravitate around these. Moreover, for our disagreement about transnational constitutional theory to be substantive and not merely semantic, we need to identify the core political value of such practices. The position defended here is that the common 'roots' of constitutional theorizing at this level—that is, the basis of a normative theory prescribing reasons for action—is the political value of transnational authority. This helps to anchor our, sometimes radical, disagreement at transnational level and helps us make advances in addressing the legitimacy questions which emerge. As such, our account of transnational constitutionalism allows us to think about disagreement at this level without foundering on the political realities of entrenched disagreement. In this regard, it provides a more attractive way of thinking about legitimacy and constitutionalism at the transnational level than alternative accounts which either do not take such disagreement seriously enough—as perhaps an idealistic blueprint for world order might—or those accounts such as disaggregated constitutionalism or GAL that capitulate to the circumstances of transnational governance and end up making (problematic) partial fixes to what are broader problems of legitimacy and authority which, moreover, can exacerbate, rather than diminish the legitimacy problems our accounts of constitutional pluralism set out to address.

However, in setting out our interpretive account of transnational constitutionalism as we have done here, we do not assume that it is the only theory of transnational legitimacy. The field of transnational normative theorizing is an exponentially expanding one and many serious contributions have been made in advancing the idea of transnational or global justice or transnational or global democracy.[230] There is, of course, an overlap between these ideas and our account of constitutionalism. In our account of constitutionalism we must expect and make room for 'best interpretations' or conceptions of legitimate political authority which are predicated on questions of justice or democracy. Indeed, these may be a core part of our understanding of the political value of legitimate political authority. Thus, our conception of constitutional pluralism shares the concerns and prescriptions of these approaches. However, where our

[230] See Gillian Brock, *Global Justice: A Cosmopolitan Account* (Oxford University Press 2009); Terry Macdonald, *Global Stakeholder Democracy: Power and Representation Beyond Liberal States* (Oxford University Press 2008); Laura Valentini, *Justice in a Globalized World: A Normative Framework* (Oxford University Press 2011).

conception departs from some of these approaches is in respect of its emphasis on a non-utopian realistic normative theory, one which makes achievable recommendations in the more immediate term based on extant practices of transnational law and governance. To the extent that theories of global justice or global democracy share these purposes, they can be considered part of the general transnational constitutional pluralist enterprise.

Index

For the benefit of digital users, indexed terms that span two pages (e.g., 52–53) may, on occasion, appear on only one of those pages.